Captivity, Forced Labour and Forced Migration in Europe during the First World War

The notion of the First World War as 'the great seminal catastrophe' (*Urkatastrophe*) of the twentieth century is now firmly established in historiography. Yet astonishingly little has been written about the fate of non-combatants in occupied and non-occupied territory, including civilian internees, deportees, expellees and disarmed military prisoners.

This volume brings together experts from across Europe to consider the phenomena of captivity, forced labour and forced migration during and immediately after the years 1914 to 1918. Each contribution offers a European-wide perspective, thus moving beyond interpretations based on narrow national frameworks or on one of the fighting fronts alone. Particular emphasis is placed on the way in which the experience of internees, forced labourers and expellees was mediated by specific situational factors and by the development of 'war cultures' and 'mentalities' at different stages in the respective war efforts. Other themes considered include the recruitment and deployment of colonial troops in Europe, and efforts to investigate, monitor and prosecute alleged war crimes in relation to the mistreatment of civilians and POWs. The final contribution will then consider the problems associated with repatriation and the reintegration of returning prisoners after the war.

This book was published as a special issue of *Immigrants and Minorities*.

Matthew Stibbe is Reader in History at Sheffield Hallam University.

D0645434

Captivity, Forced Labour and Forced Migration in Europe during the First World War

Edited by Matthew Stibbe

Routledge
Taylor & Francis Group

LONDON AND NEW YORK

First published 2009 by Routledge
2 Park Square, Milton Park, Abingdon, Oxon, OX14 4RN

Simultaneously published in the USA and Canada
by Routledge
711 Third Avenue, New York, NY 10017

First issued in paperback 2013

Routledge is an imprint of the Taylor & Francis Group, an informa business

© 2009 Edited by Matthew Stibbe

Typeset in Minion by Value Chain, India

British Library Cataloguing in Publication Data
A catalogue record for this book is available from the British Library

ISBN13: 978-0-415-44003-5
ISBN13: 978-0-415-84635-6

Contents

Notes on Contributors

Matthew Stibbe is Reader in History at Sheffield Hallam University. He has published widely in the area of First World War Studies and twentieth-century Europe more generally. His most recent work is *British Civilian Internees in Germany: The Ruhleben Camp, 1914-18* (Manchester University Press, 2008). He is currently engaged in a project on civilian internment in Austria (Cisleithania) during the First World War, as well as co-editing, with Ingrid Sharp, a collection of essays on women's movements and female activists in the aftermath of the war, 1918–23.

Heather Jones is Lecturer in International History at the London School of Economics and Political Science. She completed her Ph.D. in 2006, at Trinity College Dublin, on violence against prisoners of war during the First World War in Britain, France and Germany; this study was awarded the Eda Sagarra medal by the Irish Research Council for the Humanities and Social Sciences. A former Max Weber Fellow at the European University Institute, she has published widely on prisoner treatment. Her most recent publication is 'The German Spring Reprisals of 1917: Prisoners of War and the Violence of the Western Front' published in *German History* 26, no. 3 (2008).

Peter Gatrell is Professor of Economic History at the University of Manchester. He is the author of numerous books and articles, including *A Whole Empire Walking: Refugees in Russia during World War 1* (Indiana University Press, 1999), which won the Wayne Vucinich Prize of the American Association for the Advancement of Slavic Studies and the Alec Nove Prize of the British Association for Slavonic and East European Studies. Together with Nick Baron he is editing *Warlands: Population Resettlement and State Reconstruction in Soviet Eastern Europe, 1945-1950* (Palgrave Macmillan, forthcoming) and completing a study of World Refugee Year, 1959–60 as well as a book entitled *The Making of the Modern Refugee*.

Christian Koller is Senior Lecturer in Modern History at the University of Wales, Bangor, and Privatdozent at the University of Zurich in Switzerland. His research interests include the history of racism and nationalism, the history of peace and war (with a special focus on the First World War), sport history, historical semantics and labour history. His most important publications include '*Von Wilden aller Rassen niedergemetzelt': Die*

Diskussion um die Verwendung von Kolonialtruppen in Europa zwischen Rassismus, Kolonial- und Militärpolitik (1914–1930) (Steiner, 2001); (with F. Brändle:) *Goal! Kultur- und Sozialgeschichte des modernen Fussballs* (Orell Füssli, 2002); *Fremdherrschaft. Ein politischer Kampfbegriff im Zeitalter des Nationalismus* (Campus Verlag, 2005); and *Streikkultur. Performanzen und Diskurse des Arbeitskampfes im schweizerisch-österreichischen Vergleich (1860–1950)* (forthcoming).

Daniel Marc Segesser is Privatdozent and Collborator of the Head of the Department at the University of Bern in Switzerland. His publications include studies on the history of Australia, the military history of Belgium and France, as well as the history of the international legal debate on the punishment of war crimes in the period between 1872 and 1945 and of international law in general. His most recent work, *Recht statt Rache oder Rache durch Recht? Die Ahndung von Kriegsverbrechen in der internationalen wissenschaftlichen Debatte, 1872-1945*, is due to be published by Schöningh in Paderborn shortly.

Reinhard Nachtigal is a historian working in Freiburg im Breisgau in Germany. His many publications include a number of important works on POWs on the Eastern Front during the First World War and on British economic engagement in Russia during the same period. He has also produced a recent study of German settlers in the Don Cossack territory, *Donskiye nemcy, 1830-1930: Die Dondeutschen* (Verlag Waldemar Weber, 2007). He is currently engaged in a project on Russian military strategy in the Caucasus region during the first half of the nineteenth century.

Introduction: Captivity, Forced Labour and Forced Migration during the First World War

Matthew Stibbe

Department of History, Sheffield Hallam University, Sheffield, UK

> The citizens of Nîmes were proud of themselves for having done their duty, and more, towards the refugees. They had welcomed them with open arms, pressed them against their bosoms. There was not a single family who had not offered hospitality to these poor people. It was just a shame that this state of affairs was dragging on so unreasonably long. There was also the matter of provisions, and you can't forget either, said the townspeople, that all these poor refugees, exhausted by their journey, would be susceptible to the most terrible epidemics. There were veiled hints in the press and more open, brutal demands from other quarters, urging the refugees to leave as soon as possible. But as yet, circumstances had prevented anyone from going anywhere.[1]

So wrote the French-Russian author and Holocaust victim Irène Némirovsky in her unfinished and only recently discovered novel *Suite Française*, set in France in June 1940 at the time of the Nazi invasion and occupation. The Second World War was of course not the first conflict in twentieth-century Europe to create a large-scale crisis around displaced populations and refugees. It had all happened before, in the First World War. All over the world, during the years 1914 to 1918, people were in mass transit, much of it of an involuntary nature. France, to take one example, bore the burden of a huge wave of refugees, some of them having fled from the advancing German armies in 1914, others being compulsorily evacuated by the French army in the wake of its military operations on the western front, and others still being repatriated from occupied to non-occupied territory via neutral Switzerland.[2] By the autumn of 1918, according to one estimate, more than 2 million French civilians had been uprooted over the course of four years of fighting.[3]

Yet France was no isolated case: all of the belligerents, and even some neutrals like the Netherlands, found themselves playing host to unprecedented numbers of displaced persons during the war. In central Europe, for instance, hundreds of thousands of civilians fled or were expelled from the frontier areas of the Habsburg empire into the Austrian and Hungarian hinterland, or into surrounding countries like Serbia, Italy or Romania. Many were unable or unwilling to return to their former places of residence even after the cessation of hostilities.[4] Meanwhile, in the Balkans forced migration and deportations had already occurred on a mass scale during the wars of 1912 and 1913, and continued to blight the region thereafter.[5] But by far the largest number of refugees was to be found in Russia, where a little over 6 million people had been separated from their homes by the beginning of 1917, representing roughly 5% of the total population.[6] Most of them belonged to the non-Russian nationalities of the crumbling Tsarist empire.

On top of refugees, the 1914–18 war created a similar crisis around the treatment and eventual repatriation of up to 9 million prisoners of war, who were held in camps of varying size and quality throughout Europe. Some were recruited into labour brigades to work in industry or agriculture on the home front, or, worse still, behind the front lines. Others were exposed to political propaganda and agitation designed to persuade them to change sides and fight for their former enemies. As contemporaries knew full well, captivity of this kind was nothing new. What was unprecedented, however, was its scale, duration and brutality. Furthermore, alongside millions of soldiers captured on the battlefield, hundreds of thousands of civilians – enemy aliens, deportees or members of 'suspect' nationalities – were also interned. This was on top of hundreds of thousands of colonial peoples – mainly from Africa and Asia – who were brought to Europe to work or fight for the western Allies. They too had to be fed, clothed and housed at a distance of thousands of miles from their homelands.

The notion of the First World War as 'the great seminal catastrophe' (*Urkatastrophe*) of the twentieth century is now firmly established in historiography.[7] Yet astonishingly little has been written about the fate of non-combatants in occupied and non-occupied territory, including civilian internees, deportees, expellees and disarmed military prisoners.[8] This volume brings together experts from across Europe to consider the phenomena of captivity, forced labour and forced migration during and immediately after the years 1914 to 1918. Particular emphasis is placed on the way in which the experience of internment, exile or refugeedom was mediated by specific situational factors and by the development of 'war cultures' and 'mentalities' at different stages in the respective war efforts. Other themes considered include the recruitment and deployment of colonial troops in Europe, and efforts to investigate, monitor and prosecute alleged war crimes in relation to the mistreatment of civilians and prisoners of war (POWs). The final contribution will then consider the problems associated with repatriation and the reintegration of returning prisoners after the war.

Before proceeding, however, it is first necessary to consider why the themes developed here are of such importance to our understanding of the First World War more generally. After all, what the French officer-prisoner Georges Connes later described as the 'other ordeal' – the ordeal experienced by millions of POWs during the First World War – has only recently become the subject of systematic historical investigation, after decades of scholarly neglect.[9] The same applies to studies of civilian internees, forced migrants and refugees. Why should this be the case?

As Peter Gatrell has argued elsewhere, a number of important developments within the geopolitical and historiographical arenas are responsible for the recent 'upsurge of interest in war and forced migration' and, one might add, in wartime captivity as well.[10] Firstly, the collapse of communist rule in central and eastern Europe in 1989, and of the Soviet Union itself in 1991, opened up previously hidden archives on some of the less heroic episodes of the First World War as it was fought out on the eastern front. In the former USSR it also permitted – and legitimised – public discussion of such forgotten issues after 70 years of dictatorship in which only party-approved histories could be written. Indeed, as Reinhard Nachtigal also argues in his contribution to this work, Soviet historiography imposed a particular interpretation on the First World War, defining it as a conflict between imperialist nations which inevitably ended in the victory of communist revolution under Lenin's leadership, and of the Bolshevik Red Army in the subsequent civil war. Issues which did not fit easily within this triumphant narrative – including Soviet mistreatment of former German and Austro-Hungarian POWs, and equally of Russian POWs returning home from captivity in central Europe – were conveniently airbrushed from the historical record.

The collapse of communism also led to the violent break-up of Yugoslavia in the early 1990s, bringing with it the depopulation of formerly prosperous lands and the largest refugee crisis in Europe since the 1940s. Worse still, in both the Bosnian (1992–95) and Kosovo (1998–9) wars United Nations and Red Cross officials uncovered evidence of mass killings and other serious human rights abuses, including the establishment of special interrogation camps, concentration camps and rape camps by the Bosnian Serbs in territories they had 'ethnically cleansed'.[11] In total some

2.5 million Bosnians were uprooted during the fighting between 1992 and 1995, representing almost 60% of the 1991 population of 4.38 million. Of these, 700,000 fled, at least temporarily, to other European countries outside the former Yugoslavia.[12] Meanwhile, since 1999 the Serb minority in Kosovo, previously protected by the brutal Milošović regime in Belgrade, has itself fallen victim to several waves of violence and expulsions at the hands of ethnic Albanians and former members of the KLA (Kosovo Liberation Army).[13]

Post-colonial conflicts in other parts of the world have also created their own waves of mass forced migration, so that, for instance, 73,000 POWs and 17,000 civilian prisoners were held and 10 million people were displaced as a result of the two-week war between India and Pakistan over Bangladesh in 1971, and close to 7 million people were forced from their homes during fighting in various African states in the 1990s.[14] During the First Gulf War (1991) coalition forces detained 86,743 Iraqi officers and men, many of them deserters, while in Britain 176 Iraqis and other supposedly pro-Saddam Arabs were interned on grounds of national security, the first time such measures had been used on the mainland since 1945.[15] After its liberation in March 1991 Kuwait ordered the expulsion of some 400,000 Palestinian workers accused of having collaborated with the Iraqi occupiers, thereby adding to what was already a large-scale Palestinian refugee crisis dating back to the Arab–Israeli wars of 1948 and 1967 and the Israeli invasion of Lebanon in 1982.[16] On top of this, since 2001 the American-led 'war on terror' has given rise not only to a new refugee problem in Iraq, Afghanistan and neighbouring countries, but to the practice of 'extraordinary rendition' of terrorist suspects to any part of the world and to the establishment of a special detention camp at Guantánamo bay in Cuba to hold illegal combatants outside the auspices of the Geneva convention and the jurisdiction of United States law. The prisoners detained here are accused of fighting for a global enemy – Al Qaeda – which has no permanent territorial base, no clear goals and perhaps no permanent leadership of its own.[17]

All of these geopolitical developments have led historians to look at the First World War with new questions, particularly in relation to issues like ethnic conflict and frontier zones;[18] invasions and military occupations;[19] war crimes and atrocities committed against enemy combatants and civilians;[20] the supposed 'pleasures' of face-to-face killing;[21] the development of mass hatreds and cultures of destruction;[22] the 'politics of grief';[23] the role of religion;[24] or the impact of conflict on children and young people.[25] Some of these studies also built on earlier and important works published in the 1980s.[26] Yet the bigger picture still remains to be worked out. Indeed, as the British scholar Eric Hobsbawm noted in a paper delivered in Oslo in 2001 to mark the 100th anniversary of the Nobel Peace Prize:

> It would be easier to write about the subject of war and peace in the twentieth century if the difference between the two remained as clear-cut as it was supposed to be at the beginning of the century...[Under the Hague Conventions of 1899 and 1907] conflicts were supposed to take place primarily between sovereign states or, if they occurred within the territory of one particular state, between parties sufficiently organised to be accorded belligerent status by other sovereign states. War was supposed to be sharply distinguished from peace, by a declaration of war at one end and a treaty of peace at the other .... Non-combatants should, so far as possible, be protected in wartime.... In the course of the twentieth century, this relative clarity was replaced by confusion.[27]

Arguably some, but not all, of this confusion can be traced back to the First World War itself, as well as related conflicts such as the two Balkan wars of 1912–13 and the Russian civil war of 1918–20. This alone makes the study of captivity, forced labour and forced migration during this period of pressing and contemporary relevance. Indeed, the President of the International Commission to Inquire into the Causes and Conduct of the Balkan Wars, the French diplomat and senator Baron d'Estournelles de Constant, warned prophetically in early 1914 that the sudden redrawing of borders in south-eastern Europe, which had been accompanied by violence on all sides, might only be

> the beginning of other wars, or rather of a continuous war, a war of religion, of reprisals, of race, a war of one people against another, of man against man, brother against brother. It has become a competition as to who can best dispossess and 'denationalize' his neighbor.[28]

Yet it is not only contemporary geopolitical issues that are responsible for the renewed interest in the link between nationalism, religion, ethnicity and war. Shifts in historiography and historical methodology have been equally important. The most significant development, perhaps paralleling the end of the communist experiment in the Soviet bloc, has been the collapse of 'grand narratives' of history more generally.[29] The contention of postmodernists that all human knowledge is culturally constructed and therefore fragile and impermanent, represents both a challenge and an opportunity for scholars of the First World War. The negative side is that it may now be impossible to make any statement about the war with any degree of certainty or any guarantee of longevity. Anything that is said might be subject to sudden dissolution, just like the great empires of central, eastern and south-eastern Europe which fell apart in 1917/18, forcing people to acquire brand new nationalities and passports overnight, if not entirely new cultures and identities.[30] Yet on the other hand, the often sharply contested way in which knowledge and identity is constructed and communicated can in itself be an extremely fruitful area for investigation, particularly when applied to the war and inter-war periods.[31] This has the advantage of placing human beings once again at the centre of historical developments, rather than seeing them as passive victims of 'uncontrollable' forces, 'unchallengeable' truths or 'great' military victories.

One important response to the postmodernist challenge has been the rise of *Erfahrungsgeschichte*, translated into English as the 'history of experience'. Experience here, as Benjamin Ziemann explains in his study of rural southern Bavaria in the years 1914 to 1923, focuses on 'how individuals subjectively constitute, interpret and reinterpret social reality in a ceaseless process of communication'. It is thus distinct from the notion of discourse, which 'emphasises the objective and often inflexible aspect of this construction of reality, that is, the limits of what may be said and written about certain subjects within the public sphere'.[32]

An excellent example of the application of *Erfahrungsgeschichte* to the phenomenon of First World War captivity has been Alon Rachamimov's study of POWs on the eastern front, which makes use of letters sent to and by prisoners in Russia via the postal censorship office (*Gemeinsames Zentralnachweisbureau*) of the Habsburg Army High Command.[33] Such letters, as he demonstrates, shed light on the prisoners' subjective perception of reality, and their struggle to form new identities and loyalties against the backdrop of the disintegrating multinational Austro-Hungarian empire.[34] The captives' own experiences of encounters with Russian soldiers and civilians, or with Red Cross nurses who visited the camps, also helped to shape their somewhat idiosyncratic interpretation of unfolding events. As the war continued, loyalty to the emperor was increasingly overshadowed by the development of new social and national resentments, caused in large part by the material failure of the Austro-Hungarian relief effort. But the process of identity-formation was far less smooth or monolithic than was presented in conventional nationalist or communist historiographies after the war. For instance, it was also complicated by concerns of a personal or familial nature, and by attempts to redefine the relationship between citizen and state on the basis of contested notions of wartime 'commitment' and 'sacrifice'. In this way, Rachamimov is able to speak of a 'multiplicity of voices' among rank-and-file Habsburg prisoners, rather than a single, uniform experience.[35]

A further response to postmodernism has been the growth in transnational studies of the war. Rachamimov's work is again a prime example of this genre. Transnational in this context might mean physical movement across borders, or 'virtual' movement between different cultures and identities, or indeed both.[36] It might also involve challenging the traditional hegemony of the western front – or of the trench experience – in writings on the First World War. After all, many more soldiers were taken prisoner and many more civilians were deported or forced to flee during the course of the fighting in eastern Europe, Italy and the Balkans than in France and Belgium. Finally, rather than simply comparing the different fronts (including the home fronts), transnational history explores the many interactions and communications between them.[37] Indeed, it is arguable that the cultural history of captivity, forced labour and forced migration can only really be written from a transnational perspective, as all three involved interactions between individuals, communities and nations who were actively constituting themselves as both war victims *and* as participants in current and future wars or peace settlements.[38]

For instance, in his contribution to this volume, Peter Gatrell demonstrates that most refugees and forced migrants during the war did not actually move from one sovereign territory to another; rather, they remained subjects of the state which deported them or which had failed to protect them in the wake of foreign invasion. Yet even in these cases, refugeedom was very much about loss: loss of home, loss of land, loss of work or professional identity, in some instances loss of family or loss of faith too. On the other hand, the very fact of their displacement also brought refugees into contact with new ideas and new cultures. In central and eastern Europe it also led to a growing politicisation of the nationalities question, as different ethnic or national groups formed their own relief organisations in the face of the apparent inability of multinational states to look after them or to guarantee their swift repatriation after the war.

Those who did cross pre-war international borders, on the other hand, were often used in propaganda put out by their hosts. This could be seen, for instance, in the British condemnation of atrocities committed against 'gallant little Belgium', or the attempt by the Central Powers to recruit Ukrainian activists for the anti-Russian (and later anti-Bolshevik) cause.[39] Finally, refugeedom reinforced or helped to create new ethnic or national conflicts in post-war Europe. At Versailles in 1919, for instance, Italian negotiators repeatedly reinforced their claims to Fiume and parts of Dalmatia by claiming that the local Croat population was predominantly pro-Habsburg and pro-German and that it had collaborated in the expulsion and persecution of Italian-speaking minorities during the war. In the meantime, Croat nationalists in the disputed territories were subject to arbitrary imprisonment and deportations while, according to one British eyewitness account 'Italians only supplied food to those who signed a declaration of loyalty to Italy'.[40]

Some refugees and forced migrants also became in effect internees, forced to endure life behind barbed wire for the duration of the war and beyond. They thereby joined the ranks of hundreds of thousands of civilians who experienced captivity in one form or another in the years 1914–18. Indeed, as Matthew Stibbe shows in his essay, apart from the refugees who were dispersed to barrack camps in order to separate them from local populations, there were at least three different categories of civilian internee during the First World War. Of these enemy aliens, that is, nationals of enemy states caught on the opposing side's territory at the outbreak of war, usually enjoyed the best conditions because they were protected by the principle of reciprocity. As a rule, only men of military age were interned in this category. Some of them were also only technically aliens, having lived for many years (or even their entire lives) in the 'host' country and having married local women. Even so, they were often held in camps a long way from their homes and families, and visits, where they were allowed, were typically few and far between.

However, enemy aliens were a numerically much smaller group when compared to the mass of internees deported from or held in occupied territory as hostages, forced labourers or 'undesirables'. Often their families did not even know where they were, and all contact was thus completely severed. On top of this were those interned by their own governments as suspected spies or traitors, a fate which befell large numbers of Serb, Ruthenian and Italian subjects of the Austro-Hungarian empire, and equally large numbers of Jews, ethnic Germans and other minority nationalities in Russia. The suffering of the Serbs in particular was given widespread publicity by the London-based Serbian Relief Fund and in both the British and French press.[41] Yet as Daniel Segesser also shows in his contribution, less interest was shown in the West regarding the problems facing Russia's persecuted minorities and civilian deportees, at least until 1918.

Meanwhile, Christian Koller has looked at connections between the colonies and the western front by means of the example of some 650,000 Africans and Asians recruited by Britain and France for military deployment in Europe. As he shows, the presence of colonial troops on the battlefields of France and Belgium produced contradictory responses, both from the 'host' armies and communities on the Allied side, and from the opposing armies on the German side. Indeed, some of the racial prejudices against African soldiers in particular seemed to have transcended wartime divisions, only to reappear in a slightly different guise during the French occupation of the Rhineland in the 1920s. Yet the response of colonial soldiers themselves to their experience of contact with Europeans and European cultures was equally divided. Some North and West Africans violently resisted forcible conscription into the French army, for instance, while others were proud to fight for their colonial masters. Among African and Asian soldiers in the British army there were some who came home convinced of the supposed cultural superiority of European civilisation, and others who returned equally persuaded of the injustices of colonial rule.

Heather Jones, in her piece on prisoners of war, also draws attention to the way in which attitudes towards ethnicity and class helped to structure the policies adopted by belligerent states towards captured enemy combatants. Of these two factors, however, it was probably class that was applied more consistently and universally. Thus in virtually every scenario, with the exception of Bolshevik Russia after 1917, captured enemy officers were afforded privileges not usually granted to ordinary rank-and-file prisoners. Most crucially, officers were not required to work, meaning that boredom and depression, as opposed to hunger, physical exhaustion or exposure to life-threatening situations, was their main complaint. They were also more likely to be beneficiaries of the system of Red Cross parcel deliveries, and usually suffered milder punishments if caught attempting to escape. Class can also be seen as a key factor in Red Cross work itself. For instance, on the eastern front it was usually only women from aristocratic and diplomatic families who had the contacts and networks necessary to secure safe passage to visit camps in enemy territory.[42]

Ethnicity operated at a slightly different level. Certainly it was a factor in determining how captors perceived their prisoners, and vice versa, how prisoners viewed their captors. In Russia, in particular, those of Slavic nationality among the captured Habsburg soldiers were singled out for preferential treatment, while Germans and Hungarians were usually confronted with much worse conditions. This happened less often on the western front, where most of the prisoners taken did not belong to distinctive minority national or ethnic groups. Even so, the Germans had a special camp for Irish captives at Limburg, and the British had a similar camp for anti-Austrian Habsburg POWs at Feltham near London.

As Christian Koller's essay also emphasises, racist attitudes were commonplace throughout Europe at this time, and both sides in the war deployed racial imagery in their propaganda. German cartoonists and publicists in particular repeatedly accused Britain and France of having 'betrayed' the white race by deploying African and Asian troops on the western front.[43] The Allies in turn alleged that the Central Powers were deliberately stirring up the Islamic world against Russia and the West through their alliance with Turkey, although significantly the Armenian genocide of 1915 featured far less prominently in Allied propaganda than did the German atrocities in Belgium in 1914.[44] Meanwhile modern 'science' in the form of eugenics and 'racial hygiene' also sought to establish 'hierarchies of worth' according to supposedly 'objective' biological criteria. Often this went hand in hand with attempts to legitimise territorial expansion at the expense of 'inferior' peoples, whether Slavs and Turks in Europe or blacks and Asians overseas.[45]

Yet crucially – and in sharp contrast to the Second World War – such discourses had little impact on the actual treatment of prisoners. In practice, there was still a certain amount of room for individuality and personal choice, and some prisoners simply defied categorisation on the basis of mixed heritage, mixed marriages or mixed loyalties. Moreover, whereas class discrimination was encoded in international law, which dictated separate and superior treatment for officers, discrimination on grounds of nationality or ethnicity, where it did take place, appears to have been motivated largely by economic and political-strategic rather than racial considerations. In other words, the approach was largely utilitarian: those military prisoners who were deemed most likely to switch sides or to cause embarrassment to their home countries were treated accordingly, while those without 'political value' were more often seen from the vantage point of their 'labour potential'.[46]

Finally, Reinhard Nachtigal shows that the experience of POW repatriation also varied widely depending on which front and which identities (ethnic, class, political) an individual claimed or was deemed to have. The change of regime in Russia in October 1917 was especially important in this respect, as the new Bolshevik authorities henceforth discriminated against former POWs on class as opposed to ethnic lines. The Whites, on the other hand, continued to see Germans and Hungarians (as well as communists and Ukrainian nationalists) as their enemy. But again personal concerns could be equally important in determining an individual's fate. Thus some prisoners in Russia chose to stay where they were because they had got married or because they had been accepted by local people or communities. Others did not wish to return to countries in central Europe where they might now belong to an ethnic or national minority or be treated as 'traitors' or political suspects.

Many of the contributions to this volume have also been influenced, directly or indirectly, by the concept of 'war culture' developed by the Péronne school in France, named after the international research centre and museum, the Historial de la Grande Guerre, founded there in 1992. Thus, for scholars like Stéphane Audoin-Rouzeau and Annette Becker, the endless cycle of reprisals, confiscations, hostage-taking and arrests of French civilians by the German army after 1914 was a reflection of the war's 'brutalisation' of social relations and its 'successive breach of thresholds or degrees of violence'.[47] Conversely, in order to survive the experience of occupation, captivity, forced labour or deportation, it became necessary to hate the enemy – or at least to resist his advances.[48] This was made easier when governments – often for cynical purposes – issued sensationalist accounts of wartime atrocities which marked the enemy out as the embodiment of absolute evil and barbarity. Germans, quite simply, became 'the Hun', a brutal alien force determined to destroy the French (or British or Belgian) way of life.[49]

Such propaganda could be supported by the churches, political parties and leading figures from the academic and legal professions, as Daniel Segesser makes clear in his essay.[50] Yet it also had a wider, more popular basis within wartime societies. For instance, it could lead to public calls for reprisals and counter-reprisals, an issue also taken up Heather Jones in her contribution to this volume. Worse still, both on and off the battlefield real cases of unlawful violence against prisoners and unarmed enemy civilians were often overshadowed by internalised myths about the total depravity of the enemy-opponent, so that the violence itself was legitimised and became part of wartime (and post-war) normality. In Freiburg in south-west Germany, to take one example, city councillors were already pushing for the use of Allied POWs as human shields in 1915 in response to a series of targeted air raids on the city. The air raids themselves induced a great deal of fear and panic in the local population, partly because of their novelty (although they were still relatively limited in scope) and partly due to Freiburg's vulnerable position as a garrison town close to the front line in Alsace. In May 1917, after one particularly heavy raid, 250 British prisoners, mainly officers, were actually moved to a university-owned property close to the city centre, and the decision was made to keep this building well-lit at night, while the surrounding streets were subject to a compulsory blackout.[51] For Audoin-Rouzeau and Becker in particular, instances such as these are proof that the continual escalation of violence and accompanying hatred was 'moins un processus vertical d'endoctrine-ment des sociétés belligérantes par les cercles dirigeants qu'un processus horizontal, décentralisé, et relativement spontané d'automobilisation des "fronts intérieurs"' [less a vertical process based on the indoctrination of belligerent societies 'from above' and more a horizontal, decentralised process of relatively spontaneous self-mobilisation on the part of the home fronts themselves], although one might also add here that public opinion clearly interacted with and was influenced by official attitudes.[52] Society, in their view, never fully recovered from this 'total war' experience.

Even so, it is important to emphasise that war cultures were not always aggressive, 'totalising' or 'brutalising'. Prisoners' letters, for instance, or the development of a *Lagerkultur* in the form of camp theatres and magazines, were often more a way of communicating with the home front than aligning oneself directly with its values.[53] In some contexts *Lagerkultur* could be critical of, or at least moderately disrespectful towards, the dominant war culture of the home country. At other times it was purely escapist, or reflected the intimate concerns and internal squabbles of the camp inmates.[54] Letters written by families were also surprisingly free of bellicose or anti-enemy sentiment, as Odon Abbal has shown in his study of French prisoners in Germany.[55] Of course, as Heather Jones rightly reminds us, not all captives had access to the relative benefits of *Lagerkultur* or communications with home, particular those who worked away from the main camps in labour battalions. Prisoners who were forced to repair enemy fortifications and trenches on the front line while coming under shellfire from their own side probably had the most reason to hate their captors and to desire revenge, although only fragments of evidence survive to tell their tale.[56]

Forced migrants and refugees in various parts of Europe could equally be brutalised by their experiences, especially if they encountered a hostile reception from their host communities. In France, for instance, those who fled or were forcibly evacuated from the occupied zones were often referred to, disparagingly, as the 'boches du nord'.[57] Likewise in wartime Vienna, Jewish refugees from Galicia were faced with both official discrimination and popular hostility.[58] Yet as Peter Gatrell points out in his essay, 'the negative and demeaning image of refugeedom did not always prevail'. Indeed, in some cases, such as for Poles and Latvians displaced to various parts of the Russian empire following the German advances on the eastern front, or for Serbs driven into exile in the wake of the Habsburg and Bulgarian military occupations, the refugee experience could actually be a spur to new, more broadly-based and more confident forms of national consciousness.

Another important trend, running alongside and noticeably corresponding with the increasing violence of war, was the development of humanitarian aid programmes set up by international organisations like the Geneva-based International Committee of the Red Cross (ICRC), by national and local Red Cross societies, including those of neutral countries, and by religious or philanthropic bodies like the Quakers. As the majority of war refugees were women and children, and as many male POWs and civilian deportees had wives and children whom they could no longer support, it soon became clear that charities would have to organise themselves on an unprecedented level. Indeed providing aid (or work) for the female victims of war became a matter of priority on gender as well as humanitarian or national grounds for the many women's philanthropic groups dotted around Europe during and after the years 1914–18. Through their prominent role in national and international relief efforts women were also able, to some extent, to counteract the growing trend towards the 'rationalisation' of health care, social welfare provision and child protection in accordance with male interests and priorities as the war continued.[59]

Finally, this volume raises questions about the role of captivity, forced labour and forced migration in the process of cultural demobilisation after the war.[60] In some cases this process was relatively swift and smooth, while in others it was stymied by new national, ethnic or social hatreds. As Jones, Stibbe and Nachtigal all show, repatriation on the western front before 1918 was facilitated by diplomatic agreements which were quite generous in scope but which were slow to be implemented and subsequently abandoned under French pressure in November 1918. The withdrawal of German forces from northern France and Belgium in turn allowed the return of war refugees to these territories. Yet the French refusal to release former German POWs until the spring of 1920, and the decision to treat them instead as hostages and as a source of forced labour, created a new layer of tension and resentment. Meanwhile, even those soldiers or civilian internees on both sides who were released early, before the end of hostilities, could sometimes find that they were not very welcome when they got home, the stigma of having been a captive lasting well into the inter-war years.[61]

In post-war Austria, on the other hand, a bigger issue was what to do with refugees from the former war zones who had settled in various barrack camps or private dwellings in the hinterland and did not wish to leave. From the end of 1918 the new republic of Austria (Deutsch-Österreich) only recognised an obligation towards refugees of 'German nationality [and] Christian confession' and in March 1919 all welfare payments to non-German refugees were stopped. Even so, the republic's leaders were also conscious of the need to protect ethnic Germans in other parts of the former Habsburg empire, and were therefore anxious to make reciprocal arrangements for care and repatriation. In general, Italian, Slovene and Croat refugees left quite quickly, and relations with Italy and

Yugoslavia on these issues remained quite good. By contrast those from eastern Europe, especially Jews, Poles and Ukrainians stayed the longest, and they were joined, after 1918, by a fresh wave of people fleeing new wars and pogroms. Even so, the repatriation of large numbers of impoverished war refugees continued until 1922. This in turn led to tensions with many of Austria's former allies in the East, and with Poland in particular, which actively sought to prevent the return of Galician Jews.[62]

A further problem, which hardly assisted in the process of cultural demobilisation, was that of alleged war crimes. Here, as Daniel Segesser shows, there was no common transnational agreement as to what constituted a war crime, although the term was increasingly used in legal circles from 1918 onwards. Experts on international law in Allied countries were divided on the issue, some favouring a restricted definition which referred only to unlawful acts committed during the course of military operations, and others adopting a broader approach which took into account what happened to POWs once they had left the battlefield, and to civilians living under military occupation. After 1918 the Germans were in denial about the atrocities committed in Belgium and elsewhere, and were minded to see any attempt to put their fellow countrymen on trial as 'victors' justice'. Among the defendants at the war crimes trial held at the German Supreme Court in Leipzig in 1921 were men accused of deliberate mistreatment of prisoners of war; three of them were convicted and received short prison sentences. Yet significantly nobody was successfully prosecuted for crimes against civilian internees, deportees or refugees.

The essays which follow thus demonstrate the many contested meanings and interpretations that can be placed on the history of captivity, forced labour and forced migration during the First World War. In the public discourses of the day, these phenomena could be viewed through the lens of traditional state diplomacy, international law, military necessity, colonialism and race, the principle of reciprocity or the ideal of world revolution. They could be seen in the context of wartime violence, ethnic hatred and religious intolerance, or equally within the framework of humanitarian relief, democratic notions of citizenship and nation-state building. Understanding how the individuals, families and communities most directly affected were able to make sense of, and in some cases influence, what was happening to them, is perhaps the greatest challenge for historiography in this field. Yet what has come out of this volume in particular is (a) the importance of human agency and overlapping identities, loyalties and personal concerns in negotiating wartime experiences; and (b) the importance of enduring structures, ideas and social relations in determining the parameters of these experiences.

Or as Karl Marx once aptly wrote, men and women are capable of making their own history 'but not under conditions of their own choosing....'[63]

Acknowledgements

On behalf of all the contributors I would like to thank Jochen Oltmer for his detailed comments and suggestions on the individual essays in this volume. I would also like to express my particular gratitude to Peter Gatrell and Heather Jones for their critical and knowledgeable reading of an earlier draft of the introduction.

Notes

[1] Némirovsky, *Suite Française*, 141. For an excellent academic study of this period see also Diamond, *Fleeing Hitler*.

[2] Nivet, *Les réfugiés français*, esp. 15–16.

[3] ibid., 555.

[4] Mentzel, 'Weltkriegsflüchtlinge', 17–44.

[5] Mazower, *The Balkans*, 105–6; Marrus, *The Unwanted*, 44–8.

[6] Gatrell, *Russia's First World War*, 77.

[7] The phrase comes from the American diplomat and historian George F. Kennan who first used it in his study, *The Decline of Bismarck's European Order*, 3. See also Schulin, 'Die Urkatastrophe des zwanzigsten Jahrhunderts', 3–27.

[8] Several important collections on the First World War published in the 1990s made little or no reference to these groups. See, for example, Michalka, *Der Erste Weltkrieg*; Cecil and Liddle, *Facing Armageddon*; Kruse, *Eine Welt von Feinden*; Strachan, *World War I: A History*; and Keegan, *The First World War*. Only the pioneering work of Annette Becker in 1998, looking at occupied populations, particular in northern France, and the important studies of the Russian hinterland by Peter Gatrell and Eric Lohr in 1999 and 2003 respectively, have placed these issues more firmly on the historical agenda. See Becker, *Oubliés de la grande guerre*; Gatrell, *A Whole Empire Walking*; and Lohr, *Nationalizing the Russian Empire*. A more recent and important contribution has been Bianchi, *La violenza contro la popolazione civile*. Meanwhile, Niall Ferguson's highly acclaimed *The Pity of War* did include one chapter on POWs, but this was mainly focused on the act of surrender on the battlefield, not the experience of captivity itself. Indeed, in spite of a recent spate of monographs dealing with prisoners of war on particular fronts or in particular nations, historiography still awaits a comprehensive, transnational study of this phenomenon.

[9] Connes, *A POW's Memoir*.

[10] Gatrell, 'Introduction', 415.

[11] Some very good accounts can be found in Silber and Little, *The Death of Yugoslavia*; Honig and Both, *Srebrenica*; Simms, *Unfinest Hour*; and Giovanni, *Madness Visible*. See also Gertjejanssen, 'Sexual Violence', 358–64.

[12] Bideleux and Jeffries, *The Balkans*, 354–5.

[13] ibid., 569–70.

[14] See the entry on the 'India-Pakistan Wars (1965–1971)' in Vance, *Encyclopedia of Prisoners of War and Internment*, 192–3. Also Hobsbawm, *Globalisation, Democracy and Terrorism*, 18–19.

[15] 'The Gulf War (1990-1991)', in Vance, *Encyclopedia of Prisoners of War and Internment*, 168–9. See also Kushner and Cesarani, 'Conclusion and Epilogue', in Cesarani and Kushner, *The Internment of Aliens in Twentieth Century Britain*, 214.

[16] See bbc News, http://news.bbc.co.uk/1/hi/world/middle_east/4089961.stm (accessed 26 August 2008).

[17] Burleigh, *Sacred Causes*; and Hobsbawm, *Globalisation, Democracy and Terrorism*, 121–37.

[18] For a very useful collection of essays see Dunn and Fraser, *Europe and Ethnicity*. Studies focused on particular ethnic frontiers or border regions include Eisterer and Steininger, *Tirol und der Erste Weltkrieg*; Kramer, '*Wackes* at War', 105–22; Mazohl-Wallnig and Meriggi, *Österreichisches Italien – Italienisches Österreich?*; Wendland, *Die Russophilen in Galizien*; King, *Budweisers into Czechs and Germans*, esp. 114–52; Prusin, *Nationalizing a Borderland*; Kuprian and Überegger, *Der Erste Weltkrieg im Alpenraum*; Zahra, *Kidnapped Souls*, esp. 79–105. See also some of the contributions to Bianchi, *La violenza contro la popolazione civile*.

[19] Becker, *Oubliés de la grande guerre*; de Schaepdrijver, *De groote oorlog*; McPhail, *The Long Silence*; Liulevicius, *War Land on the Eastern Front*; Opfer, *Im Schatten des Krieges*; von Hagen, *War in a European Borderland*; Mitrović, *Serbia's Great War*; and Mayerhofer, 'Making Friends and Foes', 119–49.

[20] See the path-breaking work by Horne and Kramer, *German Atrocities 1914*. Also Kramer, 'Kriegsrecht und Kriegsverbrechen', 281–92; Jones, 'The Enemy Disarmed'; and the recent study by Pickles, *Transnational Outrage*.

[21] Bourke, *An Intimate History of Killing*. For Germany in particular, see Nelson, '"Ordinary Men" in the First World War?'.

[22] Ferguson, *The War of the World*; Hull, *Absolute Destruction*; Holquist, *Making War, Forging Revolution*; and Kramer, *Dynamic of Destruction*.

[23] Evans, *Mothers of Heroes, Mothers of Martyrs*; and Siebrecht, 'The Mater Dolorosa on the Battlefield', 259–91.

[24] Becker, 'Religion', 192–7. See also Becker, *War and Faith*.

[25] Audoin-Rouzeau, 'Kinder und Jugendliche', 135–41. See also Audoin-Rouzeau, *La guerre des enfants*, and, for the Second World War, Nicholas Stargardt's excellent study *Witnesses of War*.

[26] Particularly influential here was Marrus, *The Unwanted*, and a further collection of essays introduced by Marrus – Bramwell, *Refugees in the Age of Total War*. Important early studies on POWs and civilian internees include Davis, 'Deutsche Kriegsgefangene im Ersten Weltkrieg'; idem, 'The Life of Prisoners of War in Russia 1914–1921'; and Speed, *Prisoners, Diplomats and the Great War*.

[27] Hobsbawm, *Globalisation, Democracy and Terrorism*, 19–20.

[28] Carnegie Endowment for International Peace, *Report of the International Commission*, 15–16.

[29] Gatrell, 'Introduction', 416.

[30] See here two excellent collections of essays, Barkey and von Hagen, *After Empire*; and Roshwald, *Ethnic Nationalism and the Fall of Empires*.

[31] For one convincing illustration of this (among many others) see Wendland, 'Post-Austrian Lemberg'.

[32] Ziemann, *War Experiences in Rural Germany*, 9–10.

[33] Rachamimov, *POWs and the Great War*.

[34] Cf. the earlier study by Peter Hanák, 'Die Volksmeinung während des letzten Kriegsjahres', 58–66.

[35] Rachamimov, *POWs and the Great War*, 17.

[36] Or even movement across gender boundaries, as in the case of the men who took on female roles in camp theatre. See here Rachamimov, 'The Disruptive Comforts of Drag'.

[37] In this sense, Benjamin Ziemann's above-mentioned book *War Experiences in Rural Germany* might also be defined as a transnational study, in that it explores communications between Bavarian peasant communities and their compatriots fighting abroad as conscripts in occupied France and Belgium.

[38] For a useful set of essays which adopts this perspective, albeit within a much larger timeframe than the First World War, see Caucanas, Cazals and Payen, *Les prisonniers de guerre dans l' histoire*.

[39] Some of these Ukrainian intrigues during and after the war are dealt with in Snyder, *The Red Prince*.

[40] Cited in MacMillan, *Paris 1919*, 291. See also Afflerbach, '"... nearly a case of Italy contra mundum?"', 161.

[41] Mitrović, *Serbia's Great War*, 105. See also Peter Gatrell's contribution to this volume.

[42] See also Rachamimov, '"Female Generals" and "Siberian Angels"', 23–46.

[43] See, for example, Schütze, *Englands Blutschuld gegen die weiße Rasse*; and Stibbe, *German Anglophobia*, 38–43.

[44] Horne and Kramer, *German Atrocities 1914*, 296–7 and 528, n. 18.

[45] See Weindling, *Health, Race and German Politics*, 291–304. Also, more generally, Mosse, *Toward the Final Solution*.

[46] Running counter to this, as Mark Mazower argues in his recent book *Hitler's Empire*, is the case of occupied Europe during the Second World War, where the Nazi leadership put racial ideology very clearly above the rational exploitation of economic resources and local nationalisms.

[47] Audoin-Rouzeau and Becker, *1914–1918*, esp. 15–44. On the 'war culture' paradigm more generally, see also Purseigle, 'A very French debate'; and Winter and Prost, *The Great War in History*, 105 and 163–6.

[48] Audoin-Rouzeau and Becker, *1914–1918*, 102–3.

[49] Cf. Robert, 'Les prisonniers civils de la grande guerre'.

[50] For further evidence see Becker, 'Religion' and Jeismann, 'Propaganda'. Also Haste, *Keep the Home Fires Burning*; Buitenhuis, *The Great War of Words*; and Mommsen, *Kultur und Krieg*.

[51] Chickering, *The Great War*, 109 and 301. Miraculously none of these British hostages were killed in the ongoing air attacks. 31 German civilians nonetheless lost their lives. See also *The Great War*, 319.

[52] Audoin-Rouzeau and Becker, *La Grande Guerre*, 64. See also idem, *1914–1918*, 61–2 and 109–10.

[53] On prisoners' letters, see also Rachamimov, 'Arbiters of Allegiance', 157–77.

[54] This is one of the key findings of Stibbe, *British Civilian Internees in Germany*. For a comparative study of camp journals, which reaches similar conclusions, see also Pöppinghege, *Im Lager unbesiegt*.

[55] Abbal, *Soldats oubliés*, 176–9. Heather Jones nonetheless found a greater occurrence of bellicosity in letters sent from German families to German POWs in France in 1918, at least in the period until August to September of that year – see Jones, 'The Enemy Disarmed', 298–9.

[56] Audoin-Rouzeau and Becker, *1914–1918*, 77–9. On the brutal use of forced POW labour in similar conditions by the Russian and Austro-Hungarian armies respectively, see Nachtigal, *Russland und seine österreichisch-ungarischen Kriegsgefangenen*, 185; and Moritz, *Zwischen Nutzen und Bedrohung*, 121–7.

[57] Nivet, *Les réfugiés français*, esp. 377–421.

[58] See the evidence in Hoffmann-Holter, '*Abreisendmachung*'; Rechter, *The Jews of Vienna*; and Healy, *Vienna and the Fall of the Habsburg Empire*.

[59] See, for example, Rozenblit, 'For Fatherland and Jewish People', 199–220; and Stibbe, 'Elisabeth Rotten', 194–210. On the 'rationalisation' of welfare and the gendered and other conflicts this produced see Weindling, *Health, Race and German Politics*, 284–90; and Hong, 'World War I and the German Welfare State', 345–69.

[60] On cultural demobilisation see Historial de la Grande Guerre,'Démobilisations culturelles après la Grande Guerre', esp the intrdouction by John Horne, 45–53.

[61] Cf. Connes, *A POW' s Memoir*; and Abbal, *Soldats oubliés*, esp. 197–252. Also Pöppinghege, "Kriegsteilnehmer zweiter Klasse"?

[62] Hoffmann-Holter, '*Abreisendmachung*', esp. 143–59.

[63] Karl Marx. 'Der 18. Brumaire des Louis Napoleon' (1852). Klassiker des Marxismus-Leninismus, http://www.ml-werke.de/marxengels/me08_115.htm. (Accessed 26 August 2008).

A Missing Paradigm? Military Captivity and the Prisoner of War, 1914–18

Heather Jones

Department of International History, London School of Economics and Political Science, UK

The First World War is often understood in terms of familiar paradigms: western front trench stalemate; the brutalisation of millions of conscript soldiers; the totalisation of industrial warfare or the mass mobilisation of societies. Each of these structural processes played a role in determining the evolution of the conflict and marked an important break with the pre-1914 world. They also established new continuities: if, as the historian Omer Bartov has argued, the First World War marked *the* key moment in the development of mass, industrialised violence that facilitated the later conflict of 1939–45, then the central paradigms that framed the earlier war of 1914–18 take on an additional significance as precedents.[1] Given this context, it remains remarkable that one of the most significant paradigms of the First World War has long been overlooked – mass military captivity.

Captivity and prisoner camps still represent under-researched themes in First World War studies. It is only in the last 10 years that historians have studied captivity in any detail, and despite groundbreaking works by Annette Becker and Odon Abbal on French prisoners held by Germany, and studies by Uta Hinz and Jochen Oltmer on the German camp system, there is still no overall assessment of the way that captivity affected popular understandings of the nature of modern war or the new link that the conflict established between the existence of a 'camp' network and national security.[2] The existing historiography on prisoners of war also remains largely divided between the two principal war fronts: despite pioneering research by Reinhard Nachtigal and Alon Rachamimov into captivity on the eastern front, there is still no overview of the continual wartime process of cultural transfer that existed between eastern front and western front belligerents in relation to captivity.[3] In fact, only one historian – Richard

Speed – has attempted a comparative study of the wartime diplomatic exchanges that took place concerning prisoners.[4]

Yet, why does this missing paradigm matter? What does the experience of the prisoner of war tell us about the conflict and the precedents that it set? This contribution will attempt to sketch some preliminary answers to these questions through an overview of prisoner of war treatment – all the time bearing in mind that the sheer scale of captivity during the war makes generalisations difficult and that there is no facile, direct teleological link between the camps of 1914–18 and those of later years, but rather a series of fluctuating connections and disjunctions. It will first outline the dramatic, new mass scale of the prisoner of war phenomenon during the war; second, it will assess what common parameters existed that determined the nature of captivity and finally, it will draw some tentative conclusions about the precedents that the Great War set for the inter-war period and after.

Scale

Captivity took place on an unprecedented scale during the First World War. It entailed the indefinite confinement of millions of enemy combatants, necessitating the development of newly rationalised prisoner of war systems in belligerent countries. As the historian Alon Rachamimov has pointed out, an estimated 8.5 million soldiers were taken prisoner, 'roughly one out of every nine men in uniform', which was 'only slightly less' than the estimated 9–10 million soldiers who were killed in the conflict.[5] The vast majority of these men were taken prisoner on the eastern front, where a war of movement contributed to producing enormous numbers of captives. The disparity between eastern and western front capture rates was highly significant, mirrored in the huge variation between the number of captives held by individual belligerent states: Austria-Hungary and Germany between them captured approximately half of the war's total prisoners. Germany had captured an estimated 2.4 million prisoners in total by October 1918; the figures for the total number of prisoners of war held by Austria-Hungary vary between 1.2 and 1.86 million.[6] Russia, in turn, took 2.1 million Austro-Hungarian troops prisoner.[7] On the Italian front, mass capture also occurred, most famously at the battle of Caporetto: in total, during the war, some 600,000 Italians were taken prisoner by the Germans and Austro-Hungarians, of whom over 100,000 died in captivity.[8] In contrast, western front capture rates were lower: the French had captured 392,425 Germans *in total* by the end of the war, approximately 40% of whom entered into captivity in 1918 alone; the British took 328,020 German prisoners in the whole conflict.[9] Although atrocities against prisoners at the moment of capture did occur, the scale of battlefield shootings of captives is impossible to gauge in the absence of any systematic study.[10] Suffice to say that the large numbers captured during the war implies that prisoner-taking was generally the norm rather than the exception; however, as Niall Ferguson has pointed out 'the numbers involved mattered less than the perception that surrender was risky', a perception that stemmed from those real incidents where prisoners were killed on the battlefield.[11]

However, capture rates were strikingly low in certain specific cases, often due to different front conditions or cultural attitudes to surrender and captivity. For example, few German troops on the eastern front fell into Russian hands – between 167,000 to 170,000 found themselves in Russian captivity; the death rate among these men has been estimated at 20%.[12] Only 60,000 Ottoman troops were taken prisoner by Russia.[13] Few black prisoners appear in German prison camp sources. However, the overall number of black African, Arab and Indian colonial troops held prisoner in German camps throughout the war remains unknown. At its peak, the special prisoner of war camp at Wünsdorf near Zossen, known as the *Halbmondlager* (crescent moon camp), which was designated for British and French colonial troops, held approximately 4,000 prisoners, the majority of whom were Muslims.[14]

The differences in capture rates between fronts, in turn, shaped the national breakdown of prisoners in each country. Eastern front captives predominated in German camps: there were 1,434,529 Russian prisoners in German captivity; the number of British and French captives in German hands is acknowledged to have been far lower.[15] The most realistic estimates are those of the French Deputy Gratien Candace of 520,579 French prisoners captured by Germany, and the *Statistics of the Military Effort of the British Empire during the Great War, 1914–1920*, which calculated 175,624 British prisoners.[16] Despite their numerical preponderance, however, little research has been carried out on Russian prisoners in Germany using Russian archive sources.[17]

The huge number of prisoners captured during the opening months of the war came as a shock to many military and government officials: no country was prepared for mass captivity and all improvised, some more effectively than others. The British were unsure of what to do – one Admiralty minute looked to 'the French war at the commencement of the last century' for its precedent, in the expectation that prisoners would be exchanged.[18] Britain used ships to house additional prisoners of war; the French adapted old fortresses and barracks.[19] Many of these were quite spartan: at Lourdes, German prisoners initially slept on straw on the bare floor of a fortress.[20] All countries used cattle wagons to transport other rank prisoners – this made for an uncomfortable journey, particularly for wounded captives, and in Germany and France in 1914 prisoners were mobbed by hostile civilian crowds.[21] In Britain, such incidents were extremely rare in 1914; however, similar civilian violence towards German prisoners of war and civilian internees broke out in 1915 in the UK, after the sinking of the Lusitania.[22]

Germany and Austria-Hungary – with their massive numbers of eastern front captives in 1914 – were among the least successful at improvising a response to the situation: conditions in their camps in the winter of 1914 and the spring of 1915 were deplorable. In some cases prisoners had to sleep in open fields until they had finally built their own prisoner of war camps. According to one prisoner, Sennelager camp in September 1914 was

> an open field enclosed with wire . . . there were no tents or covering in it of any kind. There were about 2,000 prisoners in it - all British. We lay on the ground with only one blanket for three men.[23]

An escaped French prisoner, Adjutant Lucien Debond described Minden camp in September 1914 as follows:

> 13,000 prisoners, the majority from Maubeuge and also civilians from Amiens, were interned at Minden. Arriving on 11 September the prisoners were parked in a camp without any shelter . . . The men had to sleep on the wet soil in the rain, almost all without straw and many without blankets. This lasted eight days. The prisoners were then allowed to construct little shelters out of the earth, built with no tools other than iron bars [knives having been confiscated]. This situation lasted until 24 September when we were transferred into buildings made from planks. From 11 September until 24 September the prisoners had to cope with severe cold . . . some had frozen feet and others died.[24]

Overcrowding was common in the early Central Power prisoner of war camps, as well as in Russia; it was not until mid-1915 that most camps in Austria-Hungary and Germany had proper accommodation facilities, and even later in the case of Russia.

Not surprisingly sanitation was inadequate in these conditions, leading to a massive typhus epidemic in German and Austro-Hungarian camps in the spring of 1915. Thirty major German prisoner of war camps were affected between January and July 1915. These were mostly located in north Germany.[25] In March 1915, when the epidemic peaked, some 11,862 British, French, Russian and Belgian prisoners in Germany had the disease according to post-war German estimates; in total in the whole epidemic some 44,732 prisoners of war in Germany caught typhus.[26] To place this in perspective, by June 1915, Germany had captured an estimated 848,556 prisoners.[27] At the very least, therefore, the overall infection rate among prisoners can be estimated at 5.27%. In some camps the situation was particularly bad: at Cottbus camp between January and May 1915, 6,509 prisoners out of 9,400 fell ill.[28] The total number of prisoner deaths is not known, but mortality rates for individual camps were often very high in Germany and Austria-Hungary: for example, in Mauthausen camp in Austria-Hungary in January 1915, up to 186 prisoners a day died of typhus.[29] Serious typhus epidemics also broke out in Russian camps in 1915 due to overcrowding and inadequate sanitation; there was a particularly high death rate during the epidemic at Tockoe camp in the winter of 1915–16.[30]

Not only do accurate statistics on typhus deaths remain elusive, total prisoner of war death rates for the whole war are also uncertain for most countries: in the German case, in particular, estimates vary greatly. For example, between 17,000 and 38,000 French prisoners died in German captivity; in comparison, approximately 25,000 German prisoners died in France and 9,349 in British captivity.[31] Death rates also varied during different periods of the war and between different nationalities – even those held within the same captor state. For example, in the case of Germany, the annual death rate recorded in 1915 for Indian prisoners held in the special colonial prisoner camp at Wünsdorf was particularly dramatic at 16.8%.[32] Of the different nationalities in German captivity, Romanian prisoners had the highest death rate, estimated at 29%.[33] Other nationalities' overall death rates in German captivity were far lower: the German official historian Wilhelm Doegen calculated the mortality rate among British prisoners in Germany at 2.98%, and that for Germany's Italian prisoners at 5.68%.[34] However, these rates too have recently been queried: Mark Spoerer, in a demographic analysis, pointed out that mortality rates among British and Italian prisoners were actually particularly high if measured according to the length of time spent in German captivity, as the large majority of British and Italian prisoners were only captured in 1917 or 1918.[35]

Overall, across Europe, prisoner death tolls were high in eastern countries: Russia (17.6%); Serbia (25%), Romania (23%) and Turkey (13%).[36] For prisoners taken at Gallipoli or in Mesopotamia conditions were particularly difficult: British soldiers captured by the Ottoman army at Kut-al-Amara in modern day Iraq in 1915 were forced on a veritable death march. Of the 2,500 British troops captured, 1,750 died; of their 9,300 Indian comrades, 2,500 perished.[37] Little is known about the fate of the survivors and their subsequent captivity; a handful of post-war memoirs testify to very poor conditions and high levels of captor brutality.[38] A comparable horrific march was endured in Europe the same year, when the Serb army, forced to retreat across the mountains of Albania to the Adriatic sea, took some 20,000 Austro-Hungarian prisoners of war with it: one prisoner described the route as 'strewn with the bodies of prisoners who died of cold and hunger'.[39] These prisoners were eventually transferred to the custody of the Italians, who transported them to the uninhabited island of Asinara off the coast of Sardinia; between 1,500 and 7,000 died from typhus and cholera.[40] In turn, Serbs in Austro-Hungarian captivity endured very poor conditions: at least 30,000 to 40,000 had died of starvation by January 1918.[41]

If the huge number of combatants who found themselves deprived of liberty during the First World War was remarkable, the geographical scale of captivity was no less impressive. It is no exaggeration to state that a network of militarised prisoner of war and civilian internment camps was established across the world. Prisoner of war camps were to be found in locations as far flung as Utah in the United States, Templemore in Ireland, Achinsk in Siberia, and Bando in Japan – where the German soldiers captured after the fall of Tsingtau in China were held.[42] The colonial division of the globe contributed to this process: there was a network of French camps for German combatant prisoners of war across Morocco, Tunisia and Algeria by 1915, as well as a notorious internment camp for German civilians located in Dahomey; similarly, there were British camps for Turkish prisoners of war in Palestine, as well as British internment camps for German civilians in Africa and India, most notably at Ahmadabad. Conditions in North Africa were particularly difficult for German prisoners: those exchanged from North Africa to France in 1916 were suffering from anaemia, due to malaria and the almost total lack of red meat in their diet.[43] Some were repatriated with eye damage from the sun.[44] Almost all of the German prisoners sent to North Africa caught malaria.[45] The Austro-Hungarian army had special punishment camps for prisoners of war in occupied Albania and Montenegro where conditions were particularly bad. There were also prisoner of war camps in Romania, Turkey and Italy during the war – their history remains to be told.[46] The chronological span of prisoner of war camps was also significantly greater than that of the actual conflict – many prisoners of war were only repatriated from camps in France and Russia in 1920 or 1921–22; in the case of Russia many prisoners found themselves caught up in the Russian civil war – most famously Czech captives who formed their own autonomous fighting legion.[47]

In sum, the First World War marked the advent of captivity on a scale and a duration that were utterly unprecedented. The defensive techniques that were used to divide the battlefield and keep the enemy confined to his side of no-man's land – barbed wire, machine-gun emplacements and sentries – were all also rapidly adapted to create and enable a new landscape of captivity that emerged to confine the enemy within the camp. The majority of large prisoner of war camps built during the war were fortified sites, as closely associated symbolically with barbed wire during the war as the trenches were – hence the name *Stacheldrahtkrankheit* or 'Barbed-Wire-Disease' which was given to the particular form of depression which emerged among prisoners during the conflict.[48] Although by 1916, in Russia, Germany and France many prisoners were lodged in small working units near their place of employment, almost all spent some of their captivity in one of the new fortified main camps – known as *Stammlager* in Germany and Austria-Hungary. Military historians have long blamed the stalemate trench warfare of the First World War on the precocious development of defensive battlefield techniques at the expense of offensive methods; yet the corollary of this process, the fact that it enabled states and armies to create internal 'defensive' sites where large numbers of people could be held securely, has been overlooked. As on the battlefield, prisoners found that it was very difficult to develop effective offensive measures in response – the escape from the well-guarded prison camp proved extremely difficult. Although escape attempts were generally relatively mildly punished during the First World War, only a small minority succeeded in carrying them out. However, escapes remained a fundamental part of captivity mythology and later memoirs; aspiring to escape, allowed prisoners, confined in the domesticated, uniformly male, home front camp to project a sense of agency and masculinity.[49]

To some extent the camp led to a cultural disjunction: prisoners entered captivity with a proactive, virile image of soldierly masculinity, which jarred with the reality of the long-term passivity of forced imprisonment. Techniques such as floodlighting, watch towers and guard dogs modernised and rationalised the captivity landscape to an unprecedented degree, creating a series of identical, anonymous prison camp structures across Europe. In the face of this mass, uniform camp world, the individual prisoner had become anonymous, faceless; ultimately, only through the escape aspiration or attempt could a real sense of personal agency and difference be regained. In the absence of escape, however, some prisoners were able to maintain a certain level of activity and empowerment by organising cultural events such as theatre plays, concerts, religious festivals or language courses; some even produced prison camp newspapers.[50] Captives often displayed incredible levels of ingenuity and creativity in improvising this kind of camp culture; however, such activities were effectively limited to the larger, well-resourced prison camps or to officer prisoners. The increasingly harsh exploitation of prisoner labour as the war continued made it difficult for the average captive to participate in any kind of leisure events.

Parameters

Within this process of modernisation and rationalisation, it is possible to identify several key structural parameters which defined First World War captivity. The first was pre-war international law, which established the standard cultural expectations of both captors and prisoners alike, throughout Europe. As part of an overall intensification of international humanitarian activity during the late nineteenth and early years of the twentieth century, important advances had been made in international law to improve the treatment of combatants taken prisoner in war. In 1864, the first Geneva Convention had established the principle that belligerents had a duty to care for the wounded enemy on the battlefield; a second Geneva Convention was approved in 1906.[51] Most significantly, in 1907, the Hague Convention on Land Warfare set out norms for the treatment of military combatants taken prisoner. It stipulated that prisoners of war were to be treated humanely; they were not to be robbed of personal possessions, officer prisoners were not to be made work and other rank prisoners were not to be employed on work directly connected with their captor state's war effort.[52] Moreover, prisoners were to be paid a salary and were to be fed, clothed and housed to the same standard as the captor nation's own troops.[53] The existence of the Geneva and Hague Conventions meant that for the first time, there was a shared international legal framework, albeit rudimentary, for prisoner treatment; however, there was no means of punishing breaches of international law, which led to nations, in practice, falling back upon reprisals or settling prisoner treatment through bilateral wartime agreements with the enemy, such as the Hague Agreements of June 1917 and July 1918 between Germany and Britain or the two wartime Berne Accords between France and Germany. The Berne Accords were agreed too late in the war to have a significant impact – the second was only signed in April 1918.

Throughout the war there was a disjunction between the universal aspirations set out in international law and the reality on the ground; interim bilateral wartime agreements did little to rectify this. Instead, states opted for reprisals as a means of influencing enemy behaviour, resulting in an almost

constant sequence of reprisal actions against prisoners. Most reprisal cycles
were petty but a handful escalated into severe violence. An example of minor
reprisals occurred in 1915, when Britain segregated 39 German submarine
crew captured on the U-8 and U-12 in naval detention barracks rather than
in prisoner of war camps, in retaliation against the German conduct of
submarine warfare; Germany responded by placing 39 British officer
prisoners of war in solitary confinement, forcing Britain to abandon the
segregation policy.[54] From this point on, the reprisals dynamic within
prisoner diplomacy between the western front powers escalated dramatically.
In April 1916, Germany sent 30,000 French prisoners of war to Courland,
located in modern day Latvia, where they were kept in horrendous
conditions, in a reprisal to force the French to remove German prisoners
from their camps in North Africa; the reprisal worked and the German
prisoners were evacuated to France.[55] Germany also sent British prisoners to
Courland as part of a reprisal to ensure better working conditions for
German prisoners held by Britain in France.[56] In another reprisal cycle, the
French placed German officers on board hospital ships in reprisal for
German unrestricted submarine warfare in 1917.[57] In January of the same
year, the German army launched its most extreme reprisal sequence in
retaliation for poor French treatment of German prisoners who were being
forced to work on the battlefield at Verdun; it ordered that all newly captured
French other rank prisoners be kept behind the lines to carry out heavy
labour under shellfire on inadequate rations.[58] These reprisals were soon
expanded to include British prisoners as well, until the British and French
gave way and withdrew all their German prisoner workers to an agreed
distance of 30 kilometres behind the front. By 1917, there was considerable
support for extreme reprisals against prisoners in Germany; only the
socialists dissented from the policy in the Reichstag.[59] Thus the inadequacies
of international law were frequently compensated for by using a very highly
developed system of reprisals that became increasingly extreme during the
conflict.

The second key parameter that played a major role in how prisoners
were treated was class. It was taken as a given in the Europe of 1914–18
that men from the upper and middle classes, who were identified with the
military rank of officer, should not experience the kind of mass captivity
that was the norm for ordinary working-class or peasant soldiers. In all the
belligerent countries, officer prisoners were privileged, sent to relatively
comfortable small-scale camps and provided with ordinary soldiers from
their own country to act as their servant orderlies. This special status of
officer captives was even enshrined in international law: under the Hague
Convention of 1907, officer prisoners of war were exempt from the

obligation to work for their captor country, whereas other rank prisoners could be made to work in return for payment. In addition, officers enjoyed better accommodation, postal rights, food and pay than the ordinary rank and file soldier prisoner. Officer prisoners' understanding of imprisonment was thus far from representative: for example, on 1 August 1916, of the 1,625,000 prisoners held by Germany, only 19,000 (1.17%) were actually in officers' camps.[60] Despite this, after the war, officers' memoirs predominated: their accounts frequently determined the historical image of captivity. This masked the fact that the rank that a man held upon capture was a significant factor that determined his overall captivity treatment and lifestyle. Thus an older class culture was embedded in the newly developing mass, rationalised prison camp system.

The third defining parameter that determined captivity in all the belligerent states was the need for additional wartime workers, which led to a dramatic increase in the use of forced labour across Europe. This need was particularly acute in the Central Power states, which had no access to colonial resources; they rapidly mobilised prisoner labour in support of their war effort: by the second half of 1915, 60–70% of Austria-Hungary's prisoners of war were no longer held in camps but were living in work *Kommandos* – small units of prisoners sent to work in agriculture or industry.[61] In Germany, the situation was similar: by 1 August 1916, 90% of Germany's 1.6 million prisoners of war had been put to work – over 750,000 in agriculture and over 330,000 in industry.[62] By 1918, prisoners made up 16% of all miners in the Ruhr district.[63] This mobilisation involved a certain amount of localised violence to force recalcitrant captives to cooperate: as Paul Reusch, the Director of the *Gutehoffnung-shütte Aktiengesellschaft* in Oberhausen wrote, the employment of prisoners of war would be impossible if one stuck to the instructions given by the Prussian Ministry of War:

> We are in the position that we do what we consider necessary. Therefore, if a prisoner will not comply, we let him go hungry for two to three days without seeking any further instructions. This occurs with the silent approval of the military administration. It is naturally a breach of the Hague Agreement. The military administration is, however, delighted when we can enforce a little order onto the men in this way.[64]

Beating was relatively common in Germany whenever other rank prisoners tried to refuse to work for the captor state.[65] More generally, in all belligerent countries, prisoners were subject to the military law of the captor army which usually entailed some degree of corporal punishment – given this coercive legal context they had little choice but to comply.

In France, prisoner labour was also seen as essential: the captive rapidly came to be identified in terms of his value as a worker. This paralleled the increased employment of prisoners: by 18 March 1916, out of a total of some 89,841 prisoners in French captivity, there were 66,985 working on the French home front, of whom 15,997 were working in agriculture, 13,872 on transport projects, 4,654 in quarries and 1,639 in mines.[66] The rest were employed in engineering, munitions, public work projects or within the prisoner of war camps themselves, or were exempt from work due to their officer status, war injuries or sickness. Throughout Europe, the language used to describe prisoners became more utilitarian; euphemisms such as 'labour resource' or 'work units' abounded. Georges Cahen-Salvador, the Director of the Prisoner of War Service at the French Ministry for War, described the French shift in attitude in the following terms:

> German prisoners were at first considered as hostages: they were disarmed enemies whose life was matched against that of our compatriots who had fallen into the power of the enemy. Then, as the French nation progressively needed more workers, and the industries necessary for national defence had to be developed, the prisoners appeared as a permanent reserve to supplement the insufficient manual labour available. It was necessary to combine the rigours of a hard regime, imposed to obtain an improvement in the German regime for French prisoners, with the interests of French national production ... In 1914 the prisoner was merely a hostage, in 1915 and 1916 he became a tool and everything possible had to be put in train to render it productive.[67]

In contrast, Britain was remarkably slow to employ its prisoners of war in the United Kingdom – this was in no small part due to the opposition of the trade unions who feared prisoner labour would undercut the wages of British workers.[68] However, from 1916 on, Britain began to employ prisoners of war in agriculture, quarries and factories in the UK, as well as on military work for the British army in France. However, the number of prisoners employed *within* Britain remained small, in comparison to Germany or France: in September 1916, only 3,832 prisoners were working within the United Kingdom; as late as 12 May 1918, there were only 43,140 German prisoners allocated to different economic sectors, and of these only 30,480 had actually commenced work.[69] The largest number of prisoners – 9,300 – was working in agriculture; 8,850 were working in building, 3,360 in quarries, 3,250 on timber work and 2,350 on Royal Engineering tasks.[70] The remainder were manufacturing cement or working on road building. Unlike the German and the French cases, none of these prisoners was engaged in directly manufacturing munitions.

Overall, they represented a fraction of British-held German prisoners as, in reality, by 1918, the vast majority of other rank German prisoners captured by the British army were retained to work in France.

This fact illustrates one of the most significant aspects of prisoner labour during the war: the development of a dual prisoner of war camp system within a significant number of the major belligerent states – France, Germany, Britain and Austria-Hungary. In these countries, captivity was divided into two distinct systems: on the one hand, the home front camp and working unit network, and, on the other, a largely separate system of army-run prisoner of war labour companies which remained at or near the front area as a permanent labour force, working directly for armies.[71] Prisoners of war within an army labour company system were generally treated differently from those held within the home front prisoner of war network of camps and working units, and experienced a more difficult, isolated and less regulated captivity.

The prisoner of war labour company system was a direct product of the First World War. Prisoner of war labour companies were first established in the German army in 1915 using Russian prisoners captured in the east.[72] This was the first such use of prisoners of war by any army on the western front: British and French prisoner of war labour companies were only established in 1916.[73] On 22 September 1915, the German Chief of Staff announced that prisoner of war labour companies were to be used in the army zone:

> Over the coming period several prisoner of war labour battalions (each made up of 4 companies of 500 men with 1 *Landsturm* Company as guards) will be established on a trial basis. These battalions are to be set to work on non-military work (building camps and roads, agricultural work etc.). Prisoners already being used on this work … are to be organised and their number and location is to be reported.[74]

This German prisoner of war labour company system rapidly expanded: the stipulation that restricted labour company work to Russian captives was lifted and prisoner of war labour companies from spring 1917 on included French and British prisoner labourers; by 1917, Italian prisoners were also to be found working for the German army on the western front. The number of prisoners employed in these army labour companies was significant: in February 1916, an appendix to the new Reichstag Memorandum on the Economic Measures taken by the Bundesrat, stated that 'some 250,000' prisoners were employed along lines of communication.[75] By August 1916, of the 1,625,000 prisoners of war in German hands, 253,000 were working in areas behind the lines.[76] This represented 16% of the total number of prisoners held by Germany.[77] The situation was relatively similar in the Austro-Hungarian case: in spring 1917, according to figures calculated by Generaloberst Samuel Baron Hazai, Chef des Ersatzwesens, there were 295,000 prisoners working directly for the Austro-Hungarian army in prisoner of war labour companies.[78] As early as autumn 1915, the decision was taken not to allow information about these prisoners' death rates or sickness rates to be made public; by 1918, the Austro-Hungarian Ministry of War had itself stopped keeping a record of accurate statistics on prisoner deaths.[79]

In comparison, the British first established permanent prisoner of war labour companies in France in April 1916, diverting some 1,500 German prisoners of war from the UK to work in Rouen and Le Havre.[80] These British prisoner of war labour companies were created as part of a Franco-British deal, brokered by Albert Thomas, French Under-Secretary of State for Munitions, to ease congestion in French ports.[81] The British would provide a small number of prisoners to work loading and unloading French ships. In exchange the French gave the British army access to forests and quarries which helped it to overcome a tonnage crisis in spring 1916, caused by German submarine warfare and the difficulties of bringing wood and stone to the British army from the UK.[82] To exploit these forests and quarries the British government decided to form further German prisoner of war labour companies. This was formally approved by the Army Council on 11 August 1916. It stipulated that it had no objections to establishing further prisoner of war labour companies in France, provided that 'the prisoners are not employed within range of the enemy artillery and are in no case called on for any work in connection with defence or to handle munitions of war'.[83] The head of the Prisoner of War Department at the War Office, Sir Herbert Belfield also emphasised these restrictions, stating: 'I am not clear what employment at "railhead" involves. It should be clearly laid down that these prisoners shall not handle munitions'.[84] This insistence on where prisoners could work, and what tasks they could perform, was emphatic and reveals that the Army Council was keen to remain within the boundaries of international law. The British use of German prisoner labour in France rapidly expanded: by 5 October 1916, there were 28 prisoner of war labour companies and a depot company in France employing 12,300 prisoners.[85] Towards the end of the war, in October 1918, there were 303 prisoner of war labour companies comprising some 160,065 German prisoners.[86] A month later, German prisoners accounted for 44% of the British Expeditionary Force (BEF) labour force.[87]

The French introduced prisoner of war labour companies at the same time as the British, following two key decisions made by the French

Ministry of War in May 1916. The first, based on the argument that the Germans were already doing the same, rescinded the restriction, stipulated in the Hague Convention, that prisoners of war could not be employed on work directly connected to the war effort; prisoners were promptly employed to make munitions in France.[88] The second decision was that 'a certain proportion of the German prisoners would work directly for the French army at or near the front in the *Zone des Armées*, on a permanent basis, working on road building, railway lines and other tasks under the command of the *Direction de l'Arrière* at General Headquarters'.[89] The *Direction de l'Arrière* (DA) was the section that controlled operations in the area directly behind the front lines. On 10 May 1916, it requested that labour battalions be created from prisoners of war to work on urgent tasks in the *Zone des Armées*.[90] The Ministry for War in Paris agreed; on 23 May 1916, 10,600 prisoners were placed at the disposition of the Commander in Chief of the French army, who allocated them to the DA.[91] The order that these prisoners be formed into prisoner of war labour companies was issued on 9 June 1916.[92] Each company was to be made up of 400 workers, with 25 additional company workers and non-commissioned officers (NCOs), resulting in a total of 425 prisoners.[93] Prisoner labourers were to be paid 20 centimes a day in the form of vouchers or *bons* which could be exchanged for extra food or smoking materials.[94] The first of these prisoner of war labour companies were set to work on quarries, and on roads.[95] The numbers of Germans thus employed rapidly increased. By 26 January 1917, 22,915 German prisoners were working in the French prisoner of war labour companies, 5,978 of which worked for the 2nd Army at Verdun.[96]

Thus by spring 1917 there were a considerable number of prisoners of war who never left the war zone: an estimated 545,000 for the German and Austro-Hungarian armies by spring 1917 alone and at least 35,215 for the British and French by January 1917, numbers which increased rapidly. These captives, all other rank prisoners, sent straight into prisoner of war labour companies after their capture, formed an enormous labour resource, one which has been virtually ignored by historians. They also illustrated the extent to which the prisoner had become integrated into the captor's military operation and army command structure. In each case, the development of prisoner of war labour companies led to a deterioration in prisoner treatment as little effort was made to regulate army use of this labour: prisoners in labour companies were often forced to work on tasks directly connected with the captor state's war effort, such as unloading shells or digging defences; there were numerous incidents where they were forced to work under shellfire. In the German army by 1918, they were subject to frequent beatings and long hours: 12–14 hour days were not uncommon; malnutrition among these prisoners was also a major problem throughout 1918.[97] In the French army too, labour company prisoners were subject to harsh physical punishments: an order from 15 September 1916, in the French 2nd Army stated that:

> Any act of kindness, any show of consideration for a *Boche* prisoner is an act of culpable weakness and will be severely punished by commanders. Every fault by a prisoner must be punished with the utmost harshness; the punishment must be immediate and without pity. The following punishments will apply:
>
> 1st fault: dry bread for the midday meal
>
> 2nd fault: dry bread for both meals
>
> 3rd fault: 2 hours tied to a pole [*au Poteau*]
>
> 4th fault: 4 hours tied to a pole in two parts – two hours in the morning, two hours in the evening.
>
> 5th fault: in cases where prisoners try to escape, sentries or any officer can shoot at them without any warning.[98]

In other cases, German prisoners working for the French army were employed under shellfire on the Verdun battlefield. An internal French army report stated:

> It is certain that in the 2nd Army the prisoners are employed under fire ... the following losses have occurred in Prisoner Labour Company number 53: 30 November 1916: 12 killed and 5 wounded at Faubourg Pavé at Verdun. 12 December 1916: 5 wounded at Tavannes. 24 December 1916: 1 killed and 1 wounded at Douaumont.[99]

In the absence of accurate statistics, and further research, it remains impossible to estimate the total number of prisoners who died while working in the new prisoner of war labour company system in Europe during the war. In contrast to prisoner of war camps and work units on the home front, which were monitored by governments, neutral countries and international humanitarian organisations, prisoner labour companies were under the absolute control of armies alone. Deaths or abuses were often not reported. For example, in the initial post-war period the statistics on prisoner deaths provided by the German government only counted the deaths of prisoners in camps in Germany proper – those who died in labour companies in the occupied territories and the zone of operations were excluded. In addition, the German government informed the Italian Parliamentary Commission for the Investigation of Human Rights

Violations Committed by the Enemy of 'the absolute impossibility of indicating the number of dead in the labour companies'.[100] Much remains unknown about the living conditions of prisoners in British, French, German and Austro-Hungarian labour companies. As regards Russia, little is known about forced prisoner labour for the army at the front: as the historian Reinhard Nachtigal has pointed out 'most of those prisoners employed on building defences worked on the south-western and the Romanian fronts ... Their living conditions remain the least known of all working prisoners, as they were in the war zone which was also out of bounds to Russian controllers'.[101] Similarly, the British use of Turkish prisoners in labour companies has not been researched.[102] The labour company system, so long overlooked, deserves far greater historiographical attention.

This brings us to the fourth parameter which determined prisoner treatment – inspection systems. In her book *Absolute Destruction: Military Culture and the Practices of War in Imperial Germany* (2005), Isabel Hull argues that external controls were crucial to reigning in military forces and curtailing excessively destructive behaviour: 'the main effective limits to excess lay outside the military, in government, politics, law, and public opinion ... In Imperial Germany, these forces were too weak ...'[103] Hull's thesis regarding external controls is particularly evident in the case of prisoner treatment: where the military control of prisoners was tempered by inspections by external bodies, such as local civilian dignitaries, church representatives, International Committee of the Red Cross (ICRC) visits or inspections by representatives of neutral states, prisoners generally benefited from improved living conditions.

This was implicitly recognised at the time: during the war, the idea that prisoners of war should be visited and their treatment monitored by neutral delegates rapidly became widely accepted – the only group of captives excluded from this system were those working in prisoner of war labour companies directly for armies. In contrast, all prisoners who were evacuated to home front camps or work units were seen as having certain rights, defined according to both legal and cultural norms – to receive and send letters, to receive parcels, and to receive a minimum standard of clothing, shelter, food and rest time. As the war went on, additional measures were added, such as the right to repatriation for very severely wounded men whose injuries had permanently disabled them or the right to internment in a neutral country – usually Switzerland or the Netherlands – for prisoners suffering from chronic illness or wounds; these criteria were expanded in wartime agreements between France, Germany and Britain to include the right to repatriation on the basis of a prisoner's age, number of children or length of time spent in captivity. Again, here the system of neutral inspection was crucial; neutral inspectors were responsible for selecting those prisoners who qualified for repatriation or internment schemes.

The process of prisoner inspection was regulated at state level through a system of protecting powers – neutral states which represented the interests of a particular prisoner nationality to the captor nation. Thus, for example, the interests of French prisoners of war in Germany were represented by Spain and those of German prisoners in Britain were looked after by the United States until 1917, and then Switzerland. A new Weberian humanitarian bureaucracy grew out of this process – on the eastern front, representatives from the Swedish and Danish Red Cross organisations and governments inspected camps; the same role was carried out by American, Spanish, Swiss and Dutch government representatives in western Europe, as well as representatives from the ICRC in Geneva. While western front inspections were almost entirely carried out by men, women played a significant role inspecting camps in Russia; most famously, Elsa Brändström the daughter of the Swedish ambassador in Petrograd, coordinated a massive prisoner relief effort and visited prisoner of war camps in Russia throughout the conflict. Other women spent shorter four month stints inspecting Russian camps as representatives of the German, Austrian or Hungarian Red Cross societies, often exploiting pre-war aristocratic ties.[104] Thus communication channels across wartime Europe remained open – these crucially allowed prisoners to receive post from their loved ones at home. Given that prisoners often suffered a strong sense of stigma at having been captured, post was essential to counteract their frequent paranoia that their home state had 'forgotten' them. Humanitarian organisations also contributed to the considerable cultural life that developed in some prisoner of war camps; it was not unusual for large camps to have libraries, orchestras, chapels or synagogues, home-made theatres and language courses, and these developments were widely reported in Red Cross and other publications.[105] However, such facilities were only available to prisoners in the main central camps – by 1916 these represented a minority of captives in the Central Powers and in France, where prisoners had largely been relocated to much smaller, temporary local work units, with long working hours.

In this regard, the First World War marked a moment of tension between competing systems for limiting prisoner mistreatment: reciprocal reprisals, which offered one means of constraining enemy behaviour, and neutral inspections, which could be used to diffuse rumour through providing relatively accurate information to governments and the general public regarding how the enemy was actually treating its captives. Throughout the war both means were used – reprisals against prisoners and inspections by humanitarian organisations developed simultaneously, illustrating how the drive towards totalised warfare actually *interacted* with the advent of modern humanitarian norms. One consequence of this process was that charity itself became 'totalised' by 1918, as states increasingly intervened in the system of supplying their compatriot prisoners in enemy hands with food: by 1918, the British and French governments were delivering trainloads of bread and biscuit supplies to camps in Germany from Copenhagen and Bern, and had introduced systems to regulate how families sent parcels to their loved ones in enemy captivity.[106] In the West, the role of Switzerland was particularly crucial in this process: from 1915, the majority of parcels to prisoners in western Europe passed through Bern. Between September 1914 and November 1918, 1,884,914 individual parcels were forwarded to prisoners of war through the ICRC's Agency for Prisoners of War.[107]

Historians concur that these parcels were utterly essential: by 1916, British, French and Belgian prisoners in Germany were living off the food they received through the parcel system; prisoner nationalities who did not receive regular parcels, such as the Italians or the Romanians, died of malnutrition in Central Power camps.[108] Giovanna Procacci argues that the Italian government's refusal to send parcels to Italians, held prisoner by the Central Powers, in order to discourage surrenders, was a major factor in their high mortality.[109] Kai Rawe estimates that parcels raised the daily ration of prisoners working in mines in the Ruhr by between 950 and 1,200 calories.[110] Although under The Hague Convention of 1907 a captor state was responsible for feeding its prisoners, by the end of the First World War it had been largely accepted in practice that a prisoner's state of origin, as well as private charities and individuals, would supply him with food, through parcels. This overall expansion of humanitarian activity was marked by a tendency to make the camp a more accessible space – one which neutral inspectors and parcels could enter, and to universalise the camp within the context of international regulation. This process paralleled the universal development of the physically uniform prison camp landscape during the war.

However, at the same time as it universalised both the spatial landscape of captivity and humanitarian aid, the war unleashed an oppositional dynamic – to treat prisoners differently according to their nationality or ethnicity. Differentiation on the basis of a prisoner's origins became standard in most belligerent states; this was the fifth major parameter that defined a prisoner's treatment. It is important to clarify two key points here: first, where prisoners from a particular identity group benefited from privileged treatment it was usually on *political* grounds – they were treated better because the captor state wished to cultivate support among particular national or ethnic groupings. There are multiple examples of this process all across Europe: the British government established a special privileged camp at Feltham for prisoners it believed could be persuaded to change sides, such as Austro-Hungarian Slavs or ethnic minorities from the German Reich. The Germans gathered together all their Irish prisoners in 1915 at a special camp at Limburg and offered to assist them in launching a rebellion in Ireland against Britain – in exchange the Irish prisoners were to get privileged treatment and training.[111] The policy was a failure, with only 52 volunteers for Germany's planned Irish Brigade. Ethnic Germans captured fighting for the Russian army were provided with a privileged prisoner of war regime in Germany and encouraged to become naturalised German citizens.[112] In turn, the French government segregated Poles and Alsace-Lorrainers captured fighting with the German army into special camps for pro-French indoctrination; as part of this process the Russian government handed over any prisoners from Alsace-Lorraine it captured on the eastern Front to the French. Within France, different official prisoner regimes applied to different nationalities: the same prisoner treatment regime was applied to German and Turkish prisoners; Austro-Hungarian prisoners, however, were treated better and accorded more privileges.[113] The Italians had a 'policy of favoured treatment' for those Habsburg nationalities considered to be potential allies, such as the Czechs.[114] The Austro-Hungarians segregated Ukrainian, Polish and Muslim prisoners captured fighting for the Russians – the Poles were encouraged to join a Polish Corps which would then fight against Russia. However, the harsh living conditions in the special Austro-Hungarian prisoner of war camps for Polish prisoners meant the policy was unsuccessful.[115]

Second, the *discursive* backdrop to this widespread politically motivated process of discrimination was a prevalent belief that 'race' was an omnipresent marker of identity – the various peoples of Europe were believed to be different 'races'; the non-European world too was perceived in these terms. This understanding was based upon a remarkable blurring of definitions and confused borrowings from a variety of anthropological, imperialist and nationalist rhetoric, to the extent that the terms 'race' and 'nationality' were often used interchangeably. The concept of ethnicity was also largely absent, so 'race' was also often used when contemporaries discussed minority cultural groups. As a result, the term 'race' was applied indiscriminately to all prisoner nationalities or ethnicities: for example, commentators discussed Frenchmen, Bavarians, Saxons, Jews, Germans, Irish, English, Slavs, Turks, Bretons, Africans, Hungarians or Indians as different 'races' and attempted to categorise these into hierarchies – hierarchies which largely depended upon which side in the war the commentator supported.[116]

This discourse of race had an impact on how prisoners were perceived – prisoners of war came to be associated in public discourse with 'racial' identities, projected upon them by the captor state in an effort to describe cultural differences.[117] This is clear in the cultural response to prisoners: sketches of different German prisoner 'types' were produced in France.[118] In Germany, there was a general fascination with categorising prisoners according to race: the artist Hermann Struck produced a series of drawings of prisoners of war, defining them according to racial 'character'; Otto Stiehl published a series of portrait photographs of the different racial 'types' among Germany's prisoners and Wilhelm Doegen produced an inter-war anthropological study based upon his visits to prison camps.[119] In both Germany and Austro-Hungary, ambitious research projects were also established to carry out anthropological studies of different prisoner 'races': the Kaiser authorised the establishment of a Prussian Phonogram Commission to record the different dialects and songs of prisoners of war.[120] In Austria-Hungary, the President of the Vienna Anthropological Society, Carl Toldt organised similar research in prisoner camps and the anthropologist Rudolf Pöch was allowed to visit prisoners to study their songs and film their folk dances.[121] Some of this work involved measuring prisoners' skulls or taking dental moulds; however, crucially, this research had no bearing on actual prisoner treatment which was determined by military-political factors; the fascination with 'race' remained almost entirely a *discursive* phenomenon. How this discourse interacted with the actual treatment of individual groups of prisoners is difficult to assess. However, the impetus behind discriminatory treatment of different prisoner nationalities within prison camps appears to have remained overwhelmingly political-strategic, rather than racial.

This is best illustrated by the fact that one of the most powerful racial discourses in Germany did not directly morph into straightforward bad treatment of prisoners within German home front camps on the grounds of 'race'. From the outbreak of the war in 1914, German propaganda raged against the Entente use of colonial troops against white German soldiers. The language of this discourse was extreme – black and Indian troops were accused of beheading German wounded and of bestial battlefield behaviour.[122] By 1915, this racial discourse had expanded in response to rumours that the French were using colonial troops – black and Arab – to guard German prisoners held in French camps in North Africa.[123] German protests depicted this use of colonial guards in extremely racist terms; blacks and Arabs were innately cruel and violent according to official German propaganda, and their use in guarding German prisoners was depicted as an inversion of a natural racial hierarchy.

Yet, at the same time, Germany's political-strategic alliance with the Ottoman empire, and its aspirations to be a colonial empire, meant that colonial prisoners presented a particular value. Germany could use them to prove its credentials – both as a colonial power and as the protector state of Muslim freedom, in which guise it had presented itself during the immediate pre-war period.[124] Muslim prisoners, in particular, offered the chance for Germany to strengthen its alliance with the Ottomans and illustrate its willingness to assist Muslims to gain freedom from Britain and France.[125] They were also seen as a potential fighting force which could be sent to help the Ottoman army on the Mesopotamian front.

Thus in this case, racist discourse did not lead automatically to worse treatment within the German home front camp system, although it may have influenced a negative reaction to colonial prisoners on the battlefield and atrocities at the moment of surrender: in fact, Muslim prisoners were initially privileged over other captives within Germany and placed in two special camps at Wünsdorf and Weinberg, both near Zossen, where their specific cultural needs were catered for, including the provision of a mosque, the right to celebrate Muslim festivals and to prepare Halal meat. Small groups of colonial prisoners from Wünsdorf camp were even given guided tours of Berlin.[126] The inmates of the camp at Wünsdorf included Muslims from Africa and the Asian subcontinent; those held at Weinberg were largely Muslims from the Russian empire, rather than colonial troops. In addition, Sikhs, Hindus and Christians from India were sent to Wünsdorf – the hope was that they, along with the Indian Muslim and the Arab prisoners, could eventually be sent to fight with the Ottoman army.

This plan, to provide the Ottoman army with additional fighters, was largely unsuccessful, in part because Germany failed to recognise the animosity that existed between Arabs and Turks; although 1,100 Russian Muslim prisoners, 1,084 Arab prisoners and 49 Indian prisoners, in total, were kitted out, trained by the Germans and shipped to Istanbul as volunteers for the Ottoman army, the Turks were uncertain what to do with these men.[127] They were subjected to harsh conditions upon arrival – little food, no pay and beatings and eventually sent on a forced march to Baghdad, during which they experienced severe hardship; many deserted or escaped to the British lines.[128] Those Indian, African and Arab colonial prisoners who remained in Wünsdorf camp were sent to camps in Romania in 1917. According to the Army High Command and the Prussian Ministry of War this was necessary for health reasons as they believed the Romanian climate was better suited to colonial prisoners. Over 3,000 black, Arab and Indian prisoners were still working in Romania in 1918.[129] Ultimately, Germany had difficulty in getting men to change sides. Some colonial prisoners proved particularly loyal to their imperial power and had to be segregated: they were sent to a special reprisals camp at Weiler in Alsace-Lorraine. The International Committee of the Red Cross received a tip-off about this and demanded the prisoners at Weiler be examined by Swiss medical inspectors – most were found to be ill enough to qualify for repatriation, which occurred in October 1917.[130] However, overall, in the case of Germany's colonial prisoners, treatment was clearly determined by political objectives, rather than the contemporary racist discourse on colonial troops.

Thus, during the First World War, the value of a prisoner was not only determined in terms of his labour potential but also in light of whether, because of his ethnic origins, he was of *political* value to the captor state. Despite the existence of a widespread public discourse that associated prisoners of war with different racial hierarchies, the predominant, deciding factor in awarding privileges to particular groups of captives remained winning political advantage for the captor state, rather than a prisoner's perceived 'racial' worth.

Precedents

First World War captivity represented a new phenomenon – in terms of scale, duration and the parameters that defined it. Although there were clear links back to captivity during earlier wars, the rationalised, secured world of the Great War camp marked a watershed: it facilitated the establishment of mass forced labour systems, which were largely effective; as a result, the coerced enemy worker was seen as indispensable to waging the new 'total' warfare. If a key theme of Europe's twentieth century was the forced labour camp, then the First World War was a major point of departure for this process. It was in these camps during the First World War that states gained the know-how regarding how to build, house and confine large numbers of military men. Indeed, in several cases, such as Auschwitz, Mauthausen, Theresienstadt or Ohrdruf, the same sites were used for concentration camps in the Second World War. The *Stammlager, Kommando* and prisoner of war labour company systems in Germany provided both a logistical model and a vocabulary for later Second World War prisoner of war Stalags and working units. Likewise in France there was a parallel between the retention of German prisoners to work on reconstruction after the First World War and the use of German prisoners of war to rebuild France after the 1939–45 conflict – France repatriated its Great War German captives only in 1920, causing widespread public outrage in Germany.[131] It took from 1918 to 1922 to repatriate First World War eastern front prisoners; after 1945, eastern front repatriation took even longer. The earlier war provided a logistical model; not an ideological one.

There were interesting continuities at the level of personal experience too: Charles de Gaulle was a prisoner in Germany in 1914–18; Adolf Hitler served as a guard at Traunstein prisoner of war camp in Bavaria between November 1918 and late January 1919, and also worked in August 1919 on a German army propaganda course designed to re-educate German prisoners of war recently repatriated from Russia with what were termed 'Bolshevik' political tendencies.[132] The terrible condition of Russian prisoners in Bavarian camps after the Armistice may have reinforced his prejudices against Slavs. The fact that German prisoners of war were repatriated to Germany having picked up left-leaning political views in captivity may also have been a factor in his later contempt for German troops who surrendered. There was also a significant number of former prisoners of war among the 15 top officials of the German ministerial bureaucracy and the Nazi elite corps or *Schutzstaffel* (SS) who met with Reinhard Heydrich at the infamous Wannsee conference in 1942, where the escalation of the Holocaust was planned. Of the six who had served in the 1914–18 conflict, four had been prisoners of war.[133] One of those present, Dr Alfred Meyer, State Secretary at the Ministry for the Occupied Eastern Territories, had been a prisoner of the French from 1917–20. In 1942, he was a key figure in the mass deportations of Soviet forced labourers.[134]

In conclusion, the legacy of the process of rationalising captivity in 1914–18 is hard to gauge. As the historian Uta Hinz has pointed out, the process of totalisation in Germany was largely driven by the need for prisoner labour in the First World War; a process of brutalisation against prisoners, however, also played a significant secondary role with regard to those working in labour companies.[135] Certain humanitarian parameters – as we have seen – remained very powerful in mitigating prisoner mistreatment. However, several important precedent trends must be noted: first, the war established the norm that prisoners would be fed from parcels rather than, as outlined in international law, by the captor nation. This occurred once again in the Second World War when British and American prisoners lived largely off parcels sent to Germany and Italy.[136] In fact, during the Second World War, the ICRC initially adopted the patterns of 1914–18, focusing on supplying parcels to prisoner of war camps and carrying out neutral inspections – the belief that these would once again mitigate poor prisoner treatment to some extent blinded the ICRC to the changed nature of the 1939–45 conflict, in particular, the Nazi regime's genocidal policies.[137] Moreover, the First World War set the precedent of ignoring international law regarding prisoners of war when this was in the national interest, in favour of reprisals to influence the other side or when necessary to increase prisoners' labour output. What came to matter most during the 1914–18 war was reciprocity – treating one's own captives as the enemy treated its prisoners – rather than international law; this dynamic emerged again in the 1939–45 war on the eastern front and also, to some extent, in the West between Britain and Germany.[138] Thus although additional legal safeguards for prisoners were introduced in the inter-war period in the new 1929 Geneva Convention on Prisoners of War, its stipulations were widely ignored in the annihilationist war between the USSR and Germany in the Second World War.

Second, the Great War undermined the idea of a standard universal treatment for all prisoners – all belligerents favoured particular ethnicities within their camp system. Although this was on political rather than racial grounds, it weakened the idea of all prisoners having equal rights – a process of differentiation which re-emerged in the Second World War. The hugely varying death rates among prisoner nationalities held by the same captor states also set a precedent: as in the Second World War, certain prisoner nationalities died in far greater numbers than others. The First World War also saw very different patterns of prisoner taking between the eastern and western fronts, establishing different 'racial' images of prisoners in public discourse – the inter-war legacy of this process remains to be explored.

Third, the First World War gave rise to the belief in Germany that the country had wasted precious food resources on prisoners at the expense of its civilian population. In addition, right-wing German commentators argued that prisoner of war workers had sabotaged German home front agriculture – in 1939, an official German Wehrmacht publication, *Kriegsgefangene 1914/18*, reproduced documentary and photographic evidence of crop sabotage by Allied prisoners which had been gathered by the former Prussian Ministry of War.[139] Its introduction stated that the book should act as 'an admonition and a warning for every member of the *Volk*. The enemy remains the enemy'.[140] Finally, and most significantly, the First World War established the principle of the dual prisoner work system – divided between prisoner of war labour companies, where conditions were not subject to external inspection, and home front camps and working units which were subject to greater regulation.

These points made, it is important in concluding to clarify that the First World War was emphatically not the camp universe of 1939–45 – one key difference was the nature and scale of death. First World War prisoner of war camps were never designed for extermination; where mass deaths occurred among prisoners of war in 1914–18 these were largely due to negligence, leading to hunger or mass disease. The ideology of death that marked the mass Second World War concentration camp system was missing; most significantly, the majority of prisoners of war *survived* the Great War forced labour experience. However, extermination camps remained the exceptional, most extreme form of the camp in Europe's twentieth century; the norm from Stalinist Russia to Franco's Spain was the labour camp. In this respect, the First World War marked an important turning point. Its camps did not predetermine the later development of genocide in 1939–45; they did, however, set a precedent in consolidating forced labour.

Notes

[1] Bartov, *Murder in our Midst.*

[2] See Becker, *Oubliés de la grande guerre*; Abbal, *Soldats oubliés*; Hinz, *Gefangen im Großen Krieg*; Oltmer, *Bäuerliche Ökonomie*; idem, 'Zwangsmigration und Zwangsarbeit'.

[3] Rachamimov, *POWs and the Great War*; Nachtigal, *Kriegsgefangenschaft an der Ostfront.*

[4] Speed, *Prisoners, Diplomats and the Great War.*

[5] Rachamimov, 'The Disruptive Comforts of Drag', 1–4.

[6] Hinz, *Gefangen im Großen Krieg*, 238; Leidinger and Moritz, 'Verwaltete Massen', 54.

[7] Nachtigal, *Kriegsgefangenschaft an der Ostfront*, 13–16.

[8] Procacci, *Soldati e prigionieri italiani*, 168.

[9] Service Historique de L'Armée de Terre (SHAT) 16 N 525, GQG Bureau de Personnel – Pertes, Dossier no. 2, Prisonniers de Guerre, États numériques; German Reichstag, *Völkerrecht im Weltkrieg*, vol. 3, part 1, 715. Service Historique de L'Armée de Terre is hereafter referred to as SHAT.

[10] Kramer, *Dynamic of Destruction*, 63.

[11] Ferguson, 'Prisoner Taking and Prisoner Killing', 159.

[12] The higher estimate of 170,000 is from Nachtigal, *Kriegsgefangenschaft an der Ostfront*, 16; the lower figure, 167,000 is from Rachamimov, *POWs and the Great War*, 31. The death rate estimate is from Overmans, '"Hunnen" und "Untermenschen"', 343 and 348.

[13] Nachtigal, *Kriegsgefangenschaft an der Ostfront*, 16.

[14] Höpp, *Muslime in der Mark*, 44.

[15] Doegen, *Kriegsgefangene Völker*, 28–9.

[16] Gratien Candace, *Rapport fait au nom de la Commission des affaires extérieures* (Paris, 1919) no. 5676 Chambre des Deputés, onzième legislature, Session de

1919, Annexe au procès-verbal de la 2e séance du 11 février 1919; War Office, *Statistics of the Military Effort*, 632–5. Other estimates put the number of French prisoners at 600,000 or higher.

[17] One of the rare publications on this topic is Sergeev, 'Kriegsgefangenschaft aus russischer Sicht'.

[18] N.F. Oliver, D.I.D., Minute, 3 September 1914, in The National Archives, Kew, London (TNA), ADM 1/8393/304. The National Archives is hereafter referred to as TNA.

[19] Belfield, 'The Treatment of Prisoners of War'.

[20] Frerk, *Kriegsgefangen in Nordafrika*, 39.

[21] Jones, 'Encountering the "Enemy"'.

[22] Jones, 'The Enemy Disarmed', 45–6.

[23] Interview with Private Charles Brash, in TNA, WO 161/98, no. 536.

[24] SHAT, 7 N 1187, Rapports d'évadés ou rapatriés transmis par Gouv. de Boulogne, Adjutant Lucien Debond.

[25] Gärtner, 'Einrichtung und Hygiene der Kriegsgefangenenlager', 261.

[26] Ibid., 260.

[27] Doegen, *Kriegsgefangene Völker*, 28–9.

[28] Gärtner, 'Einrichtung und Hygiene der Kriegsgefangenenlager', 261.

[29] Leidinger and Moritz, 'Verwaltete Massen', 35–6.

[30] Nachtigal, 'Seuchen unter militärischer Aufsicht'; idem, 'Seuchenbekämpfung'; idem, *Kriegsgefangenschaft an der Ostfront*, 72.

[31] The higher figure for French prisoner deaths in Germany is that given by the former head of the French Service des Prisonniers de Guerre, Georges Cahen-Salvador – see Cahen-Salvador, *Les Prisonniers de Guerre*, 281, 284 and 291. The lower figure comes from the official German interwar history by Wilhelm Doegen – see Doegen, *Kriegsgefangene Völker*, 28–9. The figure for German deaths in France comes from German Reichstag, *Völkerrecht im Weltkrieg*, vol. 3, part 1, 715. See also Weiland and Kern, *In Feindeshand*, vol. 2. The figure for German deaths in British captivity is from War Office, *Statistics of the Military Effort*, 329, 352 and 632–35.

[32] Höpp, *Muslime in der Mark*, 50.

[33] Hinz, *Gefangen im Großen Krieg*, 238.

[34] Ibid.

[35] Doegen, *Kriegsgefangene Völker*, 56–7; Spoerer, 'The Mortality of Allied Prisoners of War'.

[36] Hinz, 'Kriegsgefangene', 641–6.

[37] Gilbert, *The First World War*, 248.

[38] See the accounts in Long, *Other Ranks of Kut*; and Neave, *Remembering Kut*.

[39] Kramer, *Dynamic of Destruction*, 142–3.

[40] Ibid.

[41] Ibid., 67.

[42] On the German prisoners of Tsingtau see Krebs, 'Die etwas andere Kriegsgefangenschaft', 323–8; and Powell, *Splinters of a Nation*. On German prisoners in Templemore, see D'Arcy, *Remembering the War Dead*, 198–203.

[43] SHAT, 3 H 260, Rapatriement grands blessés, prisonniers allemands du maroc, 1915-1916.

[44] Ibid.

[45] Archives du Comité International de la Croix Rouge, (ACICR) 432/II/10/c.37; Comité International de la Croix Rouge, Documents publiés à l'occasion de la Guerre Européenne, 1914-1916, *Rapports de M. le Dr A.Vernet et M. Richard de Muralt sur leurs visites aux depôts de prisonniers en Tunisie et de MM. P. Schazmann et Dr O.-L. Cramer sur leurs visites aux depôts de prisonniers en Algérie en décembre 1915 et janvier 1916* (Geneva, 1916), 57.

[46] Leidinger and Moritz, 'Verwaltete Massen', 58. As Reinhard Nachtigal has pointed out, 'research into prisoners of war taken on both sides on the Caucasus front has not yet begun' – Nachtigal, *Kriegsgefangenschaft an der Ostfront*, 13.

[47] Cf. Reinhard Nachtigal's contribution to this volume.

[48] On the wartime attempt to define this new illness see Vischer, *Barbed Wire Disease*.

[49] MacKenzie, 'The Ethics of Escape'.

[50] On prison camp newspapers see Pöppinghege, *Im Lager unbesiegt*. On camp theatre see Pörzgen, *Theater ohne Frau*; and Rachamimov, 'The Disruptive Comforts of Drag'.

[51] Cochet, *Soldats sans armes*, 11; Cahen-Salvador, *Les Prisonniers de Guerre*, 17.

[52] Brown, *The Hague Conventions and Declarations of 1899 and 1907*, 110.

[53] Ibid. See also Cahen-Salvador, *Les Prisonniers de Guerre*, 17–19.

[54] Willis, *Prologue to Nuremburg*, 17–22.

[55] d'Anthouard, *Les Prisonniers Allemands au Maroc*, 1–8. See also Jones, 'The German Spring Reprisals of 1917'.

[56] Ibid.

[57] Letter from Comité International de la Croix Rouge (CICR) to Mr le Conseiller Fédéral Hoffmann, 25 May 1917, in ACICR, 445.iv-ix.c.61.

[58] Jones, 'The German Spring Reprisals of 1917'.

[59] German Reichstag, *Verhandlungen des Reichstages*, vol. 309, 2492 (86th session, 2 March 1917).

[60] Figures from Oltmer, 'Unentbehrliche Arbeitskräfte', 71.

[61] Leidinger and Moritz, 'Verwaltete Massen', 48.

[62] Oltmer, 'Unentbehrliche Arbeitskräfte', 70.

[63] Ibid.

[64] Thiel, '*Menschenbassin Belgien*', 68, n. 60.

[65] Jones, 'The Enemy Disarmed', 88–96.

[66] SHAT, 6 N 110: Journal hebdomadaire de l'inspection générale des prisonniers de guerre, semaine du 11 au 18 mars 1916, 8.

[67] Cahen-Salvador, *Les Prisonniers de Guerre*, 43–4.

[68] House of Lords Record Office (HLRO), LG F/7/2/16, cited in Jones, 'The Enemy Disarmed', 321.

[69] Panayi, 'Normalität hinter Stacheldraht', 144; TNA, NATS 1/282, Table showing the distribution of prisoners of war in Great Britain by industry on 12 May 1918.

[70] Ibid.

[71] On prisoner treatment in German prisoner of war labour companies see Jones, 'The Final Logic of Sacrifice?'. On the establishment of prisoner of war labour companies in the German army see idem, 'The German Spring Reprisals of 1917'.

[72] Circular telegram from the Chief of the General Staff, 22 September 1915, in Bundesarchiv-Militärarchiv Freiburg (BA-MA), PH5/II/455, f. 130.

[73] TNA, WO 32/5098 1B, Formation of Prisoner of War Companies, No.A.G. b 2006/4, 27 July 1916; SHAT 16 N 2467, D.1, f. 34, 520/DA, no. 2046/DA, 9 June 1916.

[74] Circular telegram from the Chief of the General Staff, 22 September 1915 (as note 72 above). Underlining in original.

[75] TNA, MUN 4/6527.

[76] Rawe, 'Wir werden sie schon zur Arbeit bringen!', 79.

[77] Herbert, A History of Foreign Labor in Germany, 91.

[78] Leidinger and Moritz, 'Verwaltete Massen', 56.

[79] Ibid., 53.

[80] Department of Prisoners of War, WO to Sir Douglas Haig, 31 March 1916, in TNA, MUN 4/6527, 121/works/219. On British prisoner of war labour companies see Scott, 'Captive Labour'.

[81] U.F. Wintour to David Lloyd George, 12 February 1916, in HLRO, LG/D/17/6/31; Albert Thomas to David Lloyd George, 1 March 1916, in TNA, MUN 4/6527.

[82] Ferguson, The Pity of War, 283; Walter Runciman to Sir Douglas Haig, 23 March 1916, in TNA MUN 4/6527.

[83] D.P.W. to C. in C., G.H.Q., 11 August 1916, in TNA, WO 32/5098 5A.

[84] Minute no. 2, 2 August 1916., in TNA, WO 32/5098 1A Register no. 0103/8472.

[85] Scott, 'Captive Labour', 319–31.

[86] Ibid., 328.

[87] Ibid., 319.

[88] Cahen-Salvador, Les Prisonniers de Guerre, 126.

[89] Ibid., 55.

[90] SHAT, 16 N 2467, D.1, f.36, 848/DA, 15 July 1916.

[91] SHAT 16 N 2467, Index to D.A. Correspondance avec le Ministre, 1916, E.M.A. no. 8557.1/11.

[92] SHAT, 16 N 2467,D.1, f.34, 520/DA, order no. 2046/DA, 9 June 1916.

[93] It should be noted that this was the same size as the British prisoner of war labour company. See SHAT 16 N 2467, f.36, 848/DA, 15 July 1916.

[94] SHAT, 16 N 2468, Cie de P.G., D.4, f.16, 26 August 1916.

[95] SHAT, 16 N 2467, D.1, f.16, GQG, 19 June 1916.

[96] SHAT, 16 N 525, État des Prisonniers se trouvant dans la Zone des Armées le 26 janvier 1917.

[97] Jones, 'The Final Logic of Sacrifice?'.

[98] SHAT, 16 N 2468, Compagnies de prisonniers. Dossier 4, no.140, Ordre donné par Groupement ABC de la IIe Armee, copie de la note 2515, SP46, 15 September 1916.

[99] SHAT, 16 N 2468, D.5, f.47, 8 January 1917, GQG, Note relative à l'emploi des prisonniers de guerre dans la Zone des Armées.

[100] Procacci, Soldati e prigionieri italiani, 171.

[101] Nachtigal, Russland und seine österrischisch-ungarischen Kriegsgefangenen, 185.

[102] TNA, WO 95/5040, Turkish prisoner of war labour companies.

[103] Hull, Absolute Destruction, 325. See also Hinz, 'Humanität im Krieg?', 216–36.

[104] Rachamimov, POWs and the Great War, 6–7; idem., '"Female Generals" and "Siberian Angels"', 23–46.

[105] See, for example, the *Bulletin International des sociétés de la Croix-Rouge*, 1914–1918, or *The British Prisoner of War*, published by the Central Prisoners of War Committee of the British Red Cross and the Order of St. John, vol. 1, nos. 1–12 (January to December 1918).

[106] Abbal, *Soldats oubliés*, 88–9.

[107] Djurović, *L'Agence Centrale de Recherches*, 58.

[108] All the historiography concurs on the importance of parcels. See, for example, Procacci, *Soldati e Prigionieri italiani*; Hinz, *Gefangen im Großen Krieg*; Jones, 'The Enemy Disarmed', 316–20.

[109] Procacci, *Soldati e Prigionieri italiani*, 174–5.

[110] Rawe, '*Wir werden sie schon zur Arbeit bringen!*', 105–6. For contemporary evidence of the importance of parcels in German camps, see also the *Rapports des Délégués du gouvernement espagnol* (Paris, 1918).

[111] On Feltham see Württemburgisches Hauptstaatsarchiv-Militärarchiv, Stuttgart, M77/1 1024, Kriegsministerium, Nr 1280/7.18 B 4a Gef. Abschrift, Vorzugslager, 19 September 1918. On the Irish prisoners see Roth, '"The German Soldier is not tactful"'; TNA, WO 141/9, 24 R, Copy of statement from Michael O'Connor, Corporal no. 7543, 2nd Battalion, Royal Irish Regiment; Inglis, *Roger Casement*, 268.

[112] Prussian Minister of Interior to Landwirtschaft, IV.c.41247, November 1914, in Geheimes Staatsarchiv Preussischer Kulturbesitz, I. Abt., Rep. 87, B.16098, Bd. 1, Landwirtschaft. 1914, f. 71.

[113] SHAT, 7 N 1993, procès-verbal de la commission interministérielle des prisonniers de guerre – séance du 10 janvier 1916.

[114] Kramer, *Dynamic of Destruction*, 64.

[115] Leidinger and Moritz, 'Verwaltete Massen', 59–60.

[116] For a thought-provoking discussion of race and captivity see Becker, *Oubliés de la grande guerre*, 317–58.

[117] Evans, 'Capturing Race', 226–56.

[118] For example, in France the artist, Marcel Eugène Louveau-Rouveyre produced a series of sketches of German prisoners at railway stations. These can be seen at the Bibliothèque de Documentation Internationale Contemporaine, Hôtel des Invalides (BDIC, Les Invalides), Ref. Or F3 1311-1320.

[119] Struck, *Kriegsgefangene*; Stiehl, *Unsere Feinde*; Doegen, *Unter fremden Völkern*.

[120] Led by Wilhelm Doegen, the Phonographic Commission was established to record the different languages, dialects and ethnic music skills of prisoners of war in German camps. Its collection of recordings is still extant and includes an impressive range of Slavic, Yiddish, African and Asian folk music from 1915-18. See Mahrenholz, 'Zum Lautarchiv und seiner wissenschaftlichen Erschliessung', 139.

[121] Leidinger and Moritz, 'Verwaltete Massen', 60.

[122] Becker, *Oubliés de la grande guerre*, 317–58.

[123] Auswärtiges Amt, *Völkerrechtswidrige Verwendung farbiger Truppen*; Michel, '"Intoxication ou brutalisation"'.

[124] Höpp, *Muslime in der Mark*, 44.

[125] Ibid., 35.

[126] Ibid., 55.

[127] Ibid., 83–5.

[128] SHAT, 7 N 2107, Account by Moursili Ahmed, Matricule 4963 de la 2e Cie du 6ème régiment de tirailleurs algériens. See also *To Make Men Traitors: Germany's attempts to seduce her prisoners of war* (London, 1918), 1 and 20; and Höpp, *Muslime in der Mark*, 83.

[129] Doegen, *Kriegsgefangene Völker*, 12, n. 3. Höpp, *Muslime in der Mark*, 51.

[130] ACICR, 446/III/c.62, Camps de propagande et d'éliminés en France, Propagande individuelle.

[131] Jones, 'The Enemy Disarmed', 357–79.

[132] Becker, 'Charles de Gaulle, Prisonnier', 98–115. On Hitler see Kershaw, *Hitler*, vol. 1, 117 and 123.

[133] They were Otto Hofmann (1896–1982), SS Race and Settlement; Wilhelm Kritzinger (1890–1947), Reich Chancellery; Dr Roland Freisler (1893–1945), Reich Ministry of Justice; and Dr Alfred Meyer (1891–1945), Reich Ministry for the Occupied Eastern Territories. See Schoenberner and Bihaly, *House of the Wannsee Conference*, 54–67. I am grateful to Mark Jones for bringing this source to my attention.

[134] Ibid.

[135] Hinz, *Gefangen im Großen Krieg*, 353–63.

[136] Gilbert, *POW. Allied Prisoners in Europe*, 97–100.

[137] On the ICRC and the Second World War, see Favez, *The Red Cross and the Holocaust*.

[138] MacKenzie, *The Colditz Myth*.

[139] German Wehrmacht Supreme Command, *Kriegsgefangene, 1914/18*.

[140] Ibid., Preface.

Civilian Internment and Civilian Internees in Europe, 1914–20

Matthew Stibbe

Department of History, Sheffield Hallam University, Sheffield, UK

> I humbly beg to ask for your assistance. I followed my husband into war and was taken prisoner in July 1915. In December 1915 I gave birth to a baby girl at the camp at Havelberg, where I still am now. My husband is also in captivity. Unfortunately I have no means of support and therefore ask your committee to have the goodness to send my daughter and I a few items of clothing....I also humbly request that you send me a small sum of money
>
> Havelberg camp, Germany, 1 March 1916.[1]

These lines, written by a Russian woman, Nadeshda Bogdanova, to Elisabeth Rotten, head of a charity for stranded enemy aliens in Berlin, are typical of thousands of postcards sent to relief organisations and Red Cross societies across Europe during the First World War. They tell the story of a different war, the war experienced behind the barbed wire of internment camps and forced labour camps where civilian prisoners and their families lived separately or side by side with military prisoners.

The total number of civilians interned in Europe between 1914 and 1920 is not known, but certainly runs into several hundred thousand; probably around 50,000 to 100,000 were also imprisoned in countries outside Europe.[2] Some of the victims, like Frau Bogdanova, were deportees from occupied territories. Others were enemy aliens caught within the jurisdiction of the opposing state at the outbreak of the war, and others still were refugees or members of 'suspect' nationalities and ethnic groups forcibly evacuated from war zones by their own governments. Non-combatants from all the warring states were affected, including men, women and children. The uprooting and imprisonment of so many innocent civilians indeed constitutes an important aspect of the war's radical transformation of social relations and its destruction of common European values. Yet, as we shall see below, there are other aspects of this phenomenon which suggest continuity with more traditional constructions of male/female wartime activism and charity-giving stretching back into the late nineteenth century and beyond.[3]

The purpose of this essay is to examine civilian internment across the belligerent states of Europe during the years 1914–20. Above all it seeks to consider internment as an imagined experience, imagined from the inside, by the internees themselves, and from the outside, by captor nations and by friends and supporters at home. This is an issue which has received little or no coverage in mainstream publications on the war,[4] while even the relatively few studies of military POWs make scant reference to non-combatants who found themselves in enemy captivity.[5] True, a recent spate of monographs and specialist essays have shed considerable light on how and why internment took place in particular countries or regions,[6] but to date there has been no attempt to approach the subject on a transnational basis, with the partial exception of Annette Becker's influential study *Oubliés de la grande guerre* (1998). Her conclusion – that First World War captivity gave rise to a new kind of 'war culture' among occupied populations, transforming the conflict into an eschatological crusade against a hated foreign invader – must be balanced against the fact that her evidence-base is largely restricted to the experiences of French civilians in German-held territory.[7]

Internment is also occasionally mentioned in studies of the diplomacy of captivity, that is the history of international negotiations over the treatment and exchange of prisoners. Yet here again the tendency is to look at Britain, France and Germany only, with cursory attention paid to Russia and Austria-Hungary, and even less to Romania, Bulgaria or Serbia. The view that wartime diplomats 'made a serious effort to grapple with the problem', helping to negotiate exchanges and improve conditions for civilian internees, is at best a half-truth which applies to a limited number of cases only.[8] Equally dubious, though, are studies which portray the internment camps of the First World War as the starting point for the state terror practised by various European dictatorships after 1917, from Bolshevik Russia to Nazi Germany.[9] Rather, the subject deserves to be studied in its own right, and on its own terms, before bigger conclusions are drawn. As such, this essay is intended as a beginning rather than a final, definitive statement. It draws on the small but impressive body of scholarship that already exists, while also showcasing new material taken from the author's own research in British, German, Austrian and Red Cross archives.

Causes and precedents

If we accept, as has been argued, that internment practices are 'a key to understanding what was new about the [First World War]',[10] then we still need to consider some of its wider causes, as well as examining one or two precedents from earlier times. Internment, or at least the scale of it, did take many legal and political experts by surprise, but it was not entirely unexpected either. Four factors contributed to the gradual erosion of what Richard B. Speed refers to as the 'liberal tradition of captivity', namely the set of customs and practices which in previous conflicts had restricted internment to military prisoners of war (POWs) only.[11]

The first of these is the enormous growth in the scale and destructiveness of war, so that military operations became increasingly mechanised and the distinction between combatants and enemy civilians increasingly blurred. For instance, with bigger and better-equipped armies clashing in lengthy, long drawn-out battles, large numbers of civilians found themselves directly caught up in the fighting as their homes, farms and businesses were devastated, a phenomenon already evident in the American Civil War of 1861–5 and the Franco-Prussian War of 1870/1.[12] On top of this, the industrialisation of warfare led modern nation-states to place increasing emphasis on the link between citizenship and military service, whether the latter was demonstrated on the battlefield or (as was increasingly the case) on the home front. Those who were not citizens, on the other hand, were not only resented as non-participants in a national endeavour, but also came under suspicion as spies or potential recruits in the opposing army. Jörg Nagler, for instance, writes:

> The formation of nation-states lent greater emphasis to the question of citizenship, especially during wartime when it assumed central importance in relation to issues of loyalty and national security. In an administrative sense at least, it became the decisive criterion and dividing line between friend and foe. Thus documented proof of enemy nationality could lead to the imposition of restrictions on an individual's freedom and, in case of suspected disloyalty, to internment. A successful application for naturalisation, on the other hand, could prevent this from happening.[13]

Certainly this model goes some way towards explaining the internment of enemy aliens in wartime. Yet between 1914 and 1918 by no means all of the belligerents followed the French 'nation-in-arms' idea which theoretically defined all French citizens as being equally French regardless of ethnicity, and all foreign nationals as equally foreign on the same grounds. Indeed, many civilian prisoners, far from being enemy aliens, were actually subjects of the state that interned them or 'stateless persons' who refused to acknowledge citizenship of any one country in order to avoid liability for military service. This was especially the case, as we shall see below, in disputed border regions like the Italian- and Slovene-speaking areas of Habsburg Austria or parts of Alsace-Lorraine, where whole villages could find themselves deported and/or interned at great distance from their homes. Yet it is also worth noting that even in territories which belonged incontrovertibly to one nation or another, citizenship itself was no guarantee against internment. In Britain and France, for instance, 'suspect' foreign-born subjects could in some circumstances have their naturalisation certificates overturned, either under older laws or under new, more restrictive legislation introduced during the war.[14] And in Bavaria, the internment camp at Traunstein was used to hold not only enemy nationals and refugees from Alsace-Lorraine, but also German and Austro-Hungarian citizens accused of anti-war activities, Gypsies without papers, and even a random Dutchman.[15]

A second factor explaining internment is the rapid pace of globalisation from the late nineteenth century onwards, and developments in steamship and railway travel, which allowed a significant increase in the movement of people as well as goods and capital across the world.[16] In many countries, this produced a 'nativist' backlash in the form of popular resentment against outsiders, encouraging moves by governments to develop ever more sophisticated means of control and surveillance over migrants and seasonal workers. Trade unions, for instance, demanded greater protection of national labour markets from outside competition, while political parties were increasingly concerned to integrate indigenous workers into the state through granting them privileges not afforded to foreigners, such as unemployment insurance and old age pensions.[17] The growing preoccupation with state welfare and public health was also important here, as popular – and sometimes official – prejudices held impoverished refugees and immigrants responsible for the spread of contagious diseases like cholera and trachoma.[18] Thus from the 1880s onwards state and national parliaments in the USA, Britain, France and Germany were already passing new laws regulating migration and restricting the entry of non-naturalised aliens. Yet none of this really seemed to stem the flow of peoples, which continued at a great rate throughout the 1890s and 1900s and indeed was crucial to the development of regional economies and international trade during this time.[19]

Significantly, German immigrants were in a particularly vulnerable situation vis-à-vis internment as so many of them (up to 4.5 million) lived in countries which eventually found themselves at war with the new Kaiserreich, including not only Britain, France and Russia, but also the USA, Canada, China, Hong Kong, Siam, Brazil, Argentina, South Africa, Australia and New Zealand.[20] Already in 1870, at the start of the Franco-Prussian War, the French authorities forbade the 39,000 Germans resident in Paris to leave the capital, and later expelled them en masse to Germany, an episode which is often seen as a portent for what was to happen on a much larger scale in 1914.[21] Huge numbers of Germans also settled in European Russia, including farmers, industrialists, technicians and businessmen; they too faced a rising tide of nationalist resentment culminating in the Moscow riots of May 1915.[22] By the 1890s the German empire was itself a net importer of economic migrants, becoming heavily dependent on controlled flows of seasonal labour from the Low Countries and Italy and to a far greater extent from Russian and Austrian Poland.[23] Yet in 1914 there were still many more Germans in Britain and France (around 70,000 and 60,000 respectively) than French and British in Germany (around 10,000 of each). This is important because it meant that in diplomatic negotiations over exchanges of civilian prisoners after 1914 Germany was at a distinct numerical disadvantage, particularly in respect to its dealings with Britain.[24]

Thirdly, on a more general level internment was a by-product of the breakdown of multinational empires in central, eastern and south-eastern Europe, and the emergence of new, 'uncontainable' hatreds, some of which came to the surface during the Balkan wars of 1912/13 and the Armenian genocide of 1915/16.[25] Political instability throughout the region meant that conceptions as to who was a Serb, a Bulgar, a Bosnian, a Turk or a Macedonian were liable to sudden, violent change. After Romania entered the war in August 1916, for instance, both the native government and the invading armies of the Central Powers found it extraordinarily difficult to distinguish between friend and foe among the civilian population. In the words of one expert, in addition to ethnic Romanians who identified fully with the Romanian state:

> There were numerous Romanian-speaking immigrants from what was then Hungarian Transylvania (especially as after 1914 crossing the border became an easy way of avoiding military service), a mostly stateless Jewish population (although serving in the Romanian army), and Bulgarian and German-speaking minorities with Romanian citizenship next to so-called Austro-Hungarian and German 'colonies' of Central Power citizens in the cities.[26]

But it was not just in the Balkans that the nationalities' question caused such problems. In the Austrian capital Vienna, as Maureen Healy has argued, 'pre-existing ethnic tensions' and wartime food shortages made social relations equally fluid and situational, so that after 1914 refugees from the various war zones, especially Jews from the East, were treated as outsiders, as foreigners, and even as an 'enemy within':

> In the autumn of 1914, 50–70,000 Polish- and Yiddish-speaking refugees arrived from the Galician front, and refugees evacuated from areas behind the Italian front followed the next year. Some residents

imagined themselves besieged by Jews, Czechs, Hungarians and Poles, who conspired to keep bread, milk, meat and potatoes from their 'rightful' German recipients. The vocabulary of their neighbourhood arguments and street skirmishes was a war vocabulary.[27]

In this situation, again, the outbreak of war led to a new system of collective representations intimately bound up by a hatred of outsiders; the removal of refugees to reception stations and barrack camps outside Vienna was the inevitable result.[28]

A final explanation, derived from post-colonial theory, would see First World War internment as somehow related to earlier colonial episodes, in particular the use of 'concentration camps' by the Spanish General Weyler in Cuba in 1896/7 and by the British in South Africa during the Boer war of 1899–1902.[29] Thousands died in these camps from the effects of malnutrition, disease and neglect, including men, women and children who were driven from their homes in order to deprive subject peoples of shelter and support. During 1904–07, German officials in South West Africa also adopted this model for fighting colonial wars, while taking it to an even deadlier level. Instead of merely crushing the rebellious Herero tribe militarily, they carried out a deliberate policy of genocide against them, so that between 40,000 and 70,000 were murdered or left to die out of a population of less than 90,000. A further 6000 to 7000 members of the Nama tribe were also killed, reducing their numbers by around one half. Many of the deaths took place in specially constructed forced labour and extermination camps, the most notorious being that built on Shark Island, which was used between 1905 and 1907.[30]

Certainly the idea of 'concentrating' enemy civilians in one place, so that they could be closely watched, punished through food deprivation, beatings and forced labour, and used as hostages to put pressure on remaining enemy combatants, does stem from colonial practices.[31] Yet to focus exclusively on past colonial wars would be to ignore the situational peculiarities and cultural distinctiveness of First World War internment. Whereas in the former case one side was clearly much more powerful than the other, in the latter case internment was adopted by all belligerents, and on a much broader, technologically more sophisticated scale. Railways were an important enabling factor here, but so too were a series of 'historically highly specific image[s]' which determined how combatants saw the 'enemy' they were fighting – for instance the German 'spy' in Britain and France, the civilian sniper or *franc-tireur* in German-occupied Belgium and France, and the 'disorderly, filthy lands and peoples' who, in the eyes of many a German soldier, inhabited the war zones of the East.

These were the images which could lead – in specific situations or on specific war fronts – to the practice of viewing all enemy civilians as potential spies, traitors, disease-spreaders or resisters, regardless of medical and military realities.[32]

Finally, before going on to look at the different systems of internment after 1914, it is important to consider the legal – and therefore again the transnational – dimensions of the problem. Before 1914 most academic experts – as well as the International Committee of the Red Cross (ICRC) – agreed that enemy civilians ought not to be held as prisoners of war.[33] In particular the imprisonment of enemy nationals by successive French governments during the revolutionary and Napoleonic wars of 1793 to 1815 was held up as an illegitimate breach of European tradition by the predominantly conservative writers on international law during the nineteenth century. After Waterloo many of the latter returned to theories of the eighteenth-century century Swiss jurist Emerich de Vattel who argued in 1758 that 'the sovereign who declares war has not the right to detain the subjects of the enemy who are found within his state, nor their effects'.[34] Britain too was criticised for turning every war into a private 'economic war' in which it sought to outdo its closest business rivals through stealing markets, interrupting trade, imprisoning enemy merchant seamen and destroying patents; continental powers were again urged not to follow its example.[35]

The only problem was that nineteenth-century jurists increasingly qualified these general principles by suggesting that internment or other restrictive measures against aliens could be justified through appeals to overriding, albeit strictly non-commercial factors, for instance 'military necessity' or 'national security'. Furthermore, the introduction of conscription throughout most of continental Europe from the 1870s onwards led some experts to the belief that males of military age, and in particular reservists, could legitimately be detained as a means of preventing them from returning home in order to enlist in the opposing army.[36] In other words, internment was, from a legal point of view, a grey area. In 1914 this allowed most states to follow the German Chancellor Bethmann Hollweg's famous dictum that in time of war 'Not kennt kein Gebot' ('necessity knows no law').[37]

In the meantime, while military prisoners of war were guaranteed minimum standards of treatment and access to food, shelter and medical care by international treaties – most notably the Geneva and Hague conventions – civilian internees were not explicitly covered in such arrangements. All they had was a few vague clauses in the preamble to the 1907 Hague convention on land warfare (Hague IV) referring to 'usages established between civilised nations', the 'laws of humanity', and the 'requirements of public conscience'.[38] As the German jurist Franz von Liszt put it in the 10th edition of his treatise on international law, enemy civilians nonetheless enjoyed some protection against arbitrary detention and internment, in the spirit if not in the letter of the existing rules of war:

> Temporary arrest can be justified in the interests of keeping military operations secret, but there are no grounds whatsoever for long-term imprisonment....An analogy with military prisoners can be drawn in so far as civilians should not be exposed to worse treatment than their military counterparts. For this reason incarceration in conditions which are injurious to the prisoners' heath should be regarded as contrary to international law.[39]

With respect to occupied populations, Article 52 of Hague IV also expressly forbade any 'requisitions in kind and services' which might involve enemy civilians being obliged to participate in 'military operations against their own country', a clear ban on the use of forced labour close to the front line; and Article 50 stated that 'no general penalty, pecuniary or otherwise' was to be 'inflicted upon the population on account of the acts of individuals for which they cannot be regarded as jointly and severally responsible', thus in effect prohibiting the use of deportations or internment as a means of collective punishment or reprisal.[40] Yet even these more general principles were not adhered to by most of the belligerent states during the war, as we shall see below.

Conditions of internment

Conditions of internment varied enormously from country to country and region to region. They also became part of the propaganda war, waged not only between the prisoners and their captors, but also, on a much fiercer level, between enemy governments themselves, and more generally, between the rival power blocs, the Allies and the Central Powers. In other words, the 'facts' about internment were repeatedly contested, as each of the warring states represented themselves as 'civilised' and the opposite side as 'barbaric'.[41] This in turn obscured the fact that those who suffered most from internment were often the wives and children of internees, or the refugee families who were interned by their own governments. In order to understand more, it will be necessary to divide civilian POWs into different categories and to examine their experiences and their imagined wars separately and comparatively.

Enemy aliens

The first category, enemy aliens, refers to civilians of enemy nationality who were resident in the territory of a belligerent state at the outbreak of war and who were subsequently interned. Although they typically spent very long periods in captivity, sometimes quite literally for the full duration of the war and beyond, they also usually enjoyed the best conditions and the greatest opportunities for contact with the outside world. This applied in particular to men of military age who paradoxically were 'freed' from the threat of a violent and painful death on the battlefield. For them internment meant boredom, a period in their lives when 'time stood still', but also – for some at least – a period of opportunity for collective creativity and individual self-discovery.[42]

The most famous camp for enemy aliens in Germany was the so-called *Engländerlager* (English camp) at Ruhleben near Berlin. From November 1914 to November 1918 between 4000 and 5000 British males were interned at this converted racecourse, including around 1250 merchant seamen captured at Hamburg or on the high seas. Material conditions, which at first were pretty bad, gradually got better, while the camp's special mix of artists, actors, musicians, teachers and academics created the right context for the development of a sophisticated *Lagerkultur* (prison camp culture), including the development of several camp magazines, a camp theatre and a camp school.[43] Even so, conflicts arose between different groups of prisoners, especially between the pro-British majority and pro-German minority in the camp, and between the black sailors from Africa and the West Indies and some of the white prisoners who resented their presence. Class inequalities, seen in particular in the uneven distribution of gifts of food and clothes from home, further undermined the initial feelings of solidarity. As one inmate put it: 'With the coming of parcels came the school tie, the blazer [and] the club badge'.[44] Finally, the length of internment also had its impact on the physical and especially the mental health of the inmates, with many suffering from the depressive illness known as 'barbed-wire-disease' and possibly up to 100 succumbing to full-blown mental breakdowns.[45]

Germans and Austrians in Britain were interned at a number of different places on the mainland, and also in several camps on the Isle of Man. The worst detention centres, for instance the one at Newbury racecourse in Berkshire, were closed down by the end of 1914 and the inmates transferred to more suitable accommodation.[46] Some internees later recounted the trauma of their initial arrest, which – especially in the aftermath of the Lusitania riots of May 1915 – was often carried out in an alarmingly aggressive manner and to the accompaniment of hostile press coverage and verbal abuse from ordinary members of the public.[47] Yet once inside the camps, conditions were again relatively good, and there was no expectation of forced labour.[48] Camp universities, debating societies and journalism soon flourished, although again there were political and social tensions inside the camps and evidence of a gradual deterioration in the inmates' mental condition. As one concerned father wrote in a letter to the German Foreign Office in December 1916:

> My son, who has been held as a civilian prisoner at Wakefield Camp in England for over two years, and who is in as good a physical condition as the circumstances allow, nonetheless writes with increasing urgency that life in the camp is making the prisoners extraordinarily depressed and that they are gradually going mad, in spite of the many distractions, such as sports or theatrical and musical events, or [academic] lectures, on offer.[49]

The various camps for enemy aliens in the Austrian half of the Habsburg empire did not differ significantly from those in Britain and Germany, although Red Cross reports suggest that they were more variable in terms of the provision of food and the quality of accommodation.[50] Yet the key difference lay in the fact that most aliens were not detained in camps at all, but were instead confined to certain villages in Lower Austria, notably Drosendorf, Kautzen and Raabs, where they lived in privately-rented rooms and were subject to curfews and other restrictions but were not placed behind barbed wire. Some (aliens class B) were even granted the privilege of being confined in their original places of residence, usually Vienna or Prague.[51] Indeed, an important distinction was made between the minority of *Internierte* or *internés*, who were mostly without means, and the majority of *Konfinierte* or *confinés*, mainly middle class and relatively prosperous.[52] Otherwise, as one US diplomat noted in the autumn of 1915:

> The complaints of the internees in Austria bear a striking similarity to those reported in varying degree from countries where Austro-Hungarians are detained - disinclination to make complaints for fear of subsequent punishment, insufficient clothing, lack of variety of food, dilatory post etc....Since it would appear that in all probability no sensible change in their status is to be anticipated during the coming winter, it is strongly recommended that some provision be made for their mental distraction, that they be furnished with books, games [etc.] and that their friends send them additional articles of clothing to add to their comfort.[53]

Not all enemy aliens were interned, of course. In October 1915, for instance, the British and Bulgarian governments agreed to allow free passage to each other's citizens for the duration of the war, and in spite of some minor breaches on both sides, this arrangement was by and large upheld.[54] Moreover, in contrast to most other belligerents, Britain deliberately refrained from interning women, and its policy of detaining males of military age was subject to many stops and reversals in the first months of the war. Even when the move towards wholesale internment began in May 1915, the authorities discriminated in favour of Galicians, Bohemians, Alsatians, Trentino Italians and South Slavs, while giving priority to the arrest of Germans, Austrians and Hungarians.[55]

German policy towards enemy aliens (as opposed to its treatment of enemy civilians in occupied territory) was also at first fairly liberal and operated according to a strict principle of reciprocity (the so-called *Gegenseitigkeitsprinzip*). Thus early in the war agreements were signed with Britain and France for the exchange of women, children and men over 55, and with Japan and Serbia (and later with Italy) for the free departure of all civilians, regardless of age and gender.[56] As in Austria, the decision to intern British and French males of military age in November and December 1914 was presented in the German press as a legitimate 'retaliatory measure' undertaken in response to the poor treatment of German nationals in Britain and France.[57] Meanwhile, British women and children who chose to stay in Germany were not threatened with internment or expulsion at all, and as a rule only French women and children deported from the occupied territories, not those already on German soil in 1914, were deprived of their liberty. A fresh deal with France for the exchange of all women prisoners came into force in January 1916, but this failed to halt further deportations in the coming months and years.[58]

Situational and cultural factors also played a role in how enemy aliens were treated and how they perceived themselves. For instance, the British operated 'privileged camps' on the Isle of Man and at Lofthouse Park near Wakefield for those who could afford to upgrade their accommodation to the standard appropriate to a 'gentleman'. According to Paul Cohen-Portheim, Lofthouse Park

> was the true Beamtenstaat: everyone was administering and there was very little to administer; it was nearly all government and nothing much to be governed, and so really everyone administered the others by virtue of his office while being administered by them in their official capacities.[59]

Prisoners in London camps like Alexandra Palace had access to painting and sculpture studios, and were allowed frequent visits from their wives, something which was impossible for their Isle of Man counterparts.[60]

The British prisoners at Ruhleben likewise owed their relatively good conditions to the geographical location of the camp, which was easily reached from Berlin and was very much in the public limelight. They were also fortunate not to suffer from the 'franc-tireur' complex which coloured German attitudes towards French and Belgian civilians in occupied territories.[61] Like their German counterparts held in London, the British internees enjoyed monthly visits from their wives and daughters and were not completely shut off from the outside world; indeed, they were even able to acquire British newspapers which were smuggled in with the connivance of the camp censor.[62] An attempt by the Prussian Ministry of War to ration the amount of tobacco on sale in the camp in 1915 was rigorously and successfully resisted by the camp commandant, Count Schwerin, on the grounds that this was 'the one little bit of *Gemütlichkeit* permitted to the prisoners'.[63]

In Austria, the majority of British and French enemy aliens were confined rather than interned, and enjoyed limited freedom of movement, as we have seen. Yet ironically, as time went on, they were actually worse off in material terms than the internees, who at least were in regular receipt of Red Cross food parcels and did not have to pay food and rent bills at inflated prices. As one British woman who was confined with her elderly parents to the village of Raabs in Lower Austria later recalled:

> ... [W]e were exploited in every way. It was impossible to get accommodation for three people for less than K. 90-monthly-which equals about £45 a year. But most of the houses were only peasants' houses - and an Austrian peasant's house can only be described as a hole. Dirty - no comforts of any description. Added to this one has to pay for light - for a servant girl to do the dirty work if one can afford it. Nothing is free and nothing cheap. The village shops have two distinct charges - one for the inhabitants - one for the interned.[64]

For this and other reasons, it would be wrong to conclude that women living outside the camps were always better off than their male relatives inside the barbed wire. The worst affected were native-born women who had lost their citizenship upon marriage to a foreigner and were now 'enemy aliens' within their own country; destitution or total reliance on private charity often followed the internment or death of their husbands. Even those with private means found that their resources began to run out by 1916/17, particularly as wartime inflation eroded the value of savings. One German woman, whose British father was imprisoned at Ruhleben, later recalled that her mother and other 'Ruhleben wives' had regularly smuggled Red Cross parcels out of the camp to feed their families: 'it was very hard to walk out of the camp with the eyes of the guards on you, things were very heavy under their dresses'.[65] This story was probably far from untypical, and demonstrates the even graver impact that civilian internment could have on families and other dependants when compared to the internees themselves.

Deportees from war zones and occupied territories

A much larger group of civilian prisoners was made up of those who were deported from war zones or occupied territories. For instance, according to ICRC estimates, around 100,000 Belgian and French civilians were forcibly removed to Germany between 1914 and 1918, and 100,000 Germans and Austrians to Russia. The number of Ruthenian, Serb, Italian and Romanian prisoners held in the Habsburg lands was even higher, while Bulgaria, Romania and even Serbia were known to partake in the practice of deportations.[66] The conditions experienced by deportees also tended to be much worse than those faced by enemy aliens, and they were more likely to be the victims of reprisals and collective punishments, including the withdrawal of food parcels and other privileges. In the worst cases, they were deployed directly behind the front lines in mine clearing and other life-threatening duties. Alternatively they were deported to camps in the hinterland, where they were either put to work or used as hostages or bargaining tools in order to secure the release of captives held by the enemy.[67] Small wonder, then, that individual and collective representations of such prisoners tend to be framed around eschatological themes like exile, slavery and return, rather than around cultural themes, such as the development of *Lageruniversitäten* and contacts with home.[68]

The fate of civilian deportees in Europe can be illustrated by looking at the records of the Havelberg and Holzminden camps, which, apart from Ruhleben, were the two largest camps for civilian prisoners in Germany during the war. Both camps had separate compounds for men, women and children, and both camps placed a great deal of pressure on the inmates – mainly deportees from France, Belgium and Russia – to 'volunteer' for labour battalions, a policy which began as early as 1915 and was institutionalised by the Auxiliary Labour Law of December 1916.[69] By the end of 1917 regular reports were appearing in Swiss newspapers about the atrocious conditions in which the prisoners were being held,[70] and the Spanish embassy in Berlin began making its own inquiries through official channels.[71] The Prussian Ministry of War admitted that some inmates had died at Havelberg in a typhus epidemic in the summer of 1915 (278 deaths out of 1968 prisoners),[72] but otherwise it rejected complaints coming from Spanish, Swiss and Red Cross sources and issued counter-propaganda of its own. For instance, French women were only being held at Holzminden because of the French refusal to release German women from Alsace-Lorraine allegedly held against their will in non-occupied France.[73] Yet in September 1916 Dr. Frédéric Ferrière, the head of the civilian section of the ICRC's International Prisoner of War Agency, had written to Elisabeth Rotten, one of his chief contacts in Berlin, disputing these claims:

> We have passed on your observations to the [French] Minister of Interior regarding the question of reprisal measures, but we would comment that there seems to be a large imbalance between the number of women and children from Alsace who are still retained in France against their will, and the number of French women and children who wish to be returned to non-occupied France. The very extent of the territories occupied by one side and the other should suffice as a demonstration of this.[74]

In fact, the German war economy was becoming ever more dependent on the labour of enemy prisoners and deportees, as the Spanish diplomatic authorities and the ICRC knew, although they could do little about it.[75] Russian civilian prisoners suffered even more than their French and Belgian counterparts, as they received few, if any, relief parcels from home.[76] Even after the Treaty of Brest-Litovsk Russian civilians were still being held illegally at Holzminden and were sent out to work in increasingly poor conditions, as the new Bolshevik ambassador in Berlin complained in a note to the German Foreign Office on 10 May 1918: 'In spite of the peace treaty with Russia, conditions have got worse instead of better. The threat of removal to punishment camps remains in force. And the prisoners are also suffering because of periodic breakdowns in the postal service'.[77]

While the Germans were increasingly motivated by the need for forced labour,[78] in Austria-Hungary political factors also played a significant role. Thus in September 1914 around 4000 suspected 'Russophiles' from Galicia and Bukovina were deported and held in extremely harsh conditions at the Thalerhof camp near Graz, most of them members of the Ruthenian minority; and from May 1915 at least 12,000 Italian 'irredentists' were rounded up in the Trentino, Tyrol, Istria, Trieste and Dalmatia, and sent in several waves to various internment stations in Lower Austria or to the larger internment camps at Katzenau near Linz and Steinklamm near St. Pölten.[79] A total of 42,216 Italians, mainly women, children and older men, were also expelled via Switzerland to Italy, while during the year-long Austrian occupation of Italian territory which followed the battle of Caporetto in October 1917 a further 16,000 civilians were deported to and/or interned in Bohemia, Moravia and Lower Austria.[80] In all of these cases, severe punishments and humiliations were practised against the prisoners, and they were deprived of adequate food and shelter. According to one report on Thalerhof, made by British intelligence officers on the basis of interviews with escaped prisoners in Italy, the treatment of female deportees was especially inhumane:

> There was no separate latrine for them and they had to use the same as the men. Sometimes the NCOs amused themselves by pushing them into the latrines. . ..But the worst torture for them was the bath, because they had to expose themselves before the whole camp, and because . . . there were officers who came specially from Graz to see this and made the unfortunate women pose before their cameras.[81]

German civilians deported to Siberia during the brief Russian occupation of East Prussia in 1914/15 also suffered terrible conditions,[82] as did the thousands of Slovene 'suspects' who were driven from their homes, and in some cases interned, in the wake of Italian military operations on the Isonzo front between 1915 and 1917.[83] Yet the harshest treatment of all was reserved for Bosnian Serbs and for subjects of the pre-war Kingdom of Serbia arrested and imprisoned by Habsburg and Bulgarian troops during and after the invasions of 1914 and 1915. As early as November 1914 the Austrian politician Josef Redlich noted that a 'systematic policy of extermination' [*systematische Ausrottungspolitik*] had been launched by the Habsburg army on the south-eastern front, involving the murder or internment of thousands of innocent people and the depopulation of vast regions.[84] This was confirmed by an eyewitness report from the Serb lawyer and Red Cross official Dr Živko Tapalović, who spent over three years in Hungarian camps before being released in early 1918:

> Exhausted by indescribable ... privations and never ending journeys on foot to Hungary, [the deportees] reached the concentration camps haggard, bare-foot and hungry. But there were no installations ready. They found bare fields, surrounded with barbed wire. Inside those wire entanglements these men had to build themselves dwellings and barracks. But meanwhile a large proportion of them succumbed to exhaustion. Contagious disease, especially typhoid fever, claimed their holocausts. The lack of shelter and accommodation is the main reason for the extremely large loss of life during the first weeks of internment [in 1914/15].[85]

According to one source, 150,000 Serb civilians were interned in Austria-Hungary alone, with untold numbers dying; the ICRC, however, gave up trying to count and simply condemned the Habsburg military authorities for their lack of transparency in relation to Serb prisoners.[86]

In April 1917 the papal nuncio in Vienna and the Spanish government also wrote to the Habsburg Foreign Minister Count Czernin expressing their concern at the large number of civilians, including children aged 9–17, who had been deported as hostages from occupied Serbia to camps in Hungary in the period since the outbreak of war with Romania in August 1916.[87] Eventually in September 1917 the Habsburg authorities relented, agreeing to recognise the Serbian Red Cross in Geneva and to allow in relief from the London-based Serbian Relief Fund and other private charities.[88] The fate of Serbs in Bulgaria and Bulgarian-occupied Macedonia remained shrouded in mystery, however, with the Bulgarian Red Cross refusing to allow access to outside agencies or even to provide the names of the prisoners it was holding until the final collapse of its military effort in September 1918.[89] In this sense, the First World War can really be seen as a continuation of the second Balkan war of 1913 in which the two principal foes, Serbia and Bulgaria, and Serbia's allies, the Greeks, the Romanians, the Turks and the Montenegrins, 'took advantage of a military conflict to pursue long-range demographic goals' in the region, leading to enormous civilian casualties on both sides.[90] Indeed, King Ferdinand of Bulgaria explicitly mentioned the destruction of Serbia as his key war aim when entering the First World War on the side of the Central Powers in October 1915.[91]

Refugees from war zones

Meanwhile, a separate but related category of internees were refugees and forced migrants from war zones seeking shelter in the unoccupied parts of their own countries. As these were subjects of the states which deported or rehoused them they do not even appear in the Red Cross statistics as prisoners of war and were not acknowledged as such by the warring states. Yet in practice they often ended up as civilian prisoners, forced to live apart from the native population in barrack-like accommodation and/or forbidden to leave the districts in which they were billeted on pain of losing state financial support or access to rations. Jews living in the war zones of the eastern front were especially vulnerable, and were singled out for expulsions by both sides. In Russia, for instance, army commanders took the lead in sponsoring anti-Jewish violence in 1914/15, with pogroms, accompanied by arson, pillage and murder, taking place in many parts of Poland, Galicia, Lithuania and the Ukraine before, during and after the military defeats of April to October 1915. Survivors faced journeys to the interior on foot or in unheated, overcrowded cattle trucks, leading to widespread death from exposure, starvation and disease.[92]

Other groups suffered as well. Peter Gatrell, for instance, estimates that around 200,000 ethnic Germans were expelled from Russian Poland in 1914 and deported to Siberia under armed guard. Further expulsions took place from Riga, Volynia, Kiev, Podolia and the Volga region in 1915 and 1916, allegedly for the victims' 'own protection' but in reality so that their lands and property could be confiscated and handed over to imported Russian settlers.[93] On top of this, according to Alan Kramer, over 300,000 Lithuanians, 250,000 Latvians and 743,000 Poles, as well as more than half a million Jews, were forced out of their homes by retreating Tsarist forces, largely out of 'fear of betrayal by spies and deserters'.[94]

On the opposite side, Jews, Poles, Ukrainians and others who fled from the Russians into the Austrian hinterland in 1914/15 and again during the Brusilov offensive in 1916, although perhaps better protected against the threat of direct violence or starvation, also faced long journeys in cattle trucks, high mortality rates among the young, sick and old, and the possibility of hunger and/or internment when they reached their final destination.[95] Indeed Walter Mentzel found that in the Austrian/Bohemian interior, where 130,000 refugees were already living in camps by the end of 1915, policy was directed towards reducing the costs of feeding them while maximising their potential as a cheap source of labour:

> The humanitarian obligations of the state were in the meantime passed on to private welfare agencies organised on a national or confessional basis. In cases where the state did offer support, this was understood as being 'supplementary' only.[96]

These problems were all the more evident given the hostility of German Austrians towards the refugees, who they saw as spongers and shirkers rather than war victims.[97] Many were interned as 'suspects' and 'undesirables' in spite of having sufficient means to support themselves without becoming a burden on the state.[98] One of the most brutal camps in this respect was the Jewish refugee station at Deutsch-Brod in Bohemia, where inmates were routinely humiliated and abused, as well as being forced to live in unhygienic conditions which gave rise to periodic outbreaks of infectious diseases. As one inmate reported in August 1916:

> The treatment meted out to us is completely without restraint. Just like in a prison we are placed under heavy guard, in our ears echo the insults which are hurled at us by the local population: 'dirty, cursed Jews, you are worse than dogs, you'll all perish here'. But even the camp administration sees us as its playthings, and makes fun and laughter at our expense![99]

Similar trends occurred in France, where refugees from the occupied northern and eastern territories or from Alsace-Lorraine were subject to hostile encounters with local officials and a range of limitations on their freedom of movement: 'They were all promised a rapid return home and in the meantime work ... but the population was reluctant to employ them'.[100] Likewise in the neutral Netherlands the Dutch government faced local anger when it sought to house refugees, deserters and exchanged prisoners in camps outside particular towns and villages, while Dutch trade unions demanded tight restrictions on the deployment of cheaper foreign labour.[101] And even in 'liberal' Britain, where refugees were initially well received, public opinion became increasingly less sympathetic as time went on. Thus cafés owned by Belgians were suspected of being 'spy houses', while Russian Jews were subjected to verbal abuse and – in London and Leeds – physical assaults 'because the native population felt that they avoided National Service'.[102]

As for the 70,000 strong German community, the London *Daily Mail* waged a campaign from 1917 to 'send them home', calling for the expulsion of all Germans, naturalised or not, from Britain's shores in order to prevent them from 'spying on us, and stealing [our] trade'. Even those who were opposed to the German war effort should be deported, it suggested: 'They should be condemned to live in their own country until they have rescued it from the Prussian drill sergeant'.[103]

Public Opinion, private charity and the state

Clearly, then, popular resentments were harnessed across Europe to support the internment, expropriation and disenfranchisement of aliens and refugees. Jews and other persecuted minorities who had no state of their own to represent them were particularly vulnerable in this respect. Even so, we should be careful not to assume that public opinion was uniformly or consistently hostile towards enemy aliens before 1918. In fact, critics of internment emerged in all the warring states, as well as in neutral countries, and included those who came into regular contact with prisoners, such as Red Cross officials, private philanthropists, international women's organisations and representatives of the churches. Relatives of the interned also put increasing pressure on their own governments to secure the release of their loved ones, on grounds of national interest or economic hardship. From time to time they found a sympathetic voice in the press, especially at local level.

Family and community are indeed important tools for analysing the social impact of internment on European politics, particularly when we remember that large numbers of women and children were left to fend for themselves in the absence of husbands/fathers (occasionally it could be the other way round, too, as husbands were left with children when wives were deported).[104] In Britain, for instance, the Ruhleben Prisoners' Release Committee focused on this theme in a pamphlet published at the beginning of 1917, choosing to cite letters from prisoners' relatives in order to support its demands for an 'all for all' exchange of internees with Germany:

> Yorkshire, 23 January 1917:
> My son has been interned since August 4 1914. He was one of the crew of the SS — [which was] at — , in Germany, when the war broke out. I am his mother and am quite alone; 83 years of age come June. I would like to have him home if only the Government would intercede.

> London, 21 January 1917:
> Ever since he has been [at Ruhleben] I have sent [my husband] two parcels of food each week, also bread from Berne ... it does not seem fair that we should have to keep them and ourselves as well. My husband's firm allows me so much every week. Otherwise I should have to sell my home. I go out to work while the women here who are married to interned Germans are allowed 11/6 per week, and so much for each child.

> Essex, 24 January 1917
> We were living in Berlin when my husband was taken. I stayed there over a year to send him food, and paid our rent, and then had to leave so as to send food from home to him, and also money. I might say we have lost all. I have had to keep him for over two years.[105]

Alongside the family, private welfare organisations and charities also acted as mediators between the individual and the state during wartime.[106] This could be applied in the context of internment too, as seen, for instance, in the work of Elisabeth Rotten's organisation in Berlin and of like-minded groups in Britain, such as the International Women's Relief Committee and the Quaker-led Friends Emergency Committee (FEC), all of which searched for news of missing persons on behalf of anxious relatives and organised relief for civilians in captivity. Rotten's committee, the *Auskunfts- und Hilfsstelle für Deutsche im Ausland und Ausländer in Deutschland*, is particularly interesting because of the dual nature of her patriotic commitment to Germany (in spite of her Swiss parentage) and her feminist commitment to internationalism (which saw her acting as one of the German delegates to the international women's peace congress at The Hague in April–May 1915). Significantly she was able to persuade representatives of both the anti-war and pro-war wings of the German women's movement to serve on her committee, while also securing financial contributions from some of Germany's most powerful public figures, including the former diplomats Prince Lichnowsky and Prince Hatzfeldt, the newspaper proprietors Hermann Ullstein and Rudolf Mosse, and the bankers Bernhard Dernburg and Max Warburg.[107]

The idea of civilian prisoners and their families as war victims – *Opfer* – who had made a sacrifice for the common good also gradually took root in Britain and Germany from 1916 on. In both cases it was claimed that civilian internees were performing an equivalent of military service by 'holding out' against enemy propaganda.[108] French charities like the Evian-based *Secours aux rapatriés*, on the other hand, presented the war less in terms of individual or family sacrifice and more as a national crusade against a pitiless foe, a discourse which left little room for the notion of internees as a separate category of war victim. Perhaps this was because France – unlike Germany and Britain – endured four years of partial foreign occupation during the war, with all the associated religious imagery of fall and redemption that went with this.[109] Indeed, there are some interesting parallels here with the Serbian case. The lawyer Živko Tapalović, for instance, portrayed the suffering of his fellow internees in Hungary as follows:

> I am witness . . . that the largest number of our men live their days with stoical perseverance. The enemy has got hold of their bodies, but he has not succeeded in mastering their souls . . . [Yet] it is difficult and painful to think of relatives when they are known to be humilated and subjugated in the very same way. . . .Those regions which we love so much and to return to which we desire are under the heel of the conqueror. This thought is painful. One does not like to think of one's own people when they are known to be in misery and humiliation. The thoughts turn quickly to the brighter side where hope is still shining. . . .Looks turn to the representatives of free Serbia. . . .The history of our Nation in captivity has yet to be written.[110]

While internment may have helped reinforce the formation of national/religious identity in Serbia and France, in Germany and Austria-Hungary it had the opposite effect of undermining social harmony and the legitimacy of the state. Thus government officials in both of these blockaded powers found themselves increasingly on the defensive in relation to the rising cost of feeding refugees and civilian internees, many of whom did not work, or were perceived not to work by an increasingly hungry and war-weary indigenous population. The increasingly proactive stance of the Vatican on questions like civilian deportees, prisoner exchanges and peace negotiations also created problems for Catholics in the German-speaking lands, as became clear when General Ludendorff referred to Benedict XV as the 'French Pope'.[111]

In Austria the release from internment of large numbers of 'suspect' Austrian subjects from the border regions in early 1917, on the direct orders of the new emperor, led to conflicts with the military, and especially with the former chief of the general staff Conrad von Hötzendorf, who was at that point in command of Habsburg forces in Tyrol. Many of those who were released were de facto reclassified as refugees and housed in various parts of German Austria and Bohemia, albeit with restrictions on their freedom of movement. Others were allowed to return home and some were even called up into the Habsburg army.[112] Following a series of debates in the newly recalled Reichsrat (parliament), the government also introduced new legislation officially recognising all refugees as war victims with a right to state financial support. This was combined with a propaganda campaign advertising official refugee policy as an educational tool aimed at the transformation of '"uncivilised", "non-German" populations from the periphery of the Monarchy' into good, patriotic Austrians.[113] As the Ministry of the Interior put it in a letter sent to local government authorities in March 1917, efforts towards the setting up of language classes in the various barrack camps and settlements where non-German speaking Habsburg subjects were housed

> ... must from an economic and a cultural viewpoint be given the most emphatic support by the state. This is because [such projects] will promote the development of more active economic and social links between the border regions of the Monarchy and the Hinterland and strengthen the overall feeling of a harmonious belonging together.[114]

Yet after November 1918 the new law was officially allowed to lapse, and the same propaganda which had declared war refugees to be loyal, *erziehungsfähig* subjects of the Monarchy now declared them to be 'foreign nationals' (*fremde Staatsangehörige*) in need of continued detention pending repatriation or expulsion.[115] Here, as in other parts of central and eastern Europe, wartime 'expulsion fantasies' and demands for ethnic homogeneity were now brought closer to reality through the promulgation of new, more restrictive citizenship laws which redefined who was and who was not an Austrian in accordance with 'national' principles.[116]

Diplomacy and the end of internment

So far we have looked at internment as an issue in the domestic politics of the belligerent states. Yet from the beginning of the war civilian internment had also featured in international diplomacy, albeit often as a minor sub-issue linked to debates about the welfare of military POWs. Thus the Vatican sponsored a series of agreements for the exchange of sick and wounded prisoners in 1915, and the Swiss government agreed to intern limited numbers of military personnel and civilian internees from both sides under Franco-German and Anglo-German accords signed in January and May 1916.[117] On a broader level, the ICRC established a civilian section of its International Prisoner of War Agency in October 1914, under the direction of Dr Frédéric Ferrière, which facilitated communication between internees and their families and made regular visits to camps where civilians were held. Visits were also made by representatives of the Danish and Swedish Red Cross societies and by the American Young Men's Christian Association (YMCA), which meant that they too were drawn into the process of communicating ideas about the meaning and significance of internment to a broader international public.[118]

Meanwhile, through the efforts of the Swiss and Dutch governments various bilateral agreements were reached in 1917 and 1918 between France and Germany, Britain and Germany, and Austria and Serbia which allowed for the gradual release of broader categories of military and civilian prisoner. This particularly affected those who had spent more than 18 months in captivity.[119] For the first time 'barbed wire disease' was also recognised as grounds 'for release or internment in a neutral country' under the 1917 Anglo-German Hague accord, while the Dutch government followed the Swiss in agreeing to intern civilian and military personnel from both sides who were considered to be too ill to withstand the continued rigours of life in an enemy prison camp.[120] Nonetheless, by November 1918 the number of prisoners who had actually benefited from these arrangements was pitifully small, and progress towards implementation was painfully slow. Except in a few cases, diplomacy had done little for civilian prisoners.

An even bigger failure lay in efforts to prevent the use of reprisals against civilian as well as military prisoners. Part of the problem here was the refusal of belligerent states to grant access to camps in occupied territories to representatives of the ICRC or to inspection teams from neutral countries.[121] These difficulties were compounded by the fact that belligerents were reluctant to forego the right of retaliation as a means of protecting their own national interests or on grounds of 'military necessity'. Indeed, several of the bilateral and multilateral agreements regarding the treatment of prisoners negotiated in 1917 and 1918 included an explicit recognition of the right to retaliate if the other side was found to have committed violations of previous accords, albeit usually with a 'cooling off' period of a few weeks following the initial complaint.[122]

Finally, some prisoner exchanges were delayed or prevented altogether by the refusal of third parties to cooperate. For instance, an agreement between Austria-Hungary and Russia in August 1917 to release all civilians and certain categories of military prisoner failed because of the reluctance of the German naval authorities to guarantee safe passage for the returnees across the Baltic, and the simultaneous refusal of the Swedish government to allow the exchange to take place via its territory.[123]

Ultimately, civilian internment was only brought to an end by the cessation of hostilities in November 1918. Even then, the collapse of the Central Powers' war effort also led to the collapse of the *Gegenseitigkeitsprinzip* which had partially protected German and Austrian civilians living in enemy countries. Thus, as the *Revue Internationale de la Croix-Rouge* reported in January 1919, the armistice had dealt a double blow to Germans interned in France, reinforcing their position as pawns at the mercy of international developments while dashing their hopes of repatriation under the earlier Berne agreement of April 1918:

> Around 2,500 German civilians are still being held in captivity in France. Their complaints are numerous, and their situation has not only been aggravated by their strong feelings of deception, but also by the fact that their relief parcels have been stopped for several weeks now on the grounds that they are about to be released. The [International] Committee would like to see the universal adoption of the principle that 'civilians should not be taken as prisoners of war', but in the current circumstances it can do no more than rely on the clemency of the governments of the Entente.[124]

Indeed, while Britain released (and expelled) most of its internees between January and May 1919,[125] elsewhere the repatriation process was much slower, lasting until November 1919 in the French case, and even longer with respect to Soviet Russia.[126] Thus according to one estimate at least 60,000 and possibly as many as 200,000 Austro-Hungarian prisoners remained trapped in Russian territory in October 1919 with little immediate prospect of returning home.[127] Another estimate from around the same time put the number of German civilians still in Russia at 20,000, together with 25,000 to 30,000 former German POWs.[128] The worst affected were those being held in areas beyond the Urals; here repatriation could not take place until after the end of the civil war in the summer of 1920, and in the two years leading up to this many had been conscripted into the (anti-Bolshevik) Czech Legion or deported and left to die of starvation and neglect.[129]

Meanwhile, the Romanians made use of internment camps to imprison 900 civilians and several thousand military personnel deported during their invasion of Hungary in August 1919,[130] and the Slovaks likewise banished up to 2700 Hungarian communists and reservists to the former Habsburg fortress at Terezín (Theresienstadt) in the Czech lands, a policy which evoked painful comparisons with the Austrian internment camp at Thalerhof among its Czech Social Democrat critics.[131] More generally, where post-war borders were contested on ethnic grounds, for instance in the wake of the fighting between Poles, Jews and Ukrainians in 1918/19, thousands could find themselves temporarily detained as a threat to newly emerging nation-states.[132] Or, as Hannah Arendt put it, with the collapse of the Romanov and Habsburg dynasties, 'the last remnants of solidarity between the non-emancipated nationalities ... evaporated', so that 'now everybody was against everybody else, and most of all against his closest neighbo[u]rs'.[133] In the immediate period after 1918 the Slovaks, Poles and Romanians were the biggest offenders. Yet interestingly the new German government also contributed to post-war ethnic tensions in central Europe by deciding to retain Polish men of military age whose home towns and villages, formerly part of the Prussian provinces of Posen and West Prussia, were now in the new independent state of Poland. As a Swiss ICRC delegate noted in April 1919:

> In Sagan and also in Havelberg large numbers of soldiers who spilt their blood for Germany have been interned on the pretext that if they were allowed to return home they *could* fight against Germany. One has to actually listen to these unfortunate men to get a proper idea of the misery to which they are subjected. Wounded or sick, already separated from their loved ones for $4\frac{1}{2}$ years ... they were finally released from their units; and then, on the way home, they were arrested, beaten, robbed and finally sent to a prison camp, where they are now plagued by the thought: 'Can this be our reward?'.[134]

In fact, the last of these prisoners was not released until July 1920, bringing a final end to the unhappy saga of First World War civilian captivity.

Conclusion

After 1920 internment increased massively as an instrument of warfare and as a tool by which states fought so-called 'internal enemies', whether defined in terms of their nationality, political views, social class or ethnicity. The Russian Gulags, the concentration camps of Nazi Germany and Nationalist Spain, the special detention centres for Spanish republicans and other stateless communists in France in 1939/40, the British camps for German refugees from Nazism on the Isle of Man, and the deportations of German and Italian prisoners from Britain to Canada and Australia in 1940/41 are all, in their different ways, examples of this. What did governments learn from the First World War experience which may have influenced future policy and practices? In some ways it is tempting to argue that they learned that enemy civilians could be imprisoned in large numbers and at relatively little cost; that pleadings on their behalf from the ICRC, neutral governments and private charities could be ignored with impunity; that international law offered very little in the way of protection for civilian war victims; and that public and business opinion could be harnessed to support the reduction of rations for internees, or their use as forced labour. Equally it would be tempting to argue that public opinion as a whole had 'internalised' the violence of war. Or, to put it another way, internment had brought with it new, more radical and more destructive ways of imagining the 'enemy-opponent' or 'enemy within'. Such brutalised patterns of thinking in turn became inextricably linked with a '1914–18 war culture' which was only partially dismantled, if at all, after the end of hostilities.[135]

Yet this is only part of the picture. Another lesson from the war was that governments which were prepared to work through the *Gegenseitigkeit-sprinzip*, the utilitarian principle of reciprocity, could achieve a great deal in terms of helping their citizens in captivity, including securing material improvements to prisoner accommodation, regular delivery of relief parcels and increased contact with home.[136] In certain contexts the ICRC and other groups like the FEC and the *Auskunfts- und Hilfsstelle* could also help to demobilise national hatreds through publishing accounts of internment which stressed the common humanity of prisoners. The very positive Red Cross reports on British camps, published in 1915, for instance, made it very difficult for either Germany or Austria-Hungary to justify reprisal actions against British civilians held under their jurisdiction.[137] Admittedly, another factor here was the imbalance in prisoner numbers, so that whereas in 1917 Britain, together with its dominions and colonies, was holding about 36,000 Germans and 11,000 Austro-Hungarian civilians in captivity, Germany held only 3500 British civilians, and Austria-Hungary around 200.[138]

The 'forgotten victims' in the history of wartime diplomacy and humanitarian aid, on the other hand, were the wives and families of internees, and more particularly those internees who were stateless or had no government to represent them. As we have seen in the case of Austria-Hungary in particular, these captives were held not as potential combatants or even as bargaining counters, but as 'traitors' and 'suspects', unwanted, stateless persons, 'enemies of the people', 'outcasts' or (to borrow Arthur Koestler's later phrase) the 'scum of the earth'.[139] On a much larger scale, it was such people who – on account of their race, their political views or their sexual orientation – filled the concentration camps and extermination centres of Nazi-occupied Europe during the Second World War.

Notes

[1] Nadeshda Bogdanova to Elisabeth Rotten, 1 March 1916, in Evangelisches Zentralarchiv (EZA) Berlin, Bestand 51 C III g 1.

[2] Stibbe, 'The Internment of Civilians', 7–8.

[3] Quataert, 'Women's Wartime Services', 453–83; Gill, 'Calculating Compassion'; Stibbe, 'Elisabeth Rotten', 194–210.

[4] The *Enzyklopädie Erster Weltkrieg*, edited by Gerhard Hirschfeld, Gerd Krumeich and Irina Renz (Paderborn, 2003), does admittedly contain a brief entry by Uta Hinz on 'Internierung' (see 582–4), but few other surveys do the same.

[5] An important exception here is Pöppinghege, *Im Lager unbesiegt*, a book which includes civilian internees in its thorough and convincing analysis of prison camp journals.

[6] I have found the following books and essays to be the most useful: Farcy, *Les camps de concentration français*; Jahr, 'Zivilisten als Kriegsgefangene', 297–321; Lohr, *Nationalizing the Russian Empire*; Nagler, *Nationale Minoritäten*; Panayi, *The Enemy in Midst*; and de Roodt, *Oorlogsgasten*. See also my own monograph, *British Civilian Internees in Germany*.

[7] Becker, *Oubliés de la grande guerre*. See also Becker, 'Religion', 192–7.

[8] Speed, *Prisoners, Diplomats and the Great War*, 152–3.

[9] See esp. Kotek and Rigoulot, *Das Jahrhundert der Lager*, 87–97; Applebaum, *Gulag*, 18–19.

[10] Audoin-Rouzeau and Becker, *1914–1918*, 70.

[11] Speed, *Prisoners, Diplomats and the Great War*, 152.

[12] Cf. Nagler and Förster, *On the Road to Total War*.

[13] Nagler, *Nationale Minoritäten*, 13.

[14] Panayi, *The Enemy in Our Midst*, 61–7; Speed, *Prisoners, Diplomats and the Great War*, 144.

[15] Jahr, 'Keine Feriengäste', 238.

[16] For a useful overview see Osterhammel and Petersson, *Globalization*, esp. 81–98.

[17] Lucassen, 'The Great War and the Origins of Migration Control', 45–72.

[18] See, for example, Maglen, 'Importing Trachoma'.

[19] Lucassen, 'The Great War and the Origins of Migration Control', 54–5. See also Gainer, *The Alien Invasion*; Torpey, *The Invention of the Passport*, esp. 93–121; Herbert, *A History of Foreign Labor in Germany*, 18–23 and 30–7; Nathans, *The Politics of Citizenship in Germany*, esp. 139–67.

[20] The figure of 4.5 million comes from Blackbourn, 'Das Kaiserreich transnational', 302. Cf. the German Reichstag's official report, 'Die Zivilgefangenen', in *Völkerrecht im Weltkrieg*, vol. 3, part 2, 719–826.

[21] Nagler, *Nationale Minoritäten*, 52; Speed, *Prisoners, Diplomats and the Great War*, 143.

[22] See Lohr, *Nationalizing the Russian Empire*, esp. 26–7 and 31–54.

[23] Blackbourn, 'Das Kaiserreich transnational', 313; Herbert, *A History of Foreign Labor in Germany*, 9–85; Oltmer, 'Schreckbild Migration?', 141–87.

[24] See Stibbe, *British Civilian Internees in Germany*, esp. 11, 24, 31–3, 128–31 and 143.

[25] Ferguson, *The War of the World*, 138–40 and 174–84.

[26] Mayerhofer, 'Making Friends and Foes', unpublished version, 11. I am grateful to the author for permission to quote from this source.

[27] Healy, *Vienna and the Fall of the Habsburg Empire*, 1 and 4–5.

[28] Cf. Mentzel, 'Weltkriegsflüchtlinge', 17–44; and Hoffmann-Holter, 'Abreisend-machung'.

[29] Kotek and Rigoulot, *Das Jahrhundert der Lager*, 45–73; Scharnagl, *Kurze Geschichte der Konzentrationslager*, 23–41.

[30] Zimmerer, 'Kriegsgefangene im Kolonialkrieg', 277–94; idem, 'The Birth of the "Ostland" out of the Spirit of Colonialism', 197–219; Madley, 'From Africa to Auschwitz'.

[31] See also the highly disturbing evidence produced by Elkins, *Britain's Gulag*.

[32] Horne and Kramer, 'War Between Soldiers and Enemy Civilians', 163; Liulevicius, *War Land on the Eastern Front*, 159.

[33] For a broader discussion of the pre-war views see James W. Garner, 'Treatment of Enemy Aliens. Measures in Respect to Personal Liberty', *American Journal of International Law* 12, no. 1 (1918): 27–55.

[34] Emerich de Vattel, *Droit des gens, ou principes de la loi naturelle appliqués à la conduite et aux affaires des nations et des souverains* (Neuchâtel, 1758), cited in ibid., 27.

[35] Von Liszt, *Völkerrecht*, 462. Cf. Georg Cohn, 'Zur Geschichte der Einsperrung feindlicher Ausländer', *Zeitschrift für Völkerrecht*, 9 (1916), 87–8.

[36] Speed, *Prisoners, Diplomats and the Great War*, 143.

[37] Bethmann Hollweg famously used this phrase in relation to the German invasion of Belgium in his Reichstag speech on 4 August 1914. Cited in Kramer, 'Kriegsrecht und Kriegsverbrechen', 282.

[38] Durand, *From Sarajevo to Hiroshima*, 83. See also Daniel Segesser's contribution to this volume.

[39] Von Liszt, *Völkerrecht*, 461.

[40] Laws and Customs of War on Land (Hague IV) (18 October 1907). The Avalon Project at the Yale Law School. http://www.yale.edu/lawweb/avalon/lawofwar/hague04.htm (accessed 26 August 2008).

[41] See, for example, Hinz, 'Die deutschen "Barbaren" sind doch die besseren Menschen', 339–61.

[42] Cohen-Portheim, *Time Stood Still*.

[43] Stibbe, *British Civilian Internees in Germany*, esp. 79–94.

[44] Frank Stockall, unpublished memoirs, 70; cited in ibid., 95. On class and racial tensions in Ruhleben more generally see also Jahr, 'Zivilisten als Kriegsgefangene', 306–12.

[45] Ketchum, *Ruhleben*, 167–8. See also Vischer, *Barbed Wire Disease*.

[46] On Newbury camp see also the documents in The National Archives, Kew, London (TNA), FO 369/714.

[47] See, for example, Cohen-Portheim, *Time Stood Still*, 29–30; Richard Noschke, 'First World War Diaries', in Imperial War Museum, London, Department of Documents.

[48] Cf. Panayi, 'Normalität hinter Stacheldraht', 126–46.

[49] Max Hayn to the Auswärtiges Amt, 9 September 1916; cited in Stibbe, *British Civilian Internees in Germany*, 128–9.

[50] See, for example, *Rapports de MM. G. Ador, Dr. F. Ferrière et Dr. de Schultheiss-Schindler sur leurs visites à quelques camps de prisonniers en Autriche-Hongrie* (Geneva and Paris, 1915). Copy in Archive du Comité International de la

Croix-Rouge, Geneva, Groupe 400, Agence Internationale des prisonniers de guerre de Genève, 1914-18 (ACICR, C G1) 432/II/4.

[51] To date there is no published secondary literature on the treatment of enemy aliens in Austria, with the exception of the Italians. Useful archival material can nonetheless be found in TNA, FO 383/5, 383/247 and 383/364, and in Österreichisches Staatsarchiv, Vienna, Haus-, Hof- und Staatsarchiv, (ÖStA-HHStA Vienna), F 36, Karton 556, 26/2a and Karton 568, 27/2a. See also Mundschütz, 'Internierung im Waldviertel'.

[52] Cf. Ministerium des Äußerns to the Kriegsüberwachungsamt, 11 October 1914, in Österreichisches Staatsarchiv, Kriegsarchiv, Bestand Kriegsüberwachungsamt (ÖStA-KA Vienna, KÜA), Zl. 7583.

[53] Report from Mr. Grant-Smith to Mr. Penfield, US ambassador at Vienna, 5 November 1915, copy in TNA FO 383/5.

[54] See the relevant documents in TNA, FO 383/8, 383/131 and 383/254. A more limited agreement to restrict the number of internees on both sides was also reached between France and Bulgaria – see Farcy, *Les camps de concentration français*, 41.

[55] Panayi, *The Enemy in Our Midst*, 81–2. See also Stephen Hobhouse, notes on an interview with the Home Office Aliens Department, 19 May 1915, in Society of Friends Library (SFL), London, FEWVRC/CAMPS/2, no. 8. For a similar policy of favouring certain nationalities over others in France see Grandhomme, 'Internment Camps for German Civilians'.

[56] Information about these agreements can be found in Bundesarchiv (BA) Berlin, R 1501/112361-65. See also Garner, 'Treatment of Enemy Aliens', (as note 33), 49–55; Jahr, 'Keine Feriengäste', 235–7; and Wippich, 'Internierung und Abschiebung von Japanern'. Nonetheless, the German government did intern Portuguese, Romanian and Siamese nationals after the breakdown of diplomatic negotiations in 1916 and 1917 respectively. See the relevant documents in BA Berlin, R 1501/112369-70 and ÖStA-HHStA Vienna, F 36, Karton 600, 45 1/b.

[57] See, for example, *Norddeutsche Allgemeine Zeitung*, 6 November 1914 [evening edition]. Also Gottfried Prinz zu Hohenlohe-Schillingsfürst to Count Berchtold, 6 November 1914, in ÖStA-HHStA Vienna, F 36, Karton 556, 26/2a, Zl. 11.

[58] See, for example, the evidence in EZA Berlin, Bestand 51 C III g 1-3. French women were also deported as forced labourers from urban to rural parts of occupied France, particularly during the action in the Lille-Tourcoing-Roubaix area in spring 1916 – see Becker, *Oubliés de la grande guerre*, esp. 68–77; McPhail, *The Long Silence*, 166–70; and Bianchi, *La violenza contro la popolazione civile*, 440–54.

[59] Cohen-Portheim, *Time Stood Still*, 94.

[60] Panayi, *The Enemy in Our Midst*, 124 and 129.

[61] For further details see Horne and Kramer, 'War Between Soldiers and Enemy Civilians', esp. 163–8. Also idem., *German Atrocities, 1914*.

[62] Stibbe, *British Civilian Internees in Germany*, 57

[63] ibid.

[64] Dorothy Cocking, unpublished typewritten report, no date [March/April 1918], 1–2, in TNA, FO 383/364. Cf. the similar complaints in ÖStA-HHStA Vienna, F 36, Karton 556, 26/2a, Zl. 75.

[65] Ellen Prendergast, née Firth, unpublished typewritten memoirs, no date, 4; cited in Stibbe, *British Civilian Internees in Germany*, 118.

[66] Stibbe, 'The Internment of Civilians', 7. See also Bianchi, 'I civili', 62, who estimates the number of civilian internees in Austria-Hungary as being at least 200,000.

[67] Kramer, 'Deportationen', 434–5; Hinz, 'Zwangsarbeit', 978–80.

[68] Becker, *Oubliés de la grande guerre*, esp. 53–6 and 231–6.

[69] Cf. the guidelines issued to the deputy military commands by the Prussian Ministry of War and the German Army High Command, in Hauptstaatsarchiv Stuttgart, M77/1, No. 868.

[70] See, for example, 'Comment on meurt dans les camps allemands', *La Tribune de Genève*, 16 October 1917; and 'Les prisonniers au camp de Havelberg (Brandebourg)', *Le Genevois*, no. 17, 17 January 1918, copies of both in BA Berlin, R 901/84319.

[71] See the correspondence in BA Berlin, R 901/84319.

[72] See, for example, Prussian Ministry of War to the Auswärtiges Amt, 2 April 1918, in BA Berlin, R 901/84319.

[73] See, for example, *Vossische Zeitung*, 1 November 1916. On the deportation of 200 French women and men to Holzminden as hostages in November 1916 see Becker, *Oubliés de la grande guerre*, 84–6 and on German women from Alsace-Lorraine interned by the French government at Remiremont and Besançon see Becker, Oubliés de la grande guerre, 245–6, 245–6, and Farcy, *Les camps de concentration français*, 51–61.

[74] Ferrière to Rotten, 9 September 1916, in EZA Berlin, Bestand 51 C III g 1.

[75] This can be seen in the numerous reports in BA Berlin, R 901/84319 and 84337. On Germany's use of POW and enemy civilian labour more generally see Oltmer, 'Arbeitszwang und Zwangsarbeit', 96–107; Hinz, *Gefangen im Großen Krieg*, 248–318, and Thiel, '*Menschenbassin Belgien*'.

[76] See, for example, *Rapport de MM A. von Schulthess et F. Thormeyer sur leur visite aux camps de prisonniers de guerre russes en Allemagne en avril 1916* (Geneva and Paris, June 1916). Copy in ACICR, C G1/432/II/13.

[77] Verbalnote, Botschaft der Russischen Sozialistischen Sowjet-Republik, 10 May 1918, in BA Berlin, R 901/84337.

[78] There were some important exceptions here, for instance the Belgian historian Henri Pirenne, who was deported from Belgium to Germany in 1916 not for forced labour but apparently because of his role in orchestrating resistance to the German policy of Flemishisation of the University of Ghent. Numerous other 'Honoratioren' were also deported from Belgium and northern France as hostages – see Becker, *Oubliés de la grande guerre*, 83–7 and *passim*; Kramer, 'Deportationen', 434; and Thiel, '*Menschenbassin Belgien*', 11, n. 11. Also Föllmer, 'Der Feind im Salon', 7–8.

[79] On Thalerhof camp see Militärkommando Graz to the Kriegsministerium, 1 February 1918, in ÖStA-KA Vienna, Kriegsministerium 1918, Karton 2049, 10/14/3. Also Wendland, *Die Russophilen in Galizien*, 540–7, who suggests that as many as 7000 persons were eventually detained at Thalerhof, a figure which nonetheless included some Russian deserters and Galician Jews as well as 'russophile' political suspects. On Katzenau see Haller, 'Das Internierungslager Katzenau bei Linz', and on Steinklamm, which later became a refugee camp, see Mundschütz, 'Internierung im Waldviertel'. On Italian 'irredentists' or political suspects interned in Austria more generally see Cecotti, 'Internamenti di civili',

esp. 76–82; Pircher, *Militär, Verwaltung und Politik*, 64–9; Palla, *Il Trentino orientale*, 95–121; and Kramer, *Dynamic of Destruction*, 59–61.

[80] See the figures in Ermacora, 'Assistance and Surveillance', 446–7; and Kramer, *Dynamic of Destruction*, 60–1.

[81] 'Austria-Hungary: Treatment of Prisoners', 23 June 1916, in TNA FO 383/123. See also the corroborating evidence provided by Dorothy Cocking based on stories told to her by survivors of Thalerhof at Raabs confinement station in 1916/17, in TNA, FO 383/364, and the similar claims made by the Czech politician Jiří Stříbrný before the Austrian Reichsrat on 14 June 1917, in *Stenographische Protokolle des Abgeordnetenhauses des Reichsrates*, XXII. Session (Vienna, 1917), 240–50.

[82] See Tiepolato, '"... und nun waren wir auch Verbannte"'; idem, 'L'internamento di civili prussiani', 107–25; and Borck and Kölm, *Gefangen in Sibirien*.

[83] Svoljšak, 'La popolazione civile nella Slovenia occupata', 147–63. See also Cecotti, 'Internamenti di civili', 82–9; and Kramer, *Dynamic of Destruction*, 126–7.

[84] Fellner, *Schicksalsjahre Österreichs*, vol. 2, 289. Also cited in Mazower, *The Balkans*, 106.

[85] English translation of a lecture on the life of the Serbian prisoners of war and civilians interned in Austro-Hungarian camps of concentration, given on 18 May 1918 in Corfu by Dr Živko Tapalović, and forwarded to the British Foreign Office, 3, in TNA, FO 383/463. Further evidence of the exceptionally high mortality rates in the Hungarian camps at Arad and Nezsider (Neusiedl) can also be found in ÖStA-HHStA Vienna, F 36, Karton 573, 28/2a, esp. Zl. 19 and 37 a; and in Mitrović, *Serbia's Great War*, 75–8.

[86] Petrovich, *A History of Modern Serbia,* vol. 2, 625. See also *Rapport général du CICR*, 137, and Kramer, *Dynamic of Destruction*, 141.

[87] Mitrović, *Serbia's Great War*, 229; Spanish embassy in Vienna to Czernin, 10 April 1917, in ÖStA -HHStA Vienna, F 36, Karton 573, 28 2/a, Zl. 156.

[88] Baron Spiegelfeld (Austrian Red Cross) to the ICRC, 13 September 1917, in ACICR, C G1/418/III. See also Živko Tapalović's lecture (as note 85 above), 5.

[89] See, for example, Bulgarian Red Cross to the ICRC, 27 April 1916, in ACICR, C G1/418/V, and *Rapport général du CICR*, p. 138. Also the various complaints made to the British Foreign Office by Serbian representatives in London in TNA, FO 383/463. On the Bulgarian occupation of Macedonia more generally, including the treatment of Serb civilians, see Opfer, *Im Schatten des Krieges*, 114–18.

[90] Mazower, *The Balkans*, 106. Cf. Carnegie Endowment for International Peace, *Report of the International Commission*, esp. 78–108 and 148–207.

[91] Glenny, *The Balkans*, 333.

[92] See Lohr, *Nationalizing the Russian Empire*, esp. 145–50. Also Levene, 'Frontiers of Genocide', 83–117 (esp. 96).

[93] Gatrell, *Russia's First World War*, 179–80. See also Gatrell's contribution to this volume.

[94] Kramer, *Dynamic of Destruction*, 151.

[95] Hoffmann-Holter, 'Abreisendmachung', 26–9, 51–2 and 58–64.

[96] Mentzel, 'Weltkriegsflüchtlinge', 26. On the use of internees and refugees as forced labour in Austria see also Kuprian, '"Frontdienst redivivus"'.

[97] Kuprian, "'Frontdienst redivivus'", 31. Cf. Hoffmann-Holter, *'Abreisendma-chung'*, esp. 125–36.

[98] Mentzel, 'Weltkriegsflüchtlinge', 32.

[99] *Allgemeine Jüdische Zeitung*, Budapest, 15 August 1916. Copy in Österreichisches Staatsarchiv, Bestand Ministerium des Innern (ÖStA-AVA Vienna, MdI), All. Sign. 19, Zl. 52897.

[100] Farcy, *Les camps de concentration français*, 259 and 52. For further evidence see also Nivet, *Les réfugiés français*, esp. 377–421, and Grandhomme, 'Internment Camps for German Civilians'.

[101] de Roodt, *Oorlogsgasten*, esp. 282–3; Lucassen, 'The Great War and the Origins of Migration Control', 52.

[102] Panayi, *The Enemy in Our Midst*, 216. On British reactions to Belgian refugees see also Gill, 'Calculating Compassion', 170–95; and (with a slightly different emphasis) Kushner, 'Local Heroes'.

[103] 'Send them all home', *Daily Mail*, 16 February 1917.

[104] See, for example, the correspondence generated between Elisabeth Rotten and Frédéric Ferrière by the case of the Frenchman M. Michel, whose wife Louise Michel was held at Siegburg prison in the Rhineland from September 1916 with a three-year sentence for 'assisting a French soldier on the run', in EZA Berlin, Bestand 51 C III g 2/1–3.

[105] Stibbe, *British Civilian Internees in Germany*, 140–1.

[106] See, for example, the various essays in Wall and Winter, *The Upheaval of War*. Also Rozenblit, 'For Fatherland and Jewish People', 199–220.

[107] Stibbe, 'Elisabeth Rotten', 202–3.

[108] An important role here was played by the camp magazines discussed in Pöppinghege, *Im Lager unbesiegt* – these magazines were often sent by the prisoners to friends and family back home.

[109] Becker, *Oubliés de la grande guerre*, 304–5. See also idem, *War and Faith*.

[110] Živko Tapalović's lecture (as note 85 above), 14–15.

[111] Becker, 'Religion', 194. See also Thiel, *'Menschenbassin Belgien'*, 184–5.

[112] See Erlass des Kriegsüberwachungsamts, 8 March 1917, in ÖStA-KA Vienna, KÜA, Zl. 97717, and the Chief of the General Staff to the Ministry of Interior and the KÜA, 28 May 1917, in ibid., Zl. 107880. Also Stampler, 'Flüchtlingswesen in der Steiermark', 16–19; and Cornwall, *The Undermining of Austria-Hungary*, 34.

[113] Mentzel, 'Weltkriegsflüchtlinge', 28.

[114] Minister of Interior to the Landesbehörden in Wien, Linz, Salzburg, Graz, Klagenfurt, Prag, Brünn and Troppau, 14 March 1917, in Österreichisches Staatsarchiv, Archiv der Republik, Bestand Kriegsflüchtlingsfürsorge (ÖStA-AdR Vienna, KFL), Karton 15, No. VI/9.

[115] Mentzel, 'Weltkriegsflüchtlinge', 39.

[116] Cf. Healy, *Vienna and the Fall of the Habsburg Empire*, 312–13; Hoffmann-Holter, *'Abreisendmachung'*, 148–59; and more generally, Arendt, *The Origins of Totalitarianism*, 267–90.

[117] See G. Vanneufville, 'Initiatives et interventions charitables du St. Siège pendant la guerre', *Revue Internationale de la Croix-Rouge* 1, no. 7 (1919): 800–34 (here 820–1); and Speed, *Prisoners, Diplomats and the Great War*, 33–7.

[118] Stibbe, 'The Internment of Civilians', 14–15; Davis, 'National Red Cross Societies'.

[119] Further details on the Franco-German and Anglo-German agreements can be found in Speed, *Prisoners, Diplomats and the Great War*, 37–42. For the

Austro-Serbian agreement of June 1918 see also ÖStA-HHStA Vienna, F 36, Karton 572, 28 1/b, Zl. 114, and ACICR, C G1/411/XXVI.

[120] de Roodt, *Oorlagsgasten*, 278–80. For the text of the 1917 Hague accord see also ACICR, C G1/411/IX.

[121] Stibbe, 'The Internment of Civilians', 9.

[122] See, for example, the protocols of the conference in Copenhagen in November 1917 between the German, Austro-Hungarian, Turkish, Romanian and Russian governments which called for a four-week 'cooling-off' period and insisted that only the central authority for each power, and not any local authority, could authorise the use of reprisals. Copy in ACICR, C G1/411/XII. Also the similar clause built into the 1917 Anglo-German Hague accord (as note 120 above).

[123] For further details see the protocols of the conference in Stockholm between the Austrian, Russian and Swedish Red Cross societies in August 1917, in ACICR, C G1/411/X. Also *Jahresbericht der Auskunftsstelle für Kriegsgefangene des Gemeinsamen Zentralnachweisbureaus sowie des österreichischen Fürsorgekomitees für Kriegsgefangene für das Jahr 1917* (Vienna, 1918), 2. Copy in ibid., 418/III.

[124] *Revue Internationale de la Croix-Rouge* 1, no. 1 (January 1919): 50. Also cited in Stibbe, 'The Internment of Civilians', 18.

[125] Panayi, *The Enemy in Our Midst*, 96. 11,750 Germans were nonetheless given leave to remain in Britain. Cf. 'Le repatriement des prisonniers', *Revue Internationale de la Croix-Rouge* 1, no. 11 (November 1919): 1323–34.

[126] 'Le repatriement des prisonniers', *Revue Internationale de la Croix-Rouge* 1, no. 11 (November 1919): 1333–4. Military captives were also held in France until the spring of 1920. See here the contributions of Heather Jones and Reinhard Nachtigal to this volume.

[127] See 'Kriegsgefangenenstand', in *Mitteilungen der Staatskommission für Kriegsgefangenen- und Zivilinterniertenangelegenheiten*, Vienna, nos. 7–8, 11 October 1919, 7. The figures cited here include both military and civilian prisoners.

[128] Denkschrift über die Behandlung der deutschen Kriegsgefangenen, issued by the Volksbund zum Schutze der deutschen Kriegs- und Zivilgefangenen, no date [late 1919]. Copy in Bundesarchiv-Militärarchiv (BA-MA) Freiburg, MSg 200/326.

[129] See, for example, the account by Theodor Walger on the situation of German civilian POWs in Samara in the Volga district, dated 15 October 1918, in BA-MA Freiburg, MSg 200/1234. Also Borck and Kölm, *Gefangen in Sibirien*, Nachtigal, 'Die Repatriierung der Mittelmächte-Kriegsgefangenen' 239–66, and Nachtigal's contribution to this volume.

[130] 'Prisonniers de guerre hongrois en Roumanie', *Revue Internationale de la Croix-Rouge* 1, no. 9 (September 1919): 1119–20.

[131] Huebner, 'The Internment Camp at Terezín'.

[132] Marrus, *The Unwanted*, 56–7; Levene, 'Frontiers of Genocide', 98–105.

[133] Arendt, *The Origins of Totalitarianism*, 268.

[134] Major Léderrey, 'Bericht über den Besuch im Lager für posensche Gefangene zu Havelberg', 26 April 1919, in BA Berlin, R 901/84319 (emphasis in the original). According to this report there were 490 Polish prisoners at Havelberg in April 1919, including 348 demobbed soldiers who had come to the end of their periods of service in the German army, 85 soldiers who were still serving in the German army when they were arrested and 57 civilians, among them six women and one child.

[135] Audoin-Rouzeau and Becker, *1914–1918*, 102–3; Healy, *Vienna and the Fall of the Habsburg Empire*, 313.

[136] Uta Hinz has also shown this in respect to military POWs in her book *Gefangen im Großen Krieg*. Cf. Stibbe, 'Prisoners of War'.

[137] *Rapports de MM. Ed. Naville et V. van Berchem, Dr. C. de Marval et A. Eugster sur leurs visites aux camps de prisonniers en Angleterre, France et Allemagne* (Geneva and Paris, 1915), in ACICR, C G1/432/II/1. Interestingly, *In Feindeshand*, the Austrian compilation of POW memoirs published in 1931 also included a section on civilian internees which noted that the British had 'not mistreated their prisoners to the same degree as the other "cultural nations"', particularly France – see Weiland and Kern, *In Feindeshand*, vol. 2, esp. 116–19.

[138] Figures presented by British government ministers in the House of Lords and the House of Commons, 20 and 26 March 1917 respectively. See also *Rapport général du CICR*, 137.

[139] Koestler, *The Scum of the Earth*. This book provides an account of Koestler's internment in the notorious Le Vernet camp in the Ariège region of France in 1939/40. See also Hannah Arendt's use of this phrase to describe the treatment of stateless persons and refugees in inter-war Europe in *The Origins of Totalitarianism*, 267.

Refugees and Forced Migrants during the First World War

Peter Gatrell

School of Arts, Histories and Cultures, University of Manchester, Manchester, UK

Although most informed observers anticipated a short war, the First World War lasted more than four years. European armies were expected to engage in military manoeuvres, without significant costs for civilians. This vision quickly evaporated. Civilians no less than military personnel experienced war as displacement, partly because of the eruption of fighting across large swathes of territory on the European mainland, with a resulting flight of populations, but also because the fraught conditions of prolonged war disposed states to engage in the mass deportation of civilians who were believed to threaten military freedom of manoeuvre and to undermine the war effort more broadly. These crucibles of displacement stretched from Belgium to Armenia, taking in France, Italy, Austria-Hungary, the Russian empire and Serbia. The German occupation of Belgium, Poland and Lithuania provoked the flight of civilians on a large scale; so too did the Russian invasion of East Prussia in 1914. The Austrian and Bulgarian invasion of Serbia resulted in humanitarian disaster. In the Russian empire, the displacement of civilians assumed a level of intensity that took many people by surprise. Turkish troops targeted Armenian residents of the Ottoman empire, many of whom lost their lives in a terrible blood-letting, leaving the survivors struggling to escape from further danger. Nor did the cessation of hostilities bring about peace. The complex process of repatriation and resettlement affected soldiers and civilians alike and rarely took place in stable or peaceful circumstances.[1]

Beyond the scale of involuntary population displacement and the human anguish that it entailed even more was at stake. One issue related to the assistance that might be offered to refugees who were caught up in the maelstrom. What form should this support take and how would it be resourced? These apparently prosaic issues had potentially profound implications for the conduct of politics at the local, national and international level. Who counted the refugee population and how reliable were these calculations? How far should the central government be responsible for managing refugee relief or should responsibility be devolved on to voluntary agencies? To what extent might overseas communities become involved in assisting distant kin who suffered displacement and persecution? What impact would the presence of large numbers of refugees have on social and economic life in the host community? How might relations between refugees and non-refugees be managed in order to maintain wartime morale? Related issues concerned the interpretation that contemporaries placed on mass migration. For example, should it be construed as 'spontaneous' flight and, if so, what did this imply for notions of self-control? If, on the other hand, displacement derived primarily from direct military intervention, what did this suggest about attempts to mobilise the 'nation', for example by targeting groups that were deemed not to belong? Should displacement be understood as pure misery, or might it rather constitute a kind of opportunity, for example to mobilise the displaced in a new 'national cause', as happened with Poles, Latvians and other minorities in the Russian empire? Finally, what options became available as the war ended: how feasible was it to return and, if return was not an option, what other kind of provision existed for displaced persons in the aftermath of the war?

These questions have attracted little attention from historians, partly because of the great drama being played out on the battlefield and partly because historians have focused on recognised social movements and institutions such as armies, governments and political parties. Refugees are deemed to have been a transitory phenomenon. As a result, the serious historical study of displacement – and not just in relation to the First World War - has been marginalised until recently.[2]

The origins and course of displacement

'Belgium was invaded by an army; Holland was invaded by a people', wrote Ruth Fry in her account of Quaker relief work in wartime Europe.[3] Armed aggression and the loss of territory to enemy forces provided the initial basis for the displacement of civilians. Belgium felt the consequences immediately. Refugees fled from Antwerp and other towns and cities during September and October 1914. Their first destination was the Netherlands, whose population of 6.3 million was swollen by one million Belgian refugees, half of whom crossed the frontier at Noord-Brabant.[4] Around 200,000 Belgian refugees fled to France, with a similar number reaching the UK. Many refugees returned home or enlisted in the armed forces, but 160,000 Belgian refugees remained on UK registers at the end of 1916, the number dropping only slightly before the war ended. In the course of the war one in seven Belgian civilians had become a refugee.[5]

The German invasion also prompted the flight and expulsion of French civilians to 'free France'.[6] By the beginning of 1915 the total number of displaced French reached 450,000. A year later the figure stood at 710,000 and by January 1918 it climbed to more than one million, increasing sharply in the spring as a result of the German advance towards Amiens and Champagne. By July 1918 the total reached 1.53 million. Some estimates put the total considerably higher.[7]

Events elsewhere also generated large movements of population. When the Russian army invaded East Prussia around 870,000 civilians fled westwards.[8] The entry of Italy into the war in May 1915 caused around 87,000 ethnic Italian residents of the Austro-Hungarian empire, primarily workers from Trieste, Trento and Dalmatia, to flee to Italy, in order to escape conscription into the Austrian army and to lend their support to the Italian war effort. The Habsburg authorities expelled a further 42,000 civilians, mostly women, children and the elderly. Italy's advance into Austrian territory was accompanied by measures to relocate ethnic Italians from the front, affecting around 52,000 people. Several thousand others were deported on grounds of 'national security'. But by far the greatest impulse to population displacement came in October 1917, when the defeat of Italian forces at Caporetto brought about the flight of half a million civilians and one million soldiers.[9]

As a result of the Russian occupation of Galicia and Bukovina in 1914, Vienna became home to around 70,000 Jewish refugees. In Galicia the newly-installed military governor Count Georgii Bobrinskii, a devoted Russophile, decided to 'cleanse' his fiefdom prior to integrating it fully with the Tsarist empire. Local notables were arrested and deported to Siberia. Russian military commanders deported local notables and many of the remaining Galician Jews to the Russian interior, citing the need to 'protect' the non-Jewish population from the consequences of 'collaboration'.[10] In these circumstances Ukrainian activists, who enjoyed the comparatively tolerant rule of the Habsburgs before the war, wisely decided to flee to Vienna lest they feel the wrath of the new Russian administration. Jewish inhabitants of Galicia and Bukovina, fearful of the reputation of the Russian army, also fled to the relative safety of the Austrian capital.[11] Others found shelter in towns in schools, barns and other accommodation in Bohemia and Moravia. Later on the government erected refugee camps. Around 30,000 refugees fled to Hungary.[12] Some returned to their homes in the summer of 1915, following the Austrian counter-offensive, but the number of refugees grew again in 1916 following the Brusilov offensive. By the end of 1915 the Austrian Ministry of the Interior supported 290,000 refugees, of whom 75,000 were Jews; by May 1917 the corresponding figures were 430,000 and 173,000.[13]

Serbia constituted another site of displacement. The civilian population had already been exposed to displacement during the Balkan Wars in 1912–13.[14] Although the Austrian invasion of Serbia in August 1914 was initially repelled, Serbian forces were defeated in November and several thousand civilian refugees fled to the interior. Small towns of a few thousand inhabitants increased in size by a factor of 10.[15] Worse was to come in October and November 1915, when the combined Austrian and Bulgarian military intervention led to the capture of much of the country and forced the remnants of the Serbian army to retreat towards the Adriatic coast. Up to half a million civilians followed suit, in anticipation of intolerable conditions under Bulgarian occupation. A British naval commander who witnessed the evacuation at first hand commented that 'the majority of the refugees were well to do people from comfortable homes ... many of the poorer people, peasants, were clinging to their miserable homes towards the centre of the country'.[16] Contemporary descriptions described this *bezhaniya* (refugeedom) as 'Armageddon', 'the Great Retreat ... only the first stage of a Calvary which was to endure for several weeks'.[17] A British nurse who served with the Serbian Relief Unit on behalf of the Scottish Women's Hospital, and who attempted to cope with the typhus epidemic that struck Serbia, described the arduous trek through the mud south towards Monastir, in the company of wounded soldiers and civilian refugees as

> a long, slow procession of springless carts, moving deliberately at the rate of two miles an hour, day or night was all one ... The stream of the refugees grew daily greater – mothers, children, bedding, pots and pans, food and fodder, all packed into the jolting wagons ...[18]

When the Bulgarian army continued its advance her party had no choice but to cross the mountains to seek sanctuary in Albania. Others headed for Montenegro: 'many died on those pitiless mountains, and the snow fell and covered up their misery for ever'.[19] Around 140,000 Serbian refugees are thought to have died during the flight to Albania or in exile. Meanwhile the remnants of the Serbian army ended up in Corfu in the company of civilian refugees. Most refugees fled to Salonika, Corsica and France – Serbian schools were established in Nice, Tours, Grenoble and elsewhere. Others found refuge in French colonies, Tunisia, Morocco and Algeria. Some even worked on farms in East Anglia. The less fortunate faced repression and incarceration in Austrian, Hungarian and Bulgarian internment camps.[20]

The displacement of civilians in the Russian empire reached 3 million in 1915 and may have climbed to as high as 7 million by the time Russia left the war in 1917. In wartime Russia, most displaced people did not cross an internationally recognised border; they were and remained subjects of the Tsar. What gave rise to displacement on this scale? According to one explanation, 'as soon as our troops withdraw, the entire population becomes confused and runs away'.[21] Sometimes they fled, in order that they did not lose contact with relatives on Russian territory, including fathers and sons who were currently serving in the Tsarist army. This did not necessarily imply a move to distant locations; during the initial phase of retreat refugees would often stay close to Russian troops, in the hope that the army would quickly recapture land from the enemy, allowing them to go home. Civilians were also prompted to leave their homes by the fear of being terrorised by enemy troops. Nor were these fears misplaced: 'rumours are rife that the Germans have behaved abominably towards the local population'.[22] These verdicts generally supported the view that population displacement was the product of mass panic; only a minority were believed to have taken a considered decision to leave.

Yet displacement was by no means solely dictated by a fearful civilian response to punitive action by the enemy. The Russian general staff disposed of sweeping powers to enforce the resettlement of civilians, where this strategy was deemed appropriate. Army regulations permitted the military authorities to assume absolute control over all affairs in the theatre of operations. Within the extensive theatre of operations the Russian high command was accused of pursuing a scorched earth policy and driving civilians from their homes. Jews bore the brunt of this policy, but it affected Poles, Baltic farmers and others, including German settlers who had farmed in Russia for generations. In the words of one group,

> We didn't want to move, we were chased away … we were forced to burn our homes and crops, we weren't allowed to take our cattle with us, we weren't even allowed to return to our homes to get some money.[23]

In public, the Tsarist minister of the interior maintained that military behaviour had no bearing on refugeedom (*bezhenstvo*), which in his opinion was 'caused by a desire for self-preservation'.[24] Other commentators took a less coy line, openly acknowledging the routine use of compulsion. The French ambassador, Maurice Paléologue, confided in his diary: 'partout le départ a été marqué par des scènes de violence et de pillage, sous l'oeil complaisant des autorités'.[25] So widespread were the army's tactics that a leading Tsarist dignitary observed that 'refugees' constituted a minority of the displaced population, compared to the hundreds of thousands of those who had been forcibly displaced (*vyselentsy*).[26] For a while contemporaries retained the distinction between forced migration and refugeedom: 'refugeedom is something spontaneous; but forced resettlement is arbitrary behaviour' (*proizvol*), wrote a Russian doctor in April 1916, criticising the actions of the Tsarist army, adding that 'when *vyselenie* ceases we shall find it easier to combat refugeedom'.[27] But over time this distinction lost its force, as if it had become impolitic to speak of the Russian army's aggression against the Tsar's own subjects.

By far the harshest impact of the war was to be found in the Ottoman empire. Armenians became refugees by virtue of the belief, widely held amongst the Ottoman military leadership, that they either were, or had the potential to become, a fifth column that would stop at nothing to hamper the Turkish war effort. Armenian communities in Petrograd, Moscow, Odessa and elsewhere estimated that up to 100,000 Armenian refugees had fled to Russia by the end of December 1914.[28] The Russian army crossed the border in early May 1915. Held up by a Turkish counter-offensive, Russian commanders ordered troops to withdraw from the region around Van. In chaotic circumstances, some of the local Armenian population managed to flee to the relative safety of the Caucasus; others were left behind in the hasty retreat. Worse still, youthful Turkish radicals blamed Armenians for the defeats already suffered by the Ottoman army in the winter of 1914 and early 1915, and charged them with having instigated an uprising against Turkish rule. Those who remained behind after July 1915 suffered a terrible fate. Hundreds of thousands of Ottoman Armenians were butchered, or were driven from their homes and forced to endure long and humiliating marches to the south. A Russian observer was reminded of the 'Bartholomew's Day massacre'.[29] Up to 250,000 Armenians fled across the Russian border in August 1915; perhaps one-fifth of them died en route. More than 105,000 ex-Ottoman Armenians sought refuge in Erevan, a town whose population in 1914 barely reached 30,000.[30]

Comprehending the refugee

Contemporaries struggled to comprehend the circumstances that led millions of their fellow men and women to leave their homes. Some commentators blithely assumed that many refugees were opportunists who lacked the stomach to resist and who therefore took the 'easy way out'.

This lack of understanding led them to conceive of refugees as 'deserters' who had failed to demonstrate sufficient fortitude or prowess in the teeth of the enemy onslaught. A British correspondent insinuated that young Serbian refugees in Oxford deliberately evaded military service. (They were in fact too young to enlist.) Hostility towards refugees found a more acute expression in northern France where they were labelled as 'les Boches du Nord' among whom women attracted especial opprobrium, because they were thought to have slept with German soldiers. Negative views were reinforced by the belief that refugees pushed up the price of food and housing, whilst competing for jobs and driving down wages. Stories surfaced of desperate refugees who stole or damaged farmers' property, for instance when they fled from Poland to the central provinces of European Russia.[31]

Condescension and genuine concern for human suffering also found expression in contemporary views. The presence of Belgian refugees in Britain led some observers to strike a banal note: 'the 'refugee question' pervades the whole country (wrote one diarist); it is as good an opening subject for conversation as the weather once was, and like that is common to all classes'.[32] Others stressed Britain's obligation towards Belgian refugees, whose plight reflected the Allies' inability to stem the German onslaught. Sympathy for Belgian refugees who reached the UK derived from a belief that they had suffered unspeakable torment at the hands of German troops. 'Brave little Belgium' was a term much in evidence, and 'King Albert's Book' allowed British dignitaries to pay 'tribute to the Belgian king and people'.[33] The association between war, patriotic necessity and displacement operated elsewhere as well. In Austria, Jewish refugees from Galicia and Bukovina who fled to the interior in order to escape Russian rule confirmed their patriotic commitment to Habsburg rule: 'better and truer Austrians (wrote Heinrich Schreiber in July 1917) simply do not exist', although this was not enough to protect them from accusations of profiteering, which fed anti-Semitic prejudices and led to physical attacks on Jews during 1917.[34]

Other voices spoke out in support of refugees and portrayed their presence in the 'host' society in more positive terms. Local deputies from the regions most directly affected lobbied the French government for financial support for the refugees. According to L'abbé Lemire, the deputy mayor of Hazebrouck, wartime displacement had helped to forge a more united France: 'I hope that the war will have permeated the different regions of our country; we in the north have our qualities, they in the Midi have theirs ...'.[35] In Russia a refugee reported that relations between local residents and our comrades are cordial. The ordinary people regard us as sufferers who have fled the horrors of war. They give us presents, and ask after those who are most needy. Russian workers look upon us differently, as special comrades who can throw a shaft of sunlight into their dark barracks. They are very curious about our former living conditions, pay, orderliness, tidiness and so forth.[36]

Some Russian villagers complained that refugees had unrealistic expectations of village life, wanting three hot meals a day. Yet the lively debate in one peasant assembly revealed more than a little compassion and insight into the needs of refugees: 'they have nothing to wear, nothing to put on their feet and there may have been nothing for them to eat'.[37] Thus the negative and demeaning image of refugeedom did not always prevail. The dispossessed supplicant was even imbued with the capacity to impart a civilising influence on the backward village, helping for example to demonstrate new techniques of cultivation.[38]

The impulse to relieve suffering rested upon the elaboration of compelling narratives of suffering, misery and despair. Much depended on the images generated in the mass media. The role of the eyewitness as a privileged observer of refugees' condition and needs was all-important: 'only those who have actually seen the flight of the Russian population can in any way conceive the horrors that attended it'.[39] Graphic and poignant pictures of refugees underpinned the culture of humanitarianism. The 'family journal' *Rodina* published a drawing of 'Two Flights', in which the plight of the refugee family was juxtaposed with the flight of Mary, Joseph and baby Jesus to Bethlehem. Accompanying verses urged the refugees not to lose heart.[40] Editors frequently focused upon a single refugee family; some of the poses were clearly contrived to create a genre photograph of the kind that had become fashionable at the turn of the century. Other images emphasised instead the magnitude of the refugee movement; typical of these was a picture of the throng gathered outside a refugee sanctuary in Petrograd – 'people of the most diverse condition and status, *now united by the single general term, refugee*'.[41] Sometimes the photographic record drew attention not to refugees' degradation but, rather, to the impact of private benevolence upon their mood. In December 1915, for example, a picture timed for the Christmas break portrayed 'a child who has lost its refugee parents and who has found lodgings with a stranger'. Other photographs displayed refugees eating the remains of a soldier's meal, cleverly implying that the Russian soldier was the refugees' friend, not the source of their mass suffering and sorrow.[42]

Displacement was often likened to the biblical exodus. Some witnesses believed that the 'boundless ocean' of refugees could never properly be navigated. Contemporary observers used language that was directly reminiscent of disaster, of river banks being broken – thus 'flood', 'deluge' or torrent, 'wave', 'avalanche', 'deposit', 'lava', and of fertile land being laid waste by hordes of locusts. Having first described Belgian refugees as mere 'sojourners', British newspapers soon began to describe a refugee 'stream' that might yet become a 'cataract'. *The Times* called it 'a peaceful invasion'.[43] As Liisa Malkki reminds us, 'these liquid names for the uprooted reflect the sedentarist bias in dominant modes of imagining homes and homelands, identities and nationalities.' This discourse was readily embraced by an emerging patriotic intelligentsia, whose activities are discussed below.[44]

We began with a contemporary distinction between 'refugees' and 'forced migrants'. But in retrospect a more helpful distinction is between relatively prosperous refugees, who could call upon contacts and other resources and the much larger number of indigent refugees who eked out a more tenuous and vulnerable existence. Belgian relief committees in Britain complained about a dearth of 'good class' arrivals who were outnumbered by indigent refugees.[45] Ukrainian activists who fled to Berlin and middle-class Jews who entered Vienna called upon resources and contacts to sustain them in exile. Most refugees lacked these advantages – although this did not prevent unsympathetic observers from claiming that they were work-shy and idle. Eventually the distinction between rich and poor began to lose much of its meaning as displacement resulted in downward social mobility, creating a single category of refugeedom.

Relief efforts: self-help, voluntary organisations and government intervention

Against this complex background, involving large numbers of displaced persons, their abrupt departure, and the multiple interpretations given to their displacement, we can begin to trace the efforts made to deal with the consequences of wartime movements. Once basic needs had been assessed, answers had to be found to the questions that refugees posed. Children urgently sought to establish whether their parents were alive or dead. Adults wished to be reunited with children with whom they had lost contact. Refugees sought legal advice about their status and entitlements to relief. Many of them wanted the opportunity to work. Children needed to be found somewhere to continue their education. Adults wanted somewhere to meet others in the same situation. These basic needs, often accompanied by stories of dispossession and desperation, under-pinned the apparatus of relief in all theatres of war.[46]

Belgian refugees who fled to the Netherlands improvised accommodation by sheltering in makeshift structures such as greenhouses or finding emergency billets on barges and in apartments, hotels and warehouses in Maastricht, Amsterdam, Groningen and other towns. Later on, local authorities helped to erect cheap bungalows (*maisons démontables*), capable of being quickly dismantled and reassembled elsewhere. In order to appease the resident burghers in these overstretched localities, the Dutch government decided to house the refugees in camps on the outskirts of towns such as Gouda, Nunspeet and Bergen op Zoom, although the authorities preferred to designate them as 'Belgian villages', in order to avoid the negative association with erstwhile 'concentration camps' during the South African War. In a strict regime (there were regular roll calls of the camps' inhabitants) the emphasis was on health and hygiene. Refugees were expected to work hard, making toys and household goods.[47]

The arrival of Belgian refugees in England prompted widespread private philanthropy. A War Refugees Committee, launched by Dame Flora Lugard, made use of the 'hospitality lists' drawn up before the outbreak of war on behalf of the Ulster Unionist Council, whose leaders expected civil war in Ireland and a mass evacuation of women and children to England as a result. Thus, what originated as a plan to rescue likely Protestant refugees became instead a programme to assist Belgian Catholics. There were other ironies too: Herbert Samuel, a leading critic of Belgian colonial policy in the Congo at the turn of the century, found himself the minister responsible for Belgian refugees.[48] Other initiatives soon followed from local authorities in London, Manchester, Birmingham, Bradford, and Hull, where refugees found accommodation in hostels and boarding houses. By 1916 around 2,500 local refugee committees had been established. H.A. Leggett, the secretary of the War Refugees Committee, applauded the efforts both of local committees and of Belgian refugees who devoted energy to finding work:

> There were people in every country who did not care about work and who would not work if they could help it. But the vast majority of the Belgian refugees were only too ready to take every opportunity of turning their hands to something ...[49]

Government officials, anxious about 'undesirable aliens', intervened by establishing a register of the refugee population in order to keep track of them within the UK. Belgians complained that the restrictions on movement under the Aliens Restriction Act (4 August 1914), which required them to notify the police of any journey they made of more than five miles and confined them to specific areas of the country, amounted to being placed in a 'concentration camp.'[50] Meanwhile, concern about the burden on the British taxpayer, the sacrifices made by British conscripts, and anxieties about the 'disreputable' sexual conduct of Belgian women help explain why public sympathy began to diminish by 1916.[51]

The needs of refugees posed yet more of a challenge in economically less developed societies. In Italy, the Ministry of the Interior took charge of the administration of relief and the settlement of refugees. Local authorities complained that they had insufficient means to support displaced persons. As the size of the refugee population increased, the government created a central committee for refugee relief, but it had to work in tandem with Catholic and socialist organisations such as the *Opera Bonomelli* and *Umanitaria*, as well as with the Red Cross.[52]

The situation in Austria-Hungary reached its first critical juncture during the winter of 1914 and again in late 1916. Poor refugees from the shtetl usually had no independent means; officials estimated that three-quarters of the total Jewish refugee population from Galicia 'lacked means' in 1917. Even those who arrived with some belongings found that their resources soon dwindled. Their presence inflamed existing anti-Semitic sentiment among the non-Jewish residents of Vienna, who all too easily fell into the habit of berating the refugees for their bad manners and contribution to shortages. In Vienna the municipal government created a dedicated administration for refugee relief, but it faced an uphill struggle. In these circumstances, the government devolved some of the responsibility for refugee relief on to Jewish charitable organisations, chief among them the *Israelitische Allianz*, in which women played a prominent role. Middle-class Jews overcame their aversion to the *Ostjuden* and did what they could to alleviate suffering among their destitute co-religionists by funding soup kitchens and workshops, finding school fees and supporting rabbis. In Prague the equivalent committee contributed funds to supply clothing, shoes and blankets. According to one scholar, their charitable activities – sustained in part by financial support from the American Jewish Joint Distribution Committee – reflected a patriotic commitment to the Austrian cause: 'these refugees were Austrian citizens, victims of Austria's war with Russia'. But not all refugees were accommodated in towns and cities. Austrian officials despatched refugees to camps where inmates described the conditions as primitive and 'unacceptable'. Some, as in Gmünd and Leibniz, housed thousands of refugees who fell victim to infectious disease.[53]

The image of suffering Serbia encouraged dozens of international volunteers to assist the country in its time of need. 'Slav committees' in Russia collected funds to pay for medical units. The British Red Cross and

Scottish Women's Hospitals played a prominent role in this recruitment drive, noting that existing facilities could not deal with the emerging health crisis in the first winter of the war, and in particular the spread of typhus. Medical assistance was extended to civilian refugees as well as soldiers. Lady Muriel Paget – wife of a former British minister to Belgrade, and a nurse during the Balkan Wars – went to Serbia as part of the first unit of the Serbian Relief Fund (SRF). Her account is replete with detailed descriptions of medical technologies and organisation of relief and shows how population displacement facilitated the display of professional expertise.[54]

The SRF in London actively promoted the Serbian cause. As with equivalent bodies that supported displaced Poles, Armenians and Belgians, it enlisted lawyers, businessmen, archaeologists, ethnographers and historians such as R.W. Seton-Watson and G.M. Trevelyan. It sponsored 'Serbian Flag Day' and exhibitions of Serbian sculpture and handicrafts. A Serbian Relief Fund also operated in the USA.[55] Their fieldworkers distributed rice, flour and clothes to around 1000 refugees, although the crisis in the winter overwhelmed their capacity. Even so, Paget made a point of reminding her audience back home of the sentiments that Serbian troops and refugees expressed towards the SRF: 'the trust and the gratitude they give back is one of the most touching and beautiful things I have ever known, not too dearly purchased by any sacrifice'. Similar statements emanated from relief workers who were active in Armenia, Poland and Russia, sometimes moving from one country to the next, who emphasised their privileged standpoint: 'only one who has witnessed ... the thousands of refugees can have any conception of the strain that has been put upon the resources of the country'. But the unmediated voice of refugees struggled to be heard.[56]

In the Russian empire, refugees who had survived the journey from the vicinity of the front faced all manner of difficulties. Food, accommodation, sanitary needs, and fresh clothing had to be found. Zemstvos, diocesan committees, Tatiana committees and other associations – new and old – provided underwear, shoes, linen, soap and other items for refugees. Emergency accommodation was found in railway stations, schools, empty factories, breweries, hotels, bathhouses, army barracks, monasteries, synagogues, theatres, cinemas, cafés, and even prisons.[57] Towns and cities were transformed as a result. By the middle of 1916, more than one in ten inhabitants in some of Russia's largest towns were refugees; in Samara they made up almost 30%, whilst in Ekaterinoslav and Pskov refugees reached around one-quarter of the total and in Nizhnii-Novgorod 15%.[58] Some appeals for help made much of the expectation that refugees 'will not be staying long in our midst. The enemy will leave the frontiers of Russia and the refugees will once more return to their own homes'.[59] But few people probably believed this optimistic assessment, which was anyway soon overtaken by the realisation that refugees would be around for some time to come. As the journal of the union of zemstvos argued in the autumn of 1915, 'we must not lose sight of the fact that refugees are our guests – and not for a brief period either'. Some of them would wish to stay permanently.[60] Municipal authorities lost no time in trying to 'evacuate' refugees to other parts of the empire. Initial sympathy and hospitality rapidly evaporated as it became apparent that refugees had no money to pay for accommodation or food. In some places, 'there were fears of disorders and riots'.[61] Plenty of opportunities presented themselves to people who wished to exploit the vulnerability of refugees. In Russia, as elsewhere, fears of social disorder were projected on to displaced persons.

Throughout all belligerent societies the presence of refugees affected the relationship between central and local government and between the 'host' population and the newcomers. The speed and size of displacement encouraged emergency improvisation that gave way in due course to greater government intervention. Yet the growth of bureaucratic instruments did not lessen the importance of non-governmental initiatives. As the next section shows, an enlarged sphere of refugee relief had a dramatic impact on domestic politics.

Nationalising refugees

The organisation of relief along 'national' lines and the appropriation of the refugee for the national cause helped to create the possibility for a national politics in circumstances that were hitherto unpropitious. In the first place, refugeedom contributed to the sense of collective national suffering and danger. Secondly, the scale of displacement imposed an enormous strain on existing agencies. Where neither the state nor existing organisations could cope, national bodies stepped in to fill the gap. This allowed them to depict relief in national terms and to proselytise among a ready-made audience. Thirdly, diasporic groups could also be harnessed to this cause. Lastly, national consciousness might be enhanced not only by a vision of national humiliation and danger but also by new social contacts that exposed ethnic particularism.

This process was most marked in the Russian empire, where members of the patriotic intelligentsia constantly reminded their audience that invading troops had lately violated their homeland. Occupation and despoilation were bad enough, but these calamities did not exhaust the fears expressed by national leaders. Latvians and Poles, in particular, anticipated that they would suffer the terrible fate of 'national dispersion'. Yet the enforced displacement of population created an entirely new framework for belief and behaviour. When they took to the road, refugees were by definition deprived of membership in a close-knit local community. But refugeedom offered them an opportunity to gain access to a new, much broader national community, built on the foundations of a common sense of loss and the need for collective effort to regain what had been forfeited in wartime.

National spokesmen hastily improvised schools, orphanages, clubs, workshops, canteens and barracks, with funds provided by a plethora of national committees. A spokesman for the Polish national committee outlined the implications as follows:

> Only continuous and close contact with the national group, whether in the distribution of allowances, the allocation of accommodation, the supply of clothing, the search for work, the offer of medical treatment, the satisfaction of all material and spiritual needs - only this can guarantee and secure refugees on behalf of the motherland.[62]

The Tsarist state tolerated these efforts, partly as a means of lightening the burden on hard-pressed government officials and on the public purse. National committees served another purpose so far as the government was concerned: they represented an acceptable alternative to the public organisations, whose leaders had also asserted a claim to organise refugee relief and resettlement. By the autumn of 1915, contrasts were being drawn between the speed and efficiency of the national committees and the hesitant manner in which local authorities handled refugee relief.[63] Let us look at these issues in more detail.

Jews and Armenians: diaspora confirmed

Displacement had profound social and political consequences for Jewish refugees. Most dramatically, it obliged the Tsarist government to abolish the long-standing restrictions on the settlement of Jews outside the infamous Pale of Settlement. In August 1915, the government permitted Jews to move to towns and cities in the heart of the empire. To be sure, ministers insisted that Jews could not reside in Petrograd and Moscow, nor were they permitted to settle on Cossack land. Furthermore, and consistent with the official view that Jews and peasants should be kept apart in order to deter outbreaks of violence, Jewish refugees were normally forbidden to settle in villages. Government ministers believed that they could not otherwise prevent fresh pogroms. But no one could pretend that the Pale of Settlement could be re-established except at great cost.[64]

Particular tensions were thus expected to be generated by the appearance of Russian Jews in villages in and beyond the established Pale of Settlement. Government ministers extrapolated from isolated incidents to predict the imminent disintegration of public order as a consequence of the enforced proximity between local people and Jews:

> In various localities the atmosphere became more and more dangerous; the Jews were angry at everyone and everything, while the local inhabitants were angry at the uninvited guests who, moreover, were being denounced as traitors and were angered by conditions under which it became impossible to survive.[65]

Notwithstanding these comments, no widespread outbreaks of peasant protest took place against Jewish refugees, perhaps because they did not pose a significant threat to rural prosperity and had little in common with the stereotyped Jewish moneylender. However, the economic crisis in 1917 made it far more difficult to maintain this relative harmony.[66]

What of the initiatives taken by Jews themselves? In Petrograd, a group of wealthy Jewish bankers and lawyers established the central Jewish committee for the relief of victims of war (EKOPO), backed by influential organisations including the Society for the Propagation of Enlightenment among Russian Jews and the Society for Handicrafts. Jewish communities abroad were also mobilised. But these elitist bodies came up against provincial activists who challenged established divisions and modes of conduct and emphasised the need to set aside political differences. Social and cultural differences between Jews from the shtetl and the Jewish professional intelligentsia had been eroded: 'Jews who hitherto did not know or understand one another have been brought together. Mutual antagonisms have disappeared, to be replaced by excellent fraternal relations'.[67] As the official history of EKOPO put it, 'small oases have become major centres of Jewish settlement, and the newcomers have demanded the right to participate in communal life'.[68] Refugeedom thus had disruptive consequences in more than one sense.[69]

The construction of Armenian refugeedom entailed at least one set of assumptions similar to those held about Jews by Tsarist officials and the educated public alike. Like the Jews, Armenians were regarded by others as an ethnic group that had already been scattered, and whose members were predisposed to be a 'wandering' people. Leaders of the Armenian community in the Caucasus themselves alluded to the centuries-old diaspora. They had no obvious 'home', being distributed across two empires and at least two continents. Their evident proclivity to migrate and to form dispersed settlements served as an obstacle to official recognition of their plight. The reason for this was quite simple; those who constituted the Armenian diaspora were expected in due course to come to the rescue of those Armenians resident in the Transcaucasus, thereby allowing the burden of relief to be shifted from Petrograd. Allied to this went the belief that Armenians and Jews shared a common flair for business; their calling was to trade in money and manufactured goods. This perceived commercial 'guile' encouraged the view that both groups survived at the expense of others. Beliefs such as these tended to foster a more jaundiced attitude on the part of the Tsarist government towards humanitarian relief.[70]

Latvians, Lithuanians and Poles: averting diaspora

In the case of Armenians and Jews, patriotic leaders invoked the memory of torment and displacement, thereby linking past and present in a manner designed to mobilise the refugee population. This argument also held sway among the Polish patriotic intelligentsia who could draw on memories of the great revolts against Tsarist rule in 1830 and 1863. Latvian patriots found it more difficult to make a similar case. Instead they tried a different approach, arguing that the close bonds between Latvians would be severed permanently unless they resisted dispersion. The same went for Lithuanians. The alarming prospect of an enlarged Latvian diaspora was well articulated by the leading Latvian parliamentarian Jānis Goldmanis, who urged the need to find 'means of saving and preserving the Latvian people, who face the lot of the Jews - to be scattered across the entire globe'.[71] Particularly disturbing was evidence that Russian railway clerks issued travel documents that stipulated Siberia as the eventual destination earmarked for Baltic refugees. No less disquieting was the fact that others had actually nominated Siberia, because they had friends or relatives who had been exiled there. Latvian leaders urged refugees to refrain from buying or renting plots of land in Siberia, lest they forget where their 'roots' properly lay.[72]

Refugeedom might spell imminent disaster for the Latvian 'nation', but it also opened up fresh opportunities for national agitation. From its base in Petrograd, the Latvian Central Welfare Committee (LCWC) coordinated the activities of more than 100 separate Latvian welfare organisations. Like other national organisations, the LCWC maintained schools, hostels and orphanages; it made loans available to refugees who were in financial difficulty; it offered specialist legal advice; it helped Latvian refugees who were trying to establish contact with family members; and it publicised information about the activities of the cultural association 'Dzimtene'

(Homeland), which created a network of schools for Latvian-speaking children.[73] Similar considerations applied in respect of Lithuanian refugees, who were offered advice about finding work, vocational training and learning about Lithuanian culture. According to Martynas Yčas, the Lithuanian activist who later served as president of the new republic, the LCWC 'prepared the people for future action and created the foundations for a future cultural and political edifice ... It forced even non-Lithuanians to recognise that we ourselves were the masters of our country'.[74] Allowing for a degree of retrospective exaggeration, Yčas neatly encapsulated the sense of political mobilisation and the vision of national emancipation that refugeedom made possible.

Two organisations chiefly led the movement for the relief of Polish refugees. One was a 'citizens' committee' that engaged in welfare work, rapidly becoming the focus of local and national political discussion and activity. It established a network of day schools, boarding schools and orphanages in Moscow and other towns.[75] The other was the Polish Society for the Aid of War Victims (*Polski komitet pomocy ofiarom wojny*), chaired by the energetic Polish engineer and industrialist V.V. Zhukovskii. The citizens' committee divided European Russia into 38 districts and the rest of the country into five districts, with a full-time staff of more than 300 officials, not including priests, doctors, medical auxiliaries and teachers employed on the committee's behalf. The Polish committee was much larger, with a total staff of around 25,000 distributed amongst 237 offices.[76] Zhukovskii proclaimed Poland to be an 'outpost of Slavdom' whose inhabitants had made an 'incalculable sacrifice' in the interests of the Tsarist state, protecting Russia from the German onslaught at the price of becoming a wasteland. They spoke also of the destruction of Polish national wealth and a 'centuries-old culture'. Polish farmers had been forced to leave land that they had tilled for generations and now saw it being appropriated by German colonists. Poles were owed support and help from Russian citizens by virtue of the sacrifices they had made during the first year of war. Such support, however, had to take account of national needs.[77] The Russian government acknowledged the fears of the patriotic intelligentsia. Although it earmarked land for refugee settlement, the government made an exception in respect of Polish settlers who 'from a national point of view ... are lost from their homeland, which is presently undergoing such a difficult period of the greatest misfortune'.[78] There was little here to separate the official line from nationalist sentiment or, indeed, the views of refugees themselves. A correspondent for the newspaper *Sibirskaia zhizn'* (Siberian Life) wrote that the dream of Polish refugees was 'to return to their native hearth'; if asked about the possibility of settling in Siberia they replied that 'Herman can be chased off and we'll go home'.[79]

Russians as refugees

Specifically Russian organisations for refugee relief followed in the wake of other national committees. They built upon a growing sense in late 1915 and early 1916 that the Russian refugee population had been relatively neglected. One observer attacked Russia's 'public men' in general, and 'progressives' in particular, for overlooking the needs of Russian refugees in their headlong rush to attain political supremacy. Particularly significant was the All-Russian Society for the Care of Refugees formed in October 1915. It maintained more than 50 branches throughout Russia, offering shelter, clothing, footwear and schooling to 400,000 refugees.[80]

Despite these initiatives, however, complaints continued that refugees of Russian nationality found themselves at a disadvantage compared to the non-Russian population. From Ekaterinburg came the charge that Russian Orthodox refugees had been 'cheated' in comparison with Jewish refugees who received money from several sources: 'The Jewish refugee strolls around in a comfortable suit and in galoshes, whilst the Russian has to make do with cast-offs and felt boots'.[81] The right-wing nationalist Prince M. Andronikov drew attention to the prevalence of Russian refugees on the streets of Petrograd, a sure sign that they lacked the relief available to Jews, Poles, and Latvians. How could Russian society tolerate this negligent state of affairs? 'National pride' required nothing less than an adequate provision of relief to the peasant, beneath whose torn coat 'the spark of God is alight and a true Russian heart is beating'.[82] A correspondent to a provincial newspaper found it shameful that Jews and Catholics had relieved suffering amongst their flock, whereas the local Russian community displayed no such commitment: 'can we call ourselves Christians?' It was shameful to call oneself a Russian and do nothing to help.[83]

Russia lacked a diaspora that could be mobilised. But this was not the chief obstacle to assisting Russian refugees. They had first to be identified, since language, religion and customs did not make them immediately visible; on the street they were indistinguishable from the non-refugee poor. This posed a challenge to those who would assist Russian refugees. But displacement also provided them with the opportunity to assert their Russianness, because Russian culture was exposed to the powerful presence of non-Russians. In this spirit, perhaps, a priest from the Urals spoke of 'this terrible portrait of Rus' in flight', his poetic language drawing attention to a medieval past when 'Russia' did not have to contend with strangers in its midst.[84]

'Little Russians', Awkward Refugees

The situation in Ukraine was a good deal more complicated, not least given the influx of Ukrainian refugees from Galicia, where opportunities before the war for political activity had been more extensive. These refugees were now taken under the wing of the 'Russian People's Council for Carpathian Rus', a shady group whose leaders reportedly had contacts with Russia's far right. The council dedicated itself to the promotion of loyalty to Russia, opening its doors to those 'who willingly disclosed their Russian national consciousness [sic] or in some measure demonstrated that they were well disposed towards Russia and the Russian people.'[85] In reality, relief efforts fell far short of the rhetoric; one local organiser blithely told a visiting journalist that 'these are refugees after all, and they can hardly count on home comforts.'[86] Moderate and extreme Russian nationalists alike pounced on any attempt to draw attention to the Ukrainian-ness of refugees. A proposed Ukrainian society in Moscow aroused the ire of the editor of *Sputnik bezhentsa*, who demanded that it be renamed the 'Little Russian society'; to adopt the term 'Ukrainian' meant accepting that they were a 'non-Russian people'.[87] Yet his anger and unease betrayed the fact that the war facilitated the dissemination of Ukrainian views. An unsigned article, 'To flee or not to flee?' argued that there might be advantages in staying put:

> In favour of remaining behind is the centuries-old culture that previous generations have created there. Not everywhere will become a war zone. Our own culture will remain; so, too, should those people who can preserve it....Even if the enemy should strike deeper, individuals may be killed and individual property may be destroyed, but the land, its culture, its 'didivshchina', its 'bat'kivshchina' will survive.[88]

To sum up, collective action helped to bridge the gap between the educated national elite, refugee members of the national intelligentsia, and the 'common' refugee. It was no longer possible to retain the conventional sharp distinction between members of the educated intelligentsia and the 'dark' narod, because they had all been exposed to the dehumanising and debilitating consequences of refugeedom. The reiteration of a sense of loss and destruction of 'national' assets acted as a unifying device. Non-refugee members of national minorities bound themselves together with 'taxes' levied on the entire community. Diasporic communities contributed assistance as well.[89] By virtue of the disruption caused to other relationships by war, refugeedom created a situation in which nationality could assume enormous importance. Refugeedom conferred respectability upon the rhetoric of national consciousness and imparted vitality to a crusade couched in a national idiom.

Elsewhere in Europe

The situation elsewhere is more difficult to establish, although something of the repercussions of displacement for national sentiment found expression in the actions and language of Serbian exiles and supporters of the SRF. Serbian exiles in France established schools and colleges with the support of a Franco-Serbian charity ('La nation serbe en France'), in order to promote Serbian national awareness.[90] Yovanovitch lamented that the Serbian nation had been 'martyred' and 'scattered to the four winds'; worse, some refugees decided not to return when the war ended. Tatham too depicted Serbian displacement in terms of national tragedy: 'The Serbians had at last realised that the enemy were out to finish her as a nation, and the only way to save herself was to run away ...' She added in lyrical vein that 'these men had no high education to tell them how to hold themselves in this disaster. But every Serbian is a poet; how else had they kept their souls free under 500 years of the Turkish yoke?'[91] The renowned Quaker relief worker, Ruth Fry, recalled that among Serbian refugees in Corsica 'some ardent spirits likened [their plight] to the Israelites in captivity in Babylon, a nucleus whence should return a new and reunited Serbian nation'.[92] Further work is needed to establish the connection between mass displacement and the origins of Yugoslavia, but it seems likely that refugeedom played a crucial role in cementing ideas of collective suffering that helped validate the idea of national independence.

Among Belgian refugees, on the other hand, there is an intriguing suggestion that displacement, far from dissolving differences between Flemish- and French-speaking refugees, may actually have enhanced them. This too is an area where further research is needed.[93] The camps established by the Austrian government were organised along ethnic lines: Polish refugees, for example, were sent to Chotzen in Bohemia (and later on to a new camp at Auschwitz) and Jews to Nikolsburg, Phorlitz and Gaya, all in Moravia. How this segregation affected political life remains to be explored.[94]

Repatriation, return, resettlement

Repatriation took on a different aspect in different contexts. Grandiose plans drawn up in the UK to resettle Belgian refugees in Chile and

South Africa came to naught, because the Belgian authorities insisted that refugees should contribute to national reconstruction in Belgium after the war. Most of the 140,000 Belgian refugees in the UK at the Armistice returned home by 1919. Ruth Fry described a visit to Brussels and Antwerp where 'there was a strange sense of places waking up after a long bad dream', but 'Belgium was thoroughly tired of foreign charity and was anxious to stand on her own feet'.[95] The situation elsewhere was much more complicated. Serbian refugees returned home with the assistance of the SRF and Quaker relief workers, who managed orphanages and hospitals, but reconstruction took many years to complete.[96] In Austria, some Jewish refugees returned to western Galicia when the war came to an end, but they had to endure frequent pogroms. Others were prevented from returning home by the vicious conflict in the new Polish-Ukrainian borderland. Their villages had in any case often been obliterated. Non-Jewish residents of Vienna certainly did not want them to remain. Some refugees (not Jews) succeeded in enrolling at universities and gaining citizenship in the new Austrian state.[97]

The Russian Revolution and the creation of new nation-states amid the wreckage of the old continental empires established the context for repatriation and return. Many civilians who had been displaced into the Russian interior during the First World War fervently wished to return to their former abode in newly independent native lands. Others chose, or were forced, to remain where they were. Economic deprivation imposed additional burdens on displaced and settled populations. Political uncertainty in this enormous contested space only served to multiply these dilemmas and difficulties. The refugee population was swelled by newly displaced persons, the result of German military occupation of the western borderlands of the former empire. Subsequently, the prolonged dislocation of the Russian civil war, battles between Polish, Lithuanian, and Ukrainian troops, the Polish-Soviet war, and continued turmoil in the Caucasus, prompted additional displacement, to which was added large-scale emigration by Russians, Armenians, and others. Some populations stayed physically where they were, but found that borders had moved instead, effectively resulting in their political expatriation. Thus the years of war, revolution, and peacemaking between 1917 and 1921 marked renewed population displacement on a massive scale.

Only after lengthy negotiations did the states that emerged on the wreckage of the old Russian empire reach binding diplomatic agreements that paved the way for organised return. Soviet Russia finally signed a treaty with Poland on 18 March 1921, bringing the bitter Polish-Soviet war to an end. The process of return subjected individual refugees to great stress. It put pressure on government budgets. It imposed heavy demands on fledgling bureaucracies and relief workers, who were at times overwhelmed by the scale and character of population movement. As people returned, the new successor states of eastern Europe embarked on programmes to consolidate a sense of affiliation to the new national homeland, identifying those who 'belonged' by virtue of ethnicity or who might conceivably be 'nationalised' into membership of the new nation state.[98]

Of all the groups discussed earlier, Armenians faced the greatest challenge, although Serbians were not far behind. Many of those who escaped the Ottoman massacres managed to flee to neighbouring lands. Virtually uninterrupted military conflict and continuing political uncertainty thereafter deprived these refugees of any speedy or straightforward resolution of their status and security, and indeed added to their number. In the 1920s, Armenian refugees came to symbolise the condition of statelessness. A plethora of international agencies, foreign governments, religious groups, and private individuals intervened to sustain the welfare of Armenian refugees after 1917. Within Armenia itself, the new Soviet republic assumed responsibility for their upkeep. It acquitted itself reasonably well in the circumstances.[99]

There is one other aspect of displacement that deserves to be mentioned. Among the successor states, refugeedom also helped train national elites in the conduct of politics and the practicalities of administration. This became evident in the aftermath of the peace treaties and the creation of the successor states. The first cabinet to be appointed in Latvia included Mikelis Valters (Minister of the Interior), Jānis Goldmanis (Minister of Agriculture) and Jānis Zalitis (Minister of War), each of whom had played a prominent role in refugee relief work. Jānis Cakste became president of Latvia. The leader of the Lithuanian refugee relief effort in Russia, Martynas Yčas, served as finance minister in the new Lithuanian state (he boasted that the national committee 'unearthed the buried name of Lithuania' and drew attention to the 'separate and distinctive character' of the Lithuanian people). Alexander Khatisov, mayor of Tbilisi and a central figure in the Armenian relief effort, was for ten months Prime Minister of independent Armenia. Many statesmen had a background in parliamentary politics prior to the revolution but their active involvement in refugee relief brought them more closely and prominently before the public.[100]

Forgetting refugees

During the war the concerted efforts to attend to the needs of refugees prompted an outpouring of patriotic literature and eyewitness accounts, including those written by relief workers. An impressive body of artistic work supported these endeavours. Graphic artists produced posters and postcards in support of relief agencies. Composers followed suit. In December 1915 the terminally-ill French composer Claude Debussy wrote a poignant song, 'Noel des enfants qui n'ont plus de maison' that spoke affectingly of Belgian refugee children. Edward Elgar composed several orchestral pieces to accompany Belgian lyrics ('Carillon', 'Spirit of England' and 'Voice in the Desert') to show his support of the Belgian cause. Baltic artists contributed paintings and drawings in the expectation that they would be brought together to form part of the collection for the new national museums in Latvia and Lithuania.[101] During the war the English novelist Agatha Christie famously decided to create a fictional detective and asked rhetorically, 'Why not make him a Belgian? There were all types of refugees. How about a refugee police officer?'[102]

Much of the cultural and political activity discussed above betrayed a tendency to speak on behalf of the refugee, giving refugees no opportunity to articulate a sense of how displacement had affected them. The national committees that flourished in Tsarist Russia afforded little scope for ordinary refugees to express themselves. The consequences of this silencing have an eerie familiarity to a modern reader. Some refugees lamented that 'we long to become people once again'; that 'we are living people ... (with) the misfortune to have been displaced, but we are human beings all the same'.[103] Refugees in Italy submitted letters and petitions to government authorities that included statements – 'it is owed to me' – encapsulating a sense of entitlement. All too often, however, these dignified or assertive voices were drowned out.[104]

Remarkably, two attempts were made in Tsarist Russia to establish the contours of displacement. Towards the end of 1916 the Tatiana committee proposed a special exhibition designed to inform the Russian public about the living conditions and activities of refugees, who were not all 'beggars, idlers and spongers'. Four main themes were to be highlighted: conditions in Russia's borderlands before and during the war, including 'the destruction of settlements, property and artistic monuments'; their 'sorrowful journey', including the background to their displacement, the course of the refugee movement and the assistance given by government and public organisations; the living conditions in their new homes, including 'the work undertaken by refugees and their impact on the local population'; and finally the restoration of normal life in the regions cleared of enemy occupation.[105] The Tatiana committee also solicited material from refugees, who were encouraged to describe their experiences in their own words. If they needed help in formulating a coherent narrative the

Tatiana committee obligingly published a schedule of questions. The aim was to secure stories from 'simple people'. Other kinds of testimony were also sought: photographs, drawings, reports, memoirs, stories and belles-lettres; 'the material that is collected . . . will be collated and organised systematically and will form part of a projected volume of "Collected materials on the history of the refugee movement during the world war"'. The committee acknowledged 'that facts and observations, even if they seem at first to be insignificant and trivial, may prove to be of great interest . . . The most important thing is for the description to be sincere and truthful.'[106] This extraordinary initiative probably served as part of the critique of the Tsarist state that was mentioned earlier, but it made little headway before being overtaken by the upheaval of 1917.

The immediate aftermath of the First World War suggested that amnesia served a more useful political purpose than the commemoration of refugeedom. In France, Belgium and Italy the figure of the displaced refugee fitted uncomfortably with post-war attempts to play up the eventual victory over Germany and Austria-Hungary. The all-encompassing idea of national unity ('l'Union sacrée') found no room for contrary understandings of the war that might take due account of the wartime experiences of displaced civilians. In Italy, Mussolini trumpeted military prowess, not civilian suffering.[107] These attitudes also conditioned the provision that governments made for the preservation of key sites of displacement and relief. Only isolated traces of the sojourn of Belgian refugees in the Netherlands survive in cemeteries and place-names, such as Vluchtoord in Uden.[108] Such attitudes inflected political life and the dominant historiography in Poland and the Baltic states as well, even though many post-war political leaders had developed a wartime career in refugee relief. Refugees, it appeared, had served their purpose. Depressingly, the most emphatic recollection of displacement emerged in post-war Austria, where right-wing nationalists deplored the continued presence of Jewish refugees from the shtetl.[109]

Conclusions: reckoning with refugeedom

The First World War brought about momentous movements of population, ranging from the conscription and shipment of troops to and from the front line to the migration of civilians as a consequence of economic mobilisation or other forms of state intervention. But a great deal more was at stake. The history of wartime displacement is also a story of cultural contacts, the construction of new social and national identities and the demonstration of philanthropic concern. Much remains to be done to trace these processes during and immediately after the war and what they implied for the relationship between the state and its citizens.

One fruitful line of enquiry is likely to be the creation of a field for the assertion of expert knowledge. Institutions developed a vested interest in highlighting 'spontaneous' movements of people as a device that enabled them to claim the right to reorder the lives of refugees and to speak on their behalf. This moment created opportunities for newly trained lawyers, doctors, teachers, statisticians and social workers. Professional expertise was deployed wherever refugees congregated. In Vienna, the Zionist activist Anitta Müller created the *Verein soziale Hilfsgemeinschaft* that assisted pregnant refugees and young mothers and created day-care centres. It employed hundreds of middle-class women and Jewish refugees, becoming 'instrumental in the professionalisation of Jewish social work in Austria'. This example can be multiplied.[110]

If the prevailing images tended to homogenise the refugee, creating a single category of difference, nationality offered a means of drawing distinctions between refugees. Refugeedom contributed to the intensification of a sense of national identity, not because one ethnic group had been singled out – after all, displacement affected more than one nationality – but because it created the prospect that the 'nation' might be permanently displaced, uprooted and scattered. In the Russian empire, newly minted national organisations claimed the refugee for themselves. Refugees had been forced to abandon their homeland, but this did not deprive their lives of purpose. They had a responsibility to the nation, which in turn would not shirk its responsibilities to the refugee. Refugees belonged somewhere after all. The response of the Russian state to these claims is very revealing. It legitimised national committees whose leaders claimed jurisdiction over refugees, packed them into canteens and schools, showered them with literature, organised national associations, and welcomed them as members of the national club. Corralled into groups that linked welfare to national identity, the war gave them a dignity that derived from and yet transcended refugeedom. However, in Russia as elsewhere, it did not take long for this moment to evaporate and for refugees to disappear from the recorded history of the First World War.

Notes

[1]   Gatrell, 'War after the War'; Gerwarth, 'The Central European Counter-revolution'.

[2]   Marrus, *The Unwanted*, 53–81. See also Kushner and Knox, *Refugees in an Age of Genocide*, 47–63; Cahalan, *Belgian Refugee Relief*; and Becker, *Oubliés de la grande guerre*.

[3] Fry, *A Quaker Adventure*, 100.

[4] de Roodt, *Oorlogsgasten*, 147.

[5] T. de Jastrzebski, 'The Register of Belgian Refugees', *Journal of the Royal Statistical Society* 79, no. 2 (1916): 133–58.

[6] Nivet, *Les réfugiés français*. French officialdom distinguished between 'refugees', who fled in the wake of the invasion, 'evacuees', whom the German army expelled, and French 'repatriates', whom the German occupation authorities forcibly returned from countries that they invaded.

[7] Ibid., 71–2.

[8] Tooley, 'World War 1 and the Emergence of Ethnic Cleansing', 78, citing Mayer, 'Die Flüchtlingsfürsorge'.

[9] Ermacora, 'Assistance and Surveillance; Bianchi, *La violenza contro la popolazione civile*.

[10] Baron, *The Russian Jew*, 187–200. See also Prusin, *Nationalizing a Borderland*.

[11] Hoffmann-Holter, 'Abreisendmachung', 12; Rechter, 'Galicia in Vienna'; Popik, *Ukraintsi v Avstrii*, 66–85.

[12] Hoffmann-Holter, 'Abreisendmachung', 36; Rozenblit, *Reconstructing a National Identity*, 66, 193.

[13] Kazanskii, *Galitsko-russkie bezhentsy v Odesse*; Mentzel, 'Weltkriegsflüchtlinge', 17–44; Hoffmann-Holter, 'Abreisendmachung', 283.

[14] Marrus, *The Unwanted*, 44–8.

[15] Yovanovitch, *Les effets économiques et sociaux*, 30; Mitrović, *Serbia's Great War*, 71.

[16] 'The British naval mission in Serbia', in The National Archives (TNA) ADM 137/1141, quoted in Fryer, *The Destruction of Serbia*, 70. See also Mitrović, *Serbia's Great War*, 145–6.

[17] Mitrany, *The Effect of the War*, 244–5.

[18] Tatham, 'The great retreat'.

[19] Tatham, 'The great retreat in Serbia in 1915', 374–9 (quotations on pp. 374, 377).

[20] Yovanovitch, *Les effets économiques et sociaux*, 41–9, 50–56. Deaths of civilians are reported on p. 304. See also Mitrović, *Serbia's Great War*, 151–4, 222–3, 229–30, and Matthew Stibbe's contribution to this volume.

[21] I draw here on Gatrell, *A Whole Empire Walking*. The quotation is from S.I. Zubchaninov, speaking at the Special Council for Refugees, 10 September 1915, in Rossiiskii Gosudarstvennyi Istoricheskii Arkhiv (RGIA) f. 1322, op. 1, d. 1, ll.1ob.-2.

[22] Memorandum by Prince N.L. Obolenskii, 30 August 1915, in Rossiiskii Gosudarstvennyi Voenno-Istoricheskii Arkhiv (RGVIA) f. 2003, op. 2, d. 945, ll.10.

[23] *Bezhentsy i vyselentsy* (Moscow, 1915), 54. See also Nelipovich, 'V poiskakh "vnutrennogo vraga"', 59; Neutatz, *Die 'deutsche Frage' im Schwarzmeergebiet*, 405; Lohr, *Nationalizing the Russian Empire*.

[24] Prince Shcherbatov, speaking at the inaugural session of the Special Council for Refugees, in RGIA f. 1322, op. 1, d. 1, l.3.

[25] Paléologue, *La Russie des Tsars*, vol. 1, 335–6.

[26] Senator A.B. Neidgardt, quoted in Gosudarstvennyi Arkhiv Rossiiskoi Federatsii (GARF) f. 651, op. 1, d. 39, l. 25.

[27] E.M. Rozenblium, in *Trudy vneocherednogo Pirogovskogo s"ezda* (Moscow, 1917), p. 66.

[28] *Mshak*, 4 January 1915, 3.

[29] Osherovskii, *Tragediia armian-bezhentsev*, 10.

[30] Report of the governor of Erevan to MVD, 21 January 1916, in RGIA f. 1322, op. 1, d. 16, l. 38.

[31] *Oxford Chronicle*, 21 July 1916, in Seton-Watson Archives, SEW/7/20; Nivet, *Les réfugiés français*, 377–85; Governor of Mogilev province, as reported in RGVIA f. 2005, op. 1, d. 42, ll. 286–7.

[32] Cahalan, *Belgian Refugee Relief*, 4.

[33] Caine, *King Albert's Book*; Kushner and Knox, *Refugees in an Age of Genocide*, 48.

[34] Rozenblit, *Reconstructing a National Identity*, 74, 78. Schreiber was writing to a captive audience, so to speak: his comment appeared in the leading Jewish newspaper, the *Österreichische Wochenschrift*.

[35] Nivet, *Les réfugiés français*, 555.

[36] Factory worker from Riga, quoted in Netesin, *Promyshlennyi kapital Latvii*, 203.

[37] *Ezhemesiachnyi zhurnal literatury, nauk i obshchestvennoi zhizni*, 3, March 1916, 231–41.

[38] Gatrell, *A Whole Empire Walking*, 132–3.

[39] Gourko, *Memories and Impressions*, 124, emphasis added; Thurstan, *The People Who Run*.

[40] 'Dva begstva', *Rodina: illiustrirovannyi zhurnal dlia semeinogo chteniia*, 1, no. 3 January 1916, 5.

[41] *Rech'*, 207, 30 July 1915, emphasis added.

[42] *Letopis' voiny*, no. 71, 24 December 1915, 1131; no. 91, 14 May 1916, 1449.

[43] Gatrell, *A Whole Empire Walking*, 200; Cahalan, *Belgian Refugee Relief*, 4.

[44] Malkki, *Purity and Exile*, 15–16.

[45] Cahalan, *Belgian Refugee Relief*, 179–80.

[46] Polner, *Russian Local Government*, 172–3. De Roodt, *Oorlogsgasten*, 147, has photographs of Belgian children.

[47] Fry, *A Quaker Adventure*, 103–115 for vivid detail; de Roodt, *Oorlogsgasten*, 159, 173–81, 192–4.

[48] Stengers, 'Pre-war Belgian Attitudes to Britain', 35–52.

[49] de Jastrzebski, 'The Register of Belgian Refugees', 156; Cahalan, *Belgian Refugee Relief*, 13, 27–30, 170–7.

[50] Cahalan, *Belgian Refugee Relief*, 357–68.

[51] Purseigle, '"A Wave on to our Shores"'.

[52] Ermacora, 'Assistance and Surveillance'.

[53] Mentzel, 'Weltkriegsflüchtlinge', 29–34; Rozenblit, *Reconstructing a National Identity*, 59, 66–69, 193.

[54] Mitrany, *The Effect of the War*, 245; Fry, *A Quaker Adventure*, 121–32; and Paget, *With Our Serbian Allies*. Some Serbians took offence at what they felt to be a depiction of the 'apparent apathy, unpunctuality and general shortcomings of a people condemned to continuous war' (Elizabeth Christich, Valjevo, to Miss Watson, SRF, 22 September 1915, in Seton-Watson Archives, SSEES, University of London, Box SEW/7/1/2).

[55] *Report of the Work of the Serbian Relief Fund* (1918); and *Annual Report of the Serbian Aid Fund* (1918), both in Seton-Watson Archives, Box SEW/7/2/1. See also Mitrović, *Serbia's Great War*, 111–13.

[56] Paget, *With our Serbian Allies*, 39–43; Mabel Grouitch, letter to *The Times*, 14 December 1914, in Seton-Watson Archives, SEW/7/18 (Press cutting book SRF); Walter Mead, 'With a British hospital in Serbia', *World's Work*, 1 August 1915, SEW/7/19.

[57] RGIA f. 796, op. 242, d. 2790, l. 21; f. 1322, op. 1, d. 36, ll. 2, 24.

[58] *Izvestiia VZS*, 41–42, 15 June–1 July 1916, 121–2; *Izvestiia VSG*, 34, July 1916, 219.

[59] *Viatskie eparkhial'nye vedomosti*, 35, 27 August 1915, 1070–3.

[60] *Izvestiia VZS*, 27, 15 November 1915, 63.

[61] Polner, *Russian Local Government*, 175.

[62] W. Grabski, July 1916, quoted in RGVIA f. 13273, op. 1, d. 39, ll. 43–6.

[63] *Birzhevye vedomosti*, 15001, 3 August 1915.

[64] A. Kirzhnits, 'Bezhenstvo', *Bol'shaia sovetskaia entsiklopediia* (Moscow-Leningrad, 1927), vol. 5, cols. 176–8.

[65] Cherniavsky, *Prologue to Revolution*, 57.

[66] *Birzhevye vedomosti*, 14 August 1915.

[67] Chernovich, 'Problemy 'novoi cherty', pp. 10–12.

[68] Otchet tsentral'nogo evreiskogo, p. 45.

[69] Something of the same ethos and activity appears to have emerged in Austria as well, as in a speech given by Sophie Grünfeld to an audience at one of her soup kitchens: 'You were foreign to us, and your culture did not appear to be like ours. You had other customs and we approached you not with the kind of love that brothers should bring their brothers in distress. But our contact with you has brought us closer together, and the bearing and dignity with which you bear your tragedy fills us with sincere admiration'. Middle-class Jews in Prague had a much less tolerant attitude, complaining that Galician Jews were backward and even 'barbarians' and 'pestilential'. See Rozenblit, *Reconstructing a National Identity*, 75, 78–9.

[70] Gatrell, *A Whole Empire Walking*, 150–4.

[71] Quoted in *Birzhevye vedomosti*, 31 August 1915.

[72] Kristaps Bachmanis, 'Our previous mistakes', *Dzimtenes Atbalss*, nos. 18–19, 1916; *Trudovaia pomoshch'*, 1, 1916, 60; ibid., 3, 1916, 265; ibid., 5, 1916, 463.

[73] RGIA f. 1322, op. 1, d. 13, ll. 44ob.-45; *Izvestiia VSG*, 20, December 1915, 167; *Trudovaia pomoshch'*, 10, 1915, 468.

[74] Yčas, *Pirmasis nepriklausomos Lietuvos dešimtmetis*.

[75] Świętosławska-Zółkiewska, 'Działalność oświatowa polskich organizacji'.

[76] *Trudovaia pomoshch'*, 6, 1916, 46–7.

[77] Signed appeal published in *Utro Rossii*, 227, 18 August 1915.

[78] RGIA f.1322, op.1, d.1, l.46ob., 17th sitting of special council, 11 November 1915.

[79] *Trudovaia pomoshch'*, 6, 1916, 21.

[80] *Ufimskie eparkhial'nye vedomosti*, 7, 1 April 1916, 244; *Trudovaia pomoshch'*, 2, 1916, 156–7.

[81] *Ekaterinburgskie eparkhial'nye vedomosti*, 3, 17 January 1916, 61.

[82] *Golos Rossii*, 5, 3 April 1916.

[83] *Golos*, 237, 17 October 1915.

[84] M. Titov, 'Otkliki na grozu i buriu voiny', *Ekaterinburgskie eparkhial'nye vedomosti*, 37, 13 September 1915, 655–7.

[85]   RGVIA, pp. 1–14.

[86]   'Galichane v Rostove,' *Ukrainskaia zhizn'*, 11–12, December 1915, 138–50.

[87]   *Sputnik bezhentsa*, 4, 29–30 September 1915, p.1; ibid., 7, 6–7 October 1915, 1.

[88]   'Bezhat' ili ne bezhat'?' *Ukrainskaia zhizn'*, 10, October 1915, 84–5.

[89]   Gatrell, *A Whole Empire Walking*, 148, 161 for some examples.

[90]   Mitrović, *Serbia's Great War*, 169–80.

[91]   Yovanovitch, *Les effets économiques et sociaux*, 28, 33; Tatham, 'The Great Retreat in Serbia in 1915', 375, 377.

[92]   Fry, *A Quaker Adventure*, 127.

[93]   Kushner and Knox, *Refugees in an Age of Genocide*, 62.

[94]   Mentzel, 'Weltkriegsflüchtlinge', 29–30.

[95]   Fry, *A Quaker Adventure*, 118; Cahalan, *Belgian Refugee Relief*, 444–8.

[96]   Fry, *A Quaker Adventure*, 129.

[97]   Rozenblit, *Reconstructing a National Identity*, 136; Mentzel, 'Weltkriegsflücht-tlinge', 37–8.

[98]   See the essays in Baron and Gatrell, *Homelands*.

[99]   Gatrell and Laycock, 'Armenia', 179–200.

[100] Baron and Gatrell, 'Population Displacement'. Compare Zolberg, 'The Formation of New States'. My suggestion is that the refugee-generating process also helped constitute these polities.

[101] A. Kenins, 'The fund of 1917', *Dzimtenes Atbalss*, no. 7, 5 January 1917.

[102] Christie, *An Autobiography*, 256. Christie remembered Belgian refugees in her village: 'a good many of them were suspicious peasants (who) wanted to be left alone.'

[103] Bezhenets, Editorial, 2.

[104] Ermacora, 'Assistance and Surveillance'.

[105] Gatrell, *A Whole Empire Walking*, 94–5.

[106] 'Sobranie materialov o bezhenskom dvizhenii', *Izvestiia KTN*, 15, 1 January 1917, 10–11.

[107] Nivet, *Les réfugiés français*, 9, 557 and *passim*. Ermacora, 'Assistance and Surveillance', makes the same point. The Carnegie Foundation for International Peace commissioned a volume on refugees but abandoned the project; it is not known if any manuscript survives.

[108] De Roodt, *Oorlogsgasten*, 431–2.

[109] Mentzel, 'Weltkriegsflüchtlinge', 17–18.

[110] Rozenblit, *Reconstructing a National Identity*, 73; Cahalan, *Belgian Refugee Relief*, 449–50.

The Recruitment of Colonial Troops in Africa and Asia and their Deployment in Europe during the First World War

Christian Koller

School of History, Welsh History and Archaeology, Bangor University

The impact of the First World War on the colonies was profound and many-sided.[1] A conflict that began in the Balkans turned into a general European war in July and August 1914, and then took on extra-European dimensions, particularly as some of the belligerent states ranked as the most important colonial powers globally.

After the outbreak of the war, there was immediate fighting in several parts of the world as Great Britain, France, Belgium and Japan as well as the British dominions Australia, New Zealand and South Africa attacked the German colonies in Africa, Asia and the Pacific. Most of these territories were conquered by the Entente powers within a short time. Already in October and November 1914, Japanese troops occupied the German islands in Micronesia and captured the city of Tsingtau, where about 5000 Germans were made prisoners of war. Between August and November 1914 troops from Australia and New Zealand conquered Samoa, New Guinea and the Bismarck Archipelago, all of them German possessions.[2]

The German colonies in Africa were defended by so-called 'Schutztruppen', made up of German officers and African soldiers. While British and French troops overwhelmed Togo in August 1914, the fighting in Cameroon lasted until January 1916.[3] German South West Africa was attacked by South Africa on behalf of the Entente powers. This caused problems in South Africa itself, however, for about 11,500 Anglophobe Boer soldiers rebelled, some of them openly joining the German side. The South African war between the British empire and the Boers had only ended 12 years before, and many Boers had preserved their anti-British feelings. Once this rebellion was crushed, the Germans were left defenceless, for 50,000 South African soldiers faced only 5,000 men in the German colonial forces. When South African troops entered the capital city Windhuk in May 1915, they did not meet any resistance.[4]

The most important colonial theatre was German East Africa, where fighting lasted until the end of the war. German forces here were under the command of Paul von Lettow-Vorbeck and consisted of only about 7,500 men, most of them Africans. British troops, on the other hand, comprised about 160,000 soldiers and one million carriers. All the same, they were not able to defeat the Germans for more than four years, for Lettow-Vorbeck soon turned to a guerrilla strategy and escaped again and again. Furthermore, he also attacked Belgian and Portuguese colonial troops. Only in November 1918, after about 10,000 British soldiers and 100,000 carriers had died, did Lettow-Vorbeck surrender. The fighting in East Africa had a catastrophic economic as well as ecological impact. The economies of German East Africa and of bordering British colonies were deeply damaged by both sides' ongoing use of forced recruitment. Famines and epidemics spread and lasted beyond the war's end. Furthermore, migrations caused by the war led to a spread of the tsetse fly, which in turn explains the prevalence of sleeping sickness in East Africa in the following decades.[5]

However, the colonies (or some of them) were not only theatres of war, but they were also integrated into the European powers' domestic war economies. They supplied goods and some of them also made financial contributions. India, for instance, contributed £146 million to the British war costs between 1914 and 1920 and supplied products such as cotton, jute, paper and wool. In the French possessions in North Africa, the process of integration into France's war economy led to far-ranging administrative and economic reforms. Increasing demand for foodstuff at first improved the economic situation of North Africa's agriculture. In the years 1917 and 1918, however, harvests in Algeria and Tunisia were very bad, which caused famines. Furthermore, hitherto imported industrial goods were replaced by home-made ones, which promoted the development of a North African industry. However, no sustainable industrialisation process took place. After the end of the war, imports from France would destroy these nascent industries in North Africa.[6] French West Africa mainly provided palm oil, palm kernel and peanuts. However, its integration into the French war economy was chaotic rather than planned. The French colonial and military administration could not decide whether this area should be used primarily as a base for economic exploitation or whether the focus should be laid on the recruitment of soldiers.[7]

In addition to the fighting in the colonies and the increased economic exploitation of native peoples for the war effort in Europe, the First World War also witnessed migration from the colonial world to Europe on an unprecedented scale. Among the temporary migrants from the colonies and semi-colonial regions to Europe were both war workers and soldiers.

About 215,000 civilian war workers from South Africa (31,200), the West Indies (8,000), Mauritius (1,000) and the Fiji Islands (100) as well as from China (92,000) and Egypt (82,000) came to work behind the British front,[8] whilst France recruited about 220,000 workers from outside Europe, coming from Algeria (75,900), Indochina (49,000), Morocco (35,000), Tunisia (18,500) and Madagascar (5,500) as well as from China (36,700).[9] The massive presence of extra–European male war workers led to problems in France. French workers often saw these colonial migrants as rivals for jobs as well as for women, and there were numerous attacks on them, especially towards the end of the war. French trade unions were on the horns of a dilemma. On the one hand, they stressed internationalism and rejected all forms of racism. On the other hand, they were aware that the colonial workers were often misused as strike breakers. The French government, for its part, pursued a policy of strict segregation between colonial workers and French civilians and would send the former home as soon as possible after the end of the war.[10]

Even more significant in terms of both numbers and public attention was the temporary migration of colonial soldiers to Europe. The Entente powers deployed about 650,000 colonial soldiers on European battlefields. White European settlers from the colonies and dominions, who provided large contingents as well, are not included in this figure. The Central Powers, on the other hand, were not able to deploy any colonial troops in Europe.

Britain, altogether, mobilised about 1.5 million Indian soldiers during the war, of which about 90,000 were killed. Some 150,000 Indian soldiers were deployed in Europe from September 1914 on. The overwhelming majority of Indian troops, however, fought in Mesopotamia against the Ottoman empire.[11]

On the other hand, Britain did not deploy any African troops on European battlefields, although there was a group of officers and politicians with a colonial background lobbying to do so.[12] Winston Churchill, for instance, claimed in a House of Commons speech in May 1916 that not only 10–12 Indian divisions but also African units should be trained for deployment in Europe:

> Let us ... think what historians of the future would write if they were writing a history of the present time and had to record that Great Britain

was forced to make an inconclusive peace because she forgot Africa; that at a time when every man counted ... the Government of Great Britain was unable to make any use of a mighty continent ... It would be incredible; but it is taking place ... What is going on while we sit here, while we go away to dinner, or home to bed? Nearly 1,000 men – Englishmen, Britishers, men of our own race – are knocked into bundles of bloody rags every twenty-four hours ... Every measure must be considered, and none put aside while there is hope of obtaining something from it.[13]

Plenty of British African troops, however, fought in the Middle East and in Africa itself. Some battalions of the black 'British West Indies Regiment' were deployed in France, but only in ancillary functions, not as combatants.[14] Officially, this policy was justified with reference to logistical problems, but racism probably played a role as well, for after the United States had joined the war, the British army also rejected the training of African-American soldiers, who were eventually incorporated into the French army.[15]

Unlike Britain, the French deployed large numbers of African troops in Europe, including 172,800 soldiers from Algeria, 134,300 from West Africa, 60,000 from Tunisia, 37,300 from Morocco, 34,400 from Madagascar and 2100 from the Somali Coast. Another colonial contingent of about 44,000 men came from Indochina.[16] Italy, who joined the Entente side in spring 1915, tried to deploy African colonial troops in Europe as well. In August 1915, some 2,700 soldiers from Libya were shipped to Sicily. However, they did not enter the front line, because many soldiers died from pneumonia immediately after their arrival, and so, the Libyans, who were designated for Alpine warfare, were shipped home again after a short time. In the African theatres of war, however, Italy deployed plenty of Eritrean, Libyan and Somali soldiers.[17]

My contribution shall focus on three aspects of this transcontinental military migration between 1914 and 1918. In the first instance, I will analyse colonial recruitment policies and the responses they met by the colonised. Secondly, I shall consider the colonial troops' deployment on European battlefields, including two issues often discussed by contemporaries: whether colonial troops were misused as cannon fodder and whether they fought particularly cruelly. And finally, the cultural impact of military migration, especially mutual perception of Europeans and colonial soldiers, will be analysed.

Recruitment

Recruitment of colonial troops in India followed the traditional pattern of the theory of 'martial races'. The British army only recruited from the small number of castes it considered 'martial', which effectively eliminated most of the Indian population from the manpower pool. Furthermore, Indian troops were segregated by caste into companies and battalions. As such, replacements could not be assigned where needed but had to go to units restricted to their caste.[18]

Whereas the British colonial troops consisted exclusively of volunteers, the French recruitment policy in North and West Africa was a mixed one, including the enlistment of volunteers as well as conscription. In 1912, the French parliament had passed several acts enabling conscription in West Africa, Algeria and Tunisia (but not in Morocco), if the numbers of volunteers were considered to be too low. Conscription became more and more important the longer the war lasted.[19] Whilst in 1915 only 2,500 out of a total of 14,500 new recruits in Algeria were conscripts, this ratio changed dramatically in the second half of the war. In 1917, the army enlisted 6,261 volunteers and 25,925 conscripts, in the following year there were 13,942 volunteers and 34,173 conscripts.[20] During the 1915/16 recruiting campaign in West Africa, only 7,000 out of 53,000 recruits were volunteers.[21] The customary procedure was to ask local chiefs to provide potential recruits. Most often, young men from lower social strata, especially from the group of domestic slaves, were presented to French recruitment officers.

French recruitment in West Africa met all sorts of resistance, ranging from malingering and self-mutilation to flight into the bush or to Liberia, Gambia, Portuguese Guinea and the Gold Coast. In Senegal alone, some 15,000 men avoided conscription by hiding in the bush or flight. In some cases, as in Bélédougou in 1915, there was even armed resistance against French colonial administration and recruitment officers. Other rebellions such as the big uprising in Western Volta in 1915/16 and several revolts in the north of Dahomey in 1916 and 1917 were at least partially caused by French recruitment policies.[22]

In North Africa, there was resistance against forced recruitment as well. As early as the autumn of 1914, young Arabs threatened by conscription and their relatives protested against French recruitment practices in several parts of Algeria. In the winter of 1916/17, Algerian resistance against conscription climaxed in a big uprising in the southern parts of Constantinois.[23] In Tunisia, too, there were several smaller rebellions in the years 1915 and 1916.[24] Only Morocco, where there was no conscription, remained quiet.

In spite of these acts of resistance, certain military and colonial circles in metropolitan France were in favour of an expansion of colonial recruitment. In 1915, General Charles Mangin launched a propaganda campaign for the recruitment of half a million soldiers in the French colonies. Mangin was already well known as a former participant in the 1898/99 Fashoda expedition and as the most important advocate of the *force noire*, a strong African army for deployment in Europe, from 1909 on. Whilst most metropolitan newspapers supported his suggestions enthusiastically, colonial experts remained rather sceptical. So did the French government, which decided on a modest expansion of recruitment in Africa only.[25] In March 1916, ministerial attaché Paulin wrote to the colonial administration in Dakar that the colonial minister had agreed to a further enlistment campaign 'only because he was forced into it by public and parliamentary opinion, although he was never really convinced by it'.[26]

French colonial officials had first been in favour of recruitment, but, in view of African resistance, they soon changed their minds. In August 1914, William Ponty, Governor-General of French West Africa, had written to Paris that 'there would be extreme enthusiasm if people were informed that the natives were to be given the honour to fight in France'.[27] His successor Clozel, however, stated only a year later:

> The brutal and badly prepared effort demanded by Ponty, aggravated by the officers' incompetence, has completely disgusted everyone. We are exhausted. No more cadres, no more physicians to examine recruits seriously ... I shall launch another modest recruitment drive, so that, if the war continues, we can send six or seven thousand men in order to fill the holes, but this will be a terrible effort.[28]

In September 1917, Governor-General Joost van Vollenhoven obtained a temporary cessation of recruitment in French West Africa. Vollenhoven stressed that France should rather prioritise the economic exploitation of West Africa:

> This African empire is poor in men but rich in products, so let us use its miserable population for food supply during the war and for post-war times! This country has been ruined just to recruit another few thousands of men![29]

Furthermore, Vollenhoven pointed at African resistance against recruitment:

> Recruiting the Black army out of volunteers is a utopia; its creator has been mistaken, facts have proved this so dramatically that this issue can no longer be discussed ... Since the beginning of the war, recruitment has become a hunt for men ... Out of recruitment has resulted an unpopularity that has become universal from the very day when recruits were asked to serve in Europe and grim, determined, terrible revolts started against the white man, who had hitherto been tolerated, sometimes even loved, but who, transformed into a recruiting agent,

had become a detested enemy, the image of the slave hunters he had defeated and replaced himself.[30]

When the government in Paris in winter 1917/18 decided to resume recruitment in West Africa, Vollenhoven desperately wrote:

> The natives don't want to supply any more men and we won't get more by convincing them. If we really need new *tirailleurs*, we will have to recruit them forcibly, running the risk of a general revolt.[31]

Embittered, he resigned and volunteered for the front, where he fell in July 1918.[32]

In order to organise the new recruitment campaign, the French government appointed Blaise Diagne *Commissaire de la République dans l'Ouest Africain* with the powers of a Governor-General. Diagne had been the first Black African to be elected as a deputy in the French parliament in 1914. Like some African-American leaders, he considered and propagated war service as a means to obtain rights. By September 1918, he had recruited 77,000 soldiers, many more than he had been expected to do. However, most of them were not deployed before the end of the war.[33]

French officials in North Africa were less hostile towards conscription than their colleagues in West Africa. Charles Lutaud, Governor-General of Algeria, even explicitly announced an expansion of conscription of Arabs in 1916.[34] In the following year, however, he opposed governmental plans for a premature enlistment of the 1918 age group, arguing that 'even though we managed to suppress last November's uprising, the tribes' submission is far from absolute'.[35] Thereupon, the government renounced these plans and even reintroduced the system of replacements and dispensations they had, against Lutaud's will, abolished the year before. However, the government's ambition to recruit another 50,000 Algerian Arabs in 1918 by abolishing the system of dispensations again and expanding conscription to the south of Algeria, where no working colonial administration was yet in existence, was criticised by colonial officials as unrealistic. When Paris persisted, colonial administrations put the new policy into practice. However they managed to recruit far fewer soldiers than Paris had hoped for.[36]

In the second half of the war, those in favour of a strong *armée jaune* also became more and more influential and recruitment in Indochina was intensified.[37] However, Indochinese soldiers were mainly deployed in ancillary functions, for there were reservations concerning their fighting abilities. In addition to conscription in its own colonies, several proposals were made to recruit paid fighters in Ethiopia, Somalia and Yemen. The French government, however, never seriously considered these plans, which would have boosted German propaganda's allegations that the

Entente powers were cowards who preferred to rely on mercenaries to do their fighting.[38]

Deployment

Colonial troops had already entered the front line in Europe in the first months of the war. At the end of September 1914, two Indian divisions (the 3rd Lahore and the 7th Meerut division) as well as a cavalry brigade arrived in Marseilles and in October, the first Indian soldiers were deployed at Ypres. In the following months, Indian troops fought in many important battles on the western front, for instance at Festubert in December 1914 and in September 1915; in the second battle of Ypres in March 1915, where they for the first time were confronted with gas attacks; and at Loos in September 1915.

It soon became clear, however, that Indian troops were poorly prepared for modern industrialised warfare. As British policy since the 1857 mutiny had been to keep the Indian army always one generation behind in weaponry, they first had to be completely re-equipped at Marseilles where they received new rifles, ammunition, machine-guns, and both field and heavy batteries of artillery. Nevertheless, the losses of the first weeks were extremely high. Furthermore, evidence began to mount in November 1914 that men of many different battalions were shooting themselves in order to be taken out of the line. Thus, throughout the year 1915, British military leaders, who mainly attributed these failures to the climate, debated whether Indian troops would better be deployed elsewhere. The two infantry divisions were eventually withdrawn from the western front in December 1915 and shipped to extra-European theatres of war, mainly to Mesopotamia.

The Indian cavalry remained in Europe and would fight in several important battles on the western front, for instance at the Somme in July 1916. Furthermore, an Indian infantry brigade also participated in the Gallipoli operation from April 1915 to January 1916. The overwhelming majority of the Indian army, however, was deployed in the Middle East as well as in East Africa.[39]

Autumn 1914 also witnessed the first actions of African troops on the western front. Although North African units had already fought in previous European wars – in the Crimean war from 1854 to 1856, in the Italian war in 1859 and in the Franco-Prussian war in 1870/71 –, this was the first time that troops from sub–Saharan Africa had entered the front line. In September 1914, West African units fought in Picardy. In October and November, *Tirailleurs Sénégalais* were deployed at Ypres, where they suffered heavy losses.

Afterwards, a new doctrine was applied: West African troops no longer fought as independent units, but they were 'amalgamated' with European troops. Every regiment of the *troupes coloniales*, which were composed of Europeans, got a West African battalion after the historical model of amalgamation of old troops and volunteer corps during the French Revolution.[40] The same doctrine was enacted for North African troops, who were often amalgamated into so-called *régiments mixtes* together with European settlers from North Africa. This doctrine was also aimed at preventing the desertion of Muslim soldiers to the Germans, who were using their alliance with the Ottoman empire to pose as friends of Islam and even to recruit Muslim POWs to the Central Powers' cause.[41]

In the following years, African troops participated in most of the principal battles on the western front, for instance at the Marne, at the Yser, at the Somme and at Verdun.[42] Furthermore, West African troops also participated in the Gallipoli operation and fought in the Balkans from 1916 onwards. Their number grew as the war continued. Thus while 17 West African battalions fought on the western front in 1916, there were already 41 in 1917 and even 92 in the war's final year. The number of North African soldiers fighting in Europe increased considerably as well.

Two questions concerning the colonial troops' deployment in Europe were already contentious during the war itself, namely whether colonial troops were misused as canon fodder and whether they fought especially cruelly. The cannon fodder theory also entered scholarly discussions after the war.[43]

Charles Mangin, the most important promoter of the *force noire*, had already propagated the deployment of African units as shock troops in pre-war times. Mangin had argued that because of its demographic development, France would have to rely on colonial forces to a much higher degree in the future. For historical as well as racial reasons, West African warriors would be especially well-suited to fill the gap. They had already been held in high esteem by Arab and Ottoman rulers as very martial people. In addition, Mangin argued, they were especially suitable for modern warfare because of their underdeveloped nervous system and their hereditary fatalism that would allow them to sleep in the trenches in the midst of a battle, if they were ordered to do so.[44]

On the western front, African troops were indeed often deployed as shock troops. Thus, French soldiers used to interpret the emergence of African troops as an unmistakable sign that an attack was imminent. Henri Barbusse, for instance, in his literary war diary *Le Feu*, described Moroccan soldiers as follows:

One looks at them and is silent. One would not speak to them. They are imposing and even frighten a bit....Of course they are heading for the front line. This is their place, and their arrival means we are about to attack. They are made for attacking.[45]

French propaganda also developed similar themes:

From the very first hour on, African regiments had the privilege to occupy the most dangerous posts, which permitted them to enrich their book of traditions and past glory.[46]

Colonel Petitdemange, responsible for West Africans' training in the camp of Fréjus in southern France, wrote in a letter in January 1918 to a colleague that African soldiers were 'cannon fodder, who should, in order to save whites' lives, be made use of much more intensively'.[47] And even Prime Minister Georges Clemenceau, in a speech delivered to the French Senate on 20 February 1918, stated:

We are going to offer civilisation to the Blacks. They will have to pay for that.... I would prefer that ten Blacks are killed rather than one Frenchman – although I immensely respect those brave Blacks –, for I think that enough Frenchmen are killed anyway and that we should sacrifice as few as possible![48]

Thus it is clear that there was at least the intention to assign colonial troops to especially dangerous tasks. The question remains, however, whether this doctrine caused significantly higher casualty rates than with European troops. After the war, Mangin published the following casualty rates for the French army:

Colonial soldiers: 20.0%
European soldiers: 15.8%
European officers: 22.0%.[49]

These figures have repeatedly been interpreted in scholarly debates on the cannon fodder thesis.[50] However, any attempt to verify or challenge this thesis by interpreting casualty rates is problematic for several reasons. Firstly, there is an issue with the statistics themselves. For the whole period, French casualties were registered for the different ranks, but not for the soldiers' origin. The figures most commonly quoted come from a report by Baron Lyons de Feuchin, published in 1924 on behalf of the army committee of the French parliament. According to this report, 22% of deployed West African soldiers fell in the war, 13% of North Africans and 7% of other French colonial troops. In total, the casualty rate of French colonial troops was 14%, while that for European combatants in the French army reached 18%.[51]

Yet there is much confusion over the casualty rates of African troops. In the official *Histoire militaire de l' A. O. F.*, published in 1931, as well as in a 1936 publication by the *Ministère des Pensions*, West Africans' casualty rate was slightly lower than in Feuchin's report. According to a 1919 study by the *Direction des Troupes Coloniales*, it was even considerably lower, reaching only 19%.[52] On the other hand, according to non-official figures, West Africans' real casualty rate was considerably higher. Colonial officer Edouard de Martonne published a figure of 65,000 West Africans killed in action, which would equal a casualty rate of 48%.[53] For the casualty rates of North African contingents there is confusion as well. The number of Moroccan soldiers killed in action ranges between 2500 and 9000 or between 7% and 24%.[54] The most frequently cited figure for fallen Algerians is 19,000 or 11%. Immediately after the war, however, reported Algerian dead reached up to 56,000 or 32.5%.[55] Some scholars even claim that 100,000 Algerians were killed.[56]

Yet, even if the statistics were more reliable, it would be too simplistic to base any judgment of the cannon fodder thesis on global figures of killed and wounded alone, for this neglects the temporal dimension of deployment. The overwhelming majority of Indian troops, for instance, were only in Europe for 15 months and their time spent at the front was probably shorter than that of European soldiers. West African troops used to be withdrawn from the front and transferred to camps in southern France during the winter months, because French officials thought they could not bear cold weather. Furthermore, the overwhelming majority of North and West Africans only came to Europe in the second half of the war. Thus, casualty rates should not be compared to overall figures of deployed soldiers, but to average figures.

Joe Harris Lunn, analysing annual casualty rates of West Africans, concludes that in the last two and-a-half years of the war, when their deployment in Europe reached its peak, the rate of killed and wounded West African soldiers was twice that of French infantrymen. Given the fact that West Africans used to be withdrawn from the front in the winter months, the probability of a West African soldier being killed during his time at the front was two and-a-half times as high as for a French infantryman. For the members of ethnic groups considered 'martial', such as the Wolof, Tukulor and Serer, it was even three times as high.[57]

Another approach is to analyse casualty rates for individual battles. This can be done, thanks to figures provided by Marc Michel, for the battle of Reims (July 1917), the offensive at Villers-Cotterêt (July 1918) and the battle at Avre (July/August 1918). In all these battles, the rate of killed, wounded and missed was higher for West Africans than for French infantrymen (Reims: 29.0% to 27.5%; Villers-Cotterêt: 33.6% to 23.6%; Avre: 19.8% to 17.5%).[58] There are also figures for several battles where Indian and British troops fought together. Here, there is hardly any difference between colonial and metropolitan soldiers. In the second battle of Ypres, the rate of killed, wounded and missing reached 30.4% for Indians and 29.8% for British soldiers.[59] In the battle of Neuve Chapelle, the casualty rate for British soldiers was even higher than for Indians (21% compared to 19%).[60]

On balance, the canon fodder thesis can neither be entirely verified nor falsified by interpreting statistics. As far as West Africans are concerned, however, not only the doctrine of deployment, but also Lunn's analysis contradicts Marc Michel's statement that the cannon fodder thesis was just a legend.[61]

The second question linked to the deployment of colonial troops in Europe is whether they fought especially cruelly. The allegation that Africans and Indians engaged in brutal practices which were not in accordance with international law soon became a standard topic in German propaganda.[62] Alleged atrocities committed by colonial soldiers included violations of international regulations on the treatment of wounded combatants and prisoners captured on the battlefield, the hunt for trophies such as fingers, ears and heads, and the use of allegedly unlawful weapons such as the *coupe-coupe* (long bush knives), in close combat.

Did these allegations have any substance? First, it is striking that German propaganda repeatedly told the same atrocity stories involving colonial soldiers. Thus, if these stories, which hardly number a dozen, were based on reality at all, they were obviously isolated events. On the other hand, in German propaganda publications dealing with alleged Entente violations of international law in general, cases involving colonial troops did not appear more frequently than average.[63] As far as close combat is concerned, the use of the *coupe-coupe* cannot be denied,[64] yet this was by no means unlawful and it is doubtful whether the use of these knives was more 'barbaric' than the use of bayonets and spades in close combat. The stories about the cutting off of ears and heads were probably the German response to Entente propaganda concerning German atrocities in Belgium, where the cutting off of Belgian children's hands was a standard topic.[65]

Yet the notion that some of the atrocity stories were at least partly true cannot be dismissed out of hand. Some of the French colonial troops indeed originated from areas where the hunt for heads as trophies had been an important element of traditional warfare.[66] Furthermore, there are also French sources – albeit hostile to the deployment of colonial troops in Europe – which talk about colonial soldiers proudly displaying heads and ears.[67] In general, however, colonial troops' methods of warfare did not differ significantly from those of European units.[68]

Cultural impact

The deployment of more than half a million African and Asian soldiers in Europe had a strong cultural impact. Never before had so many Europeans been confronted with so many Africans and Asians – as comrades in arms, as enemies at the front, or as prisoners of war. This produced discourses about the colonial soldiers, which included exoticism, racism and paternalism.[69] On the other hand, never before had so many men from the colonies been directly exposed to the realities of European culture and society. The experience had an impact on their perceptions of their colonial masters and on the long-range, changed colonial relationships.

European images of African and Asian soldiers evolved in different ways on both sides of the western front. In Germany, representation further developed along the line of racist pre-war imagery, even reaching the extremes of representing colonial soldiers as beasts. In summer 1915, the German Foreign Office put into circulation a pamphlet with the title *Employment, Contrary to International Law, of Coloured Troops upon the European Theatre of War by England and France*, in which, as mentioned above, many atrocities were attributed to colonial soldiers, such as the poking out of eyes and the cutting off of the ears, noses and heads of wounded and captured German soldiers.[70] The colonial troops were labelled with expressions that negated their quality as regular military forces, for example 'a motley crew of colours and religions', 'devils', 'dehumanised wilderness', 'dead vermin of the wilderness', 'Africans jumping around in a devilish ecstasy', 'auxiliary rabble of all colours'. Other idioms used included 'an exhibition of Africans', or 'an anthropological show of uncivilised or half civilised bands and hordes', 'black flood' or 'dark mud', and finally the catchphrase 'the black shame' [*schwarze Schmach*] which quickly rose to common usage in the early 1920s.[71]

However, another image – diametrically opposed to the above – was to be found in publications trying to justify the German practice of recruiting Muslim prisoners of war (POWs) for the Ottoman army or in propaganda attempting to prove the cannon fodder thesis. Thus German propaganda sought to profit from the alliance with the Ottoman empire and to present the Central Powers as friends of Islam, for instance by arranging the publication of several texts by the Algerian officer Rabah Abdallah Boukabouya, who had deserted in 1915.[72] Muslim deserters and prisoners of war were interned in the so-called 'crescent camp' (*Halbmondlager*) at Wünsdorf near Zossen, which comprised a mosque erected at the Kaiser's expense.[73] As for German civilians, some of them developed a more exotic view than official propaganda and met African and Asian POWs with curiosity and fascination, albeit often tinged with fear.

Another recurrent theme in German propaganda against the deployment of colonial troops on European battlefields was its alleged impact on the future of the colonial system and the supremacy of the 'white race'. If African and Asian soldiers were trained in the handling of modern arms, if they were brought to Europe and saw the white nations fighting against each other, and if they were even allowed to participate in these battles and experience the vulnerability of the white man, then they would lose their respect once and for all. After the war, they would turn their weapons against their own masters and remove colonial rule. Thus German propaganda argued that the French and British policy of deploying colonial troops in Europe was a flagrant breach of white solidarity and should be condemned by every civilized nation.[74]

Entente propaganda countered these allegations within the patterns of pre–World War argumentation, albeit with some modifications. In the first months of the war, representations of colonial troops in the French press did not differ much from German propaganda images. Two weeks after the outbreak of the war, the *Dépêche Coloniale* portrayed African soldiers as *démons noirs* who would carry over the Rhine, with their bayonets, the revenge of civilization against modern barbarism.[75] In February 1915, the Marseilles-based journal *Midi Colonial* published a cartoon showing a Muslim soldier wearing a necklace with German soldiers' ears. The subtitle ran: 'Be silent, be careful, enemy ears are listening!'.[76]

Beginning in 1915/16, officials propagated a modified image of infantile and devoted savages. The colonial soldiers were depicted as belonging to *races jeunes* and as absolutely obedient to the white masters because of the latter's intellectual supremacy.[77] Alphonse Séché, for instance, stated in the weekly *L'Opinion*:

> For the black man, the white man's orders, the chief's orders are summarised in one word that he repeats again and again 'y a service'.... He won't discuss; he does not try to understand. He would kill his father, mother, wife, child, in order to obey to the order he received. He is not responsible; a superior's will is more important than his own one.... In all the blacks' acts, we find this mixture of childlike innocence and heroism.... The Senegalese is brave by nature; as a primitive being, he does not analyse.... For the Senegalese, his officer

is everything; he replaces the absent chief of his village, his father. If the Senegalese has confidence in his chief, he does not do anything without consulting him . . .[78]

This image also appeared in two special issues of the *Depêche Coloniale Illustrée* in January 1916 and in February 1917 as well as in Lieutenant Gaillet's book *Coulibaly: Les Sénégalais sur la terre de France* (published in 1917).[79] In pictorial representations, the images of the bloodthirsty *brute* and of the infantile savage were alternating.[80] The infantile savages in French wartime propaganda – often described as *grands enfants* – appeared as naive and almost sexless. Therefore, they were a danger neither to white supremacy in the colonial world, nor to the French metropolitan population.

This propaganda was produced to counter German propaganda as well as to calm the French population's reservation about the African troops' presence in France. Large parts of the French population seem to have shared the image of colonial troops as bloodthirsty savages that was omnipresent in the German propaganda. When the first units from West Africa arrived in France, large crowds welcomed them shouting: 'Bravo les tirailleurs sénégalais! Couper têtes aux allemands!'[81]

This image also seems to have caused a latent popular opposition against stationing African soldiers at the Côte d'Azur. Lucie Cousturier, who had been acquainted with several wounded Senegalese soldiers in the military hospital at Fréjus during and after the war, wrote about the French population's feelings towards the Africans in her book *Des Inconnus chez moi* (1920):

> In April and May of 1916 we were very anxious about our future friends. . . . There was simply no crime that one could put beyond them: . . . drunkenness, theft, rape, epidemics . . . 'What will become of us?' the farmers' wives moaned. . . ' We cannot let our little daughters go out alone any more because of those savages. We do not even risk going out alone ourselves any more . . . Imagine! If you were in the hands of those gorillas!'[82]

Below the level of official French propaganda, for instance in trench journals, images very similar to those of German propaganda were also to be found as far as sexuality was concerned. A postcard depicting an African grasping a white French woman's breast with the cry 'Vive les Teutons' has to be seen in this context.[83] Thus to some extent German propaganda on this topic seems to have reflected the French *poilu's* fears.

The French military administration promoted the image of primitive savages, too. For instance, African soldiers were given boots from the French arsenals that were far too big for them, as their feet were supposed to have enormous dimensions because of permanent barefooted walking.[84] As late as in 1917, there was a proposal that West African soldiers should fight barefoot, because with French boots, 'those agile apes are loosing one of their best infantry qualities, namely their elasticity at marching'.[85]

French propaganda also again and again stressed the alleged identity of interests between France and its colonised peoples. The *Revue de Paris*, for instance, stated in 1915:

> Their existence, their destiny is connected to ours. It is our task to elevate them to a superior life and to protect them from German rule that everywhere has been very hard for indigenous peoples and that considers its colonies only as a field of exploitation. So, we have got the right – and not only the master's right – to request our subjects' help, for their interests are mingled with ours.[86]

According to the journal *Afrique Française*, the *grands enfants joyeux* wanted to prove by their disciplined heroism their gratitude towards the 'glorious country that civilised them'.[87] In June 1917, a *Journée de l'Armée d'Afrique et des troupes coloniales* was celebrated in order to demonstrate the ties between motherland and colonies.[88]

On balance, this stress on the colonial soldiers' bravery and loyalty was intended not only to counter German propaganda concerning France's supposed 'betrayal' of white solidarity, but also to offset objections from French military circles and especially colonial administrations. Yet, despite the utter contrary lines of argument in German and Entente propaganda, basic common structures can be delineated. Both sides held a similar view of colonial soldiers as fundamentally different and inferior, which implies a common European racism.

But how did colonial soldiers perceive Europe and the Europeans? Several scholars have examined this question by analysing letters and memoirs as well as by conducting studies based on oral history. As for Indian soldiers, there exist several articles on war letters.[89] These show a far from uniform strategy on the part of Indian soldiers coping with the experience of a completely foreign world.

Some of the Indian soldiers obviously were able to integrate what they experienced in Europe into their cognitive background. They enjoyed honour gained on the battlefields and were proud of the English king's power. Thus, a wounded Garhwali wrote to a friend in India in February 1915:

> England is a superb country with an excellent climate. Think it a great honour that we have an opportunity of showing our loyalty to our great Emperor by the sacrifice of our bodies and by the favour that is accorded to us of being present on the field of battle. . . . If our ancestors

help us and God shows us favour, if we die on the battlefield in the service of our King, this is equal to entering heaven.... My prayer is that the great God will quickly make me well and give me an opportunity of showing my loyalty.[90]

Soldiers from this group even thought it possible to marry a European woman, albeit following Indian customs.

For a second group, there was a large gap between what they were used to in India and what they experienced in Europe. Comparing these two worlds, they arrived at a rejection of their own customs and habits and an unconditional admiration for the European social, economic and gender order. A Hindu military surgeon stationed in England, for instance, stated in a letter to a friend in Peshawar at the beginning of the year 1915:

> When one considers this country and these people in comparison with our own country and our own people one cannot be but distressed. Our country is very poor and feeble and its lot is very depressed. Our people copy the faults of the British nation and leave its good qualities alone. We shall never advance ourselves merely by wearing trousers and hats and smoking cigarettes and drinking wine. In fact they have a real moral superiority. They are energetic. We are poor and hunger for ease. They limit their leisure, do their work justly and do it well. They do not follow their own inclinations, but obey their superior officers and masters. They avoid idle chatter. Their delight is cleanliness. Even a sweeper will not remain in a bare house. He will adorn it with some green plants and flowers and will take pains to improve his condition. Never under any circumstances do they tell lies. As for shopkeepers, everything has a fixed price. You may take it or leave it as you please.[91]

Muslim soldier Shah Nawaz even wrote in a letter from Marseilles in September 1915:

> The Creator has shown the perfection of his benefice in Europe, and we people have been created only for the purpose of completing the totality of the world. In truth, it has now become evident that the Indian is not fit to stand in any rank of the world. You may be sure that India will not rise to the pitch of perfection of Europe for another two thousand years. The French nation is highly civilised, and they have great soldiers to an extent of which we are not – and never could be – worthy.[92]

A third group of Indian soldiers tried to defend their cultural identity, to meet their religious duties and traditional expectations as men and warriors. However, it was particularly soldiers from this third group who went on to suffer despair and resignation.

As for West African soldiers, the two key sources available are Bakary Diallo's memoirs[93] and an extensive oral history study conducted by Joe Harris Lunn in the 1980s.[94] Bakary Diallo's memoirs entitled *Force–bonté* were published in 1926 as the first book in French authored by a Black African. Diallo had obviously strongly adhered to French colonial ideologies. He first describes himself and his comrades as being on the same level as French children, who then gradually reached the higher stages of French civilisation thanks to military service, until they were completely assimilated and started even to dream in French.

Diallo's war experience, however, differed from that of most of his comrades in several respects. He had volunteered for the French army as early as 1911, so he did not experience the forced conscription between 1914 and 1917 that traumatised West African populations. Diallo's experience at the front was not representative either. He had only been at the front for a relatively short time. Already on 3 November 1914, he was wounded and afterwards promoted. He gained a distinction for bravery and was even granted French citizenship in 1920. After the war, he would remain in France until 1928.

Thanks to Lunn's oral history study, we are also informed about the war experience of a larger group of West Africans. Lunn interviewed 85 Senegalese veterans in 1982/83, about half of the veterans still living at that time. His book shows, that important cultural changes in Franco-Senegalese relations took place in the years from 1914 to 1918. West Africans would no longer think of the French as almighty 'devils', as they had done before. This would promote their self-consciousness in the post-war period.

Conclusion

On balance, the deployment of colonial troops in Europe proved to be a dramatic experience for all contemporaries. Forced recruitment in the colonies met several forms of resistance, including even armed rebellions. Deployment in Europe would then change many Africans' and Asians' perceptions of their colonial masters and of Europeans in general. Europeans, on the other hand, whilst preserving racist stereotypes, became aware of the precariousness of their global dominance. However, the impact of colonial troops' deployment in Europe in the First World War on the colonial system is still debated. In particular, the colonial veterans' digestion of their European experience was far from uniform.

The use of colonial troops would remain an issue in the early 1920s, when France (unlike Britain) deployed many African and Asian soldiers as occupation troops in the German Rhineland. German propaganda now altered the bloodthirsty beast into ' lusty coloured murderers' who raped; the poster *Jumbo* became famous showing an enormous black soldier wearing nothing but a helmet and pressing white women to his belly. Although the vast majority of African occupation troops on the Rhine came from Morocco and Algeria, people generally spoke of the 'black shame' and the 'black horror' in a propaganda campaign lasting more than two years and backed by all political parties with the exception of the extreme left.[95] In the aftermath of the Franco-Belgian invasion of the Ruhr in January 1923, the German propaganda campaign against the 'black shame' evidently decreased. Apparently, in the eyes of the Germans the French had discredited themselves so deeply before the international community that further topical reference to 'colonial troops' was no longer needed.

In the Second World War, colonial troops were deployed on European battlefields once again.

During the western campaign, the German leadership planned a similar propaganda initiative as in the previous war. On 23 May 1940, the section *Wehrmachtpropaganda* of the *Oberkommando der Wehrmacht* (OKW) passed an urgent directive that all propaganda channels should 'quickly take photographs showing particularly good-looking German soldiers with particularly bestial-looking Senegalese Negroes and other coloured prisoners of war … Sharp racial contrasts are of special importance'.[96] Because of the western campaign's brevity, the propaganda in the spring of 1940 was not as intense as in the years 1914–23. This time, however, the perception of colonial soldiers as inferior beings was not restricted to pamphlets and posters. German troops, when they captured French units, sometimes systematically sought out African soldiers and shot them immediately. At least 3000 soldiers are estimated to have died in this way.[97] In the last months of the war German propaganda again represented black French soldiers as murderers and rapists.[98] The colonial troops' last battles did not take place in Europe, however, but in the decolonisation wars of the 1950s and 60s, where troops from one colony would often be deployed to fight against anti-colonial uprisings in another.[99]

Notes

[1] For an overview see Waites, 'Peoples of the Underdeveloped World', 596–614.

[2] See Burdick and Moessner, *The German Prisoners-of-War in Japan*; Krebs, 'Die etwas andere Kriegsgefangenschaft', 323–37, and Hermann Joseph Hiery, *The Neglected war*.

[3] See Grove, 'The First Shots of the Great War'; and Krech, *Die Kampfhandlungen in den ehemaligen deutschen Kolonien*.

[4] See Davenport, 'The South African Rebellion, 1914'; Garson, 'South Africa and World War I'; Katzenellenbogen, 'Southern Africa and the War of 1914–1918',

107–121; and Krech, *Die Kampfhandlungen in den ehemaligen deutschen Kolonien*.

[5] See von Lettow-Vorbeck, *Meine Erinnerungen*; Deppe, *Mit Lettow-Vorbeck*; Buhrer, *L'Afrique orientale allemande*; Paice, *Tip and Run*; Samson, *Britain, South Africa and the East Africa Campaign*; Anderson, *The Forgotten Front*; Strachan, *The First World War in Africa*; Gardner, *German East*; Bradley, 'The 1914–18 Campaign', 27–36; Greenstein, 'The Impact of Military Service'; Hodges, *The Carrier Corps*; Krech, *Die Kampfhandlungen in den ehemaligen deutschen Kolonien*; Miller, *Battle for the Bundu*; Mundro and Savage, 'Carrier Corps Recruitment'; Hodges, 'African Manpower Statistics'; Iliffe, *A Modern History of Tanganyika*, 240–72; and Michels, 'Askari – treu bis in den Tod?', 171–86.

[6] See Bernard, *L'Afrique du Nord*; Meynier, *L'Algérie révélée*; and Goldstein, *Libération ou annexion*.

[7] See Michel, *L'appel à l'Afrique*.

[8] See War Office, *Statistics of the Military Effort*, 772; Carrington, 'The Empire at War', 642; Beckett, 'The Nation in Arms', 13–14; Grundy, *Soldiers without Politics*, 54; Besson and Perreau-Pradier, *L'Effort Colonial des Alliés*, 121–2; Willan, 'The South African Native Labour Contingent'; Smith, *Jamaican Volunteers in the First World War*; Schulze, *Die Rebellion der ägyptischen Fallahin*, 120–1; and Summershill, *China on the Western Front*; Wou, *Les travailleurs chinois*.

[9] See Nogaro and Weil, *La main-d'œuvre étrangère et coloniale*; Varet, *Du concours apporté à la France*, 41–5; Boussenot, *La France d'outre-mer*, 67–73; Schor, *Histoire de l'immigration en France*, 40–4; Sarraut, *La mise en valeur*, 43; Duomg, *L'Indochine pendant la Guerre de 1914–1918*, 107–132; Ray, *Les Marocains en France*, 48–59; Meynier, *L'Algérie révélé*, 405–13 and 459–84; Talha, *Le salariat immigré*, 63–78; Ageron and Julien, *Histoire de l'Algérie contemporaine*, 1157–60; Stora, *Ils venaient d'Algérie*, 14–15; Chen, *Chinese Migrations*; and Wang, 'Chinesische Kontraktarbeiter', 440–3.

[10] See Stovall, 'The Color Line behind the Lines'.

[11] See Greenhut, 'The Imperial Reserve'; Ellinwood and Pradham, *India and World War 1*; Merewether and Smith, *The Indian Corps in France*; Willcocks, *With the Indians in France*.

[12] See Killingray, 'The Idea of a British Imperial African Army'.

[13] *Parliamentary Debates*, 5th series, vol. 82, 2023–5. ˋ

[14] See Smith, *Jamaican Volunteers in the First World War*.

[15] See Pershing, *My Experiences in the World War*, vol. 2, 64.

[16] Sarraut, *La mise en valeur*, 44; see also Fogarty, *Race and War in France*.

[17] Hill, *The Marcus Garvey and Universal Negro Improvement Association Papers*, vol. 9, 588.

[18] See Greenhut, 'The Imperial Reserve'.

[19] See Echenberg, 'Paying the Blood Tax'; Michel, 'Le recrutement des tirailleurs'; Clarke, *West Africans at War*.

[20] Meynier, *L'Algérie révélée*, 405.

[21] Michel, *L'appel à l'Afrique*, 84.

[22] See Cornevin, *La République populaire*, 418–23; de Rivières, *Histoire du Niger*, 224–30; Michel, *L'appel à l'Afrique*, 50–7, 100–16, 118–20 and 127–30; Lunn, *Memoirs of the Maelstrom*, 33–58; Fournier, *Historique du 2ᵉ Régiment de Tirailleurs Sénégalais*, 169–89; Echenberg, 'Les Migrations militaires'; Asiwaju,

'Migration as revolt', 577–94; Hebert, 'Révoltes en Haute Volta'; Garcia, 'Les mouvements de résistance'; Johnson and Summers, 'World War I: Conscription and Social Change in Guinea'; D'Almeida-Topor, 'Les populations dahoméens'; Lombard, *Structures de type féodal*, 412–28; Suret-Canale, *Schwarzafrika*, vol. II, 183–91; Loth, *Geschichte Afrikas*, vol. II, 119–22; Kouandété, *Un aspect de l'insurrection nationaliste*; Mercier, *Tradition, changement, histoire*, 435–48; and Gnankambary, 'La révolte bobo de 1916'.

[23]   See Ageron and Julien, *Histoire de l'Algérie contemporaine*, 1142–3 and 1150–7; Meynier, *L'Algérie révélée*, 569–98.

[24]   See Lejri, *L' histoire du mouvement national*, 157–63.

[25]   See Michel, *L'appel à l'Afrique*, 73–81; Margueritte, *L'immense effort*, 127–33.

[26]   Cited in Delafosse, *Maurice Delafosse*, 310.

[27]   Cited in Michel, *L'appel à l'Afrique*, 43.

[28]   Cited in Delafosse, *Maurice Delafosse*, 310.

[29]   Cited in Michel, *L'appel à l'Afrique*, 132.

[30]   Cited in Ibid., 133.

[31]   Cited in Delafosse, *Maurice Delafosse*, 338.

[32]   See Echenberg, *Colonial Conscripts*, 44; *Une ame de Chef*, 27–8 and 264–6.

[33]   See Glinga, 'Ein koloniales Paradoxon', 21–37; Crowder, 'Blaise Diagne and the Recruitment of African Troops', 104–21; Lunn, *Memoirs of the Maelstrom*, 73–81; Michel, *L'appel à l'Afrique*, 223–38; idem, 'La genèse du recrutement'.

[34]   See Ageron, *Les Algériens musulmans*, vol. 2, 1146–7.

[35]   Cited in Ibid., 1162.

[36]   Ibid., 1064–5.

[37]   See Fernand Farjenel, 'Une armée jaune', *Revue de Paris* 23 (1916): 112–37.

[38]   See Mangin, *Lettres de Guerre*, 125–6; Ageron, *Les Algériens musulmans*, 1164; idem, 'Clemenceau et la question coloniale', 80.

[39]   See Merewether and Smith, *The Indian Corps in France*; Willcocks, *With the Indians in France*; Greenhut, 'The Imperial Reserve'; Omissi, *The Sepoy and the Raj*, 38–40, 65–6, 78–82, 114–23 and 160–2; Mason, *A Matter of Honour*, 412–21; Smith, *Britain's Brigade of Gurkhas*, 42–51 and 72–84; Tuker, *Gorkha*, 192–200; MacMunn, *The Martial Races of India*, 318–40; Farwell, *The Gurkhas*, 86–104; idem, *Armies of the Raj*, 248–66; Bolt, *Gurkhas*, 90–6; Trench, *The Indian Army*, 31–66; Mollo, *The Indian Army*, 139–44; Banskota, *The Gurkha Connection*, 122–30; *History of the 5th Royal Gurkha Rifles*, 217–71 and 310–17; Besson and Perreau-Pradier, *L'Effort Colonial des Alliés*, 123–4; Pradhan, 'The Indian Army and the First World War', 49–67; idem, 'The Sikh Soldier in the First World War', 177–211; Ellinwood, 'Ethnicity in a Colonial Asian Army', 89–144; and Latter, 'The Indian Army in Mesopotamia', 92–102, 160–79 and 232–46.

[40]   See Balesi, *From Adversaries to Comrades-in-Arms*, 99.

[41]   See Bernard, *L'Afrique du Nord*; Horne, *The Price of Glory*, 111–12. Also Heather Jones's contribution to this volume.

[42]   See, for example, Michel, *L'appel à l'Afrique*; Bekraoui, 'Les soldats marocains'; and Kamian, *Des tranchées de Verdun*.

[43]   See, for example, Horne, *The Price of Glory*, 100–101; Goldstein, *Libération ou annexion*, 176–7; Crowder, 'The 1914–1918 European War and West Africa', 494.

[44]   See Paul Mangin, 'Troupes noires', *Revue de France* 16 (1909): 61–80 and 383–98; idem, 'Soldats Noirs en Europe', *Questions Diplomatiques et Coloniales* 13 (1909):

449–60.; idem, *La Force Noire*; idem, 'Troupes noires', *Revue de Paris* 18 (1911): 484–94; idem, 'De l'emploi des troupes noires', *Revue anthropologique* 21 (1911): 113–28.

[45] Barbusse, *Le Feu*, 48–9.

[46] Boussenot, *France d' outre-mer*, 43.

[47] Cited in Michel, *L'appel à l'Afrique*, 323.

[48] Cited in Ageron, *Clemenceau et la question coloniale*, 80.

[49] Paul Mangin, 'Comment finit la guerre', *Revue des Deux Mondes* 57 (1920): 794.

[50] See Barrows, ' L'influence des conquêtes algériennes et coloniales', 111; and Lunn, 'Kande Kamara Speaks', 39.

[51] Cited in Becker, *Les Français dans la Grande Guerre*, 316 as well as in Michel, *L'appel à l'Afrique*, 408.

[52] Michel, *L'appel à l'Afrique*, 407–8.

[53] Edouard de Martonne, 'La Vérité sur les Tirailleurs Sénégalais', *Outre-Mer: Revue Générale de Colonisation* 7 (1935): 41.

[54] See Bidwell, *Morocco under Colonial Rule*, 297.

[55] See Recham, *Les musulmans algériens*, 23–4.

[56] Benamrane, *L'émigration algérienne*, 28; and Ruf, 'Politische und ökonomische Ursachen', 68.

[57] Lunn, *Memoirs of the Maelstrom*, 140–7.

[58] Michel, *L'appel à l'Afrique*, 329–30.

[59] See Merewether and Smith, *The Indian Corps in France*, 332.

[60] See Greenhut, 'The Imperial Reserve', 65.

[61] Michel, *L'appel à l'Afrique*, 337.

[62] See, for example, Auswärtiges Amt, *Employment, Contrary to International Law, of Coloured Troops*; Belius, *Die farbigen Hilfsvölker*.

[63] See, for example, *Frankreich und die Genfer Konvention*, 2 vols. (1917); German Reichstag, *Völkerrecht im Weltkrieg*.

[64] See Deroo and Champeaux, *La Force Noire*, 62–5.

[65] Horne and Kramer, 'German "Atrocities"'; idem, 'War between Soldiers and Enemy Civilians'; idem, *German Atrocities, 1914*.

[66] See Sterckx, *La tête et les seins*, 79–81.

[67] See, for example, Marthe Bigot, 'Armée Noire', *Humanité*, 31 October 1920: 1.

[68] See also Read, *Atrocity Propaganda*, 4.

[69] See Koller, *'Von Wilden aller Rassen niedergemetzelt'*; idem, 'Enemy Images', 139–57; Kettlitz, *Afrikanische Soldaten*; Lunn, '"Les Races Guerrières"'; Lüsebrink, '"Tirailleurs Sénégalais"', 57–71; Martin, 'German and French Perceptions'; and Melzer, 'The "Mise–en–Scène" of the "Tirailleurs Sénégalais"', 213–44.

[70] Auswärtiges Amt, *Employment, Contrary to International Law, of Coloured Troops*.

[71] Rosen, *England*, 96 and 98; Valois, *Nieder mit England!*, 7; Borchardt, 'Der Krieg und die deutsche Selbsteinkehr', 243; Lisbeth Dill, 'Die Gefangenenlager bei Merseburg', *Gartenlaube* 63 (1915): 7–9; *Ein Dutzend englischer Sünden wider das Völkerrecht: Tatsachen und Feststellungen* (1916): 5; *Kriegschronik. Kriegstagebuch, Soldatenbriefe, Kriegsbilder*, June 1915: 48; *Illustrierte Geschichte des Weltkrieges*, vol. 5 (Stuttgart, 1916) 307; and Baer, *Der Völkerkrieg.*, vol. 3, 217 and vol. 10,107.

[72] Rabah Abdallah Boukabouya, *L'Islam dans l'armée française* (Constantinople, 1915); idem, 'Die marokkanischen Kaids unter der französischen Herrschaft', *Korrespondenzblatt der Nachrichtenstelle für den Orient*, 3 (1916): 220–2, 271–3

and 328–30; idem, 'Der General Gourand als Generalresident von Marokko', *Korrespondenzblatt der Nachrichtenstelle für den Orient*, 3 (1916): 419–20; idem, 'Das Protektorat über Marokko. General Lyautey und seine Islampolitik', *Islamische Welt*, 1, no. 3 (1917): 57–8 and 1, no. 4 (1917): 253–4; idem, 'Die "Weissen Väter"', *Islamische Welt*, 1, no. 6 (1917): 352–3; idem, 'Der zukünftige Friede und die algerischen Muslims', *Islamische Welt*, 1, no. 9 (1917): 557–9. On Boukabouya see also Müller, *Islam, gihad ('Heiliger Krieg') und Deutsches Reich*, 270, 292–6, 341–47.

[73] See Höpp, *Muslime in der Mark*; Kahleyss, *Muslime in Brandenburg*; and Hinz, 'Die deutschen "Barbaren" sind doch die besseren Menschen', 339–61.

[74] See, for example, Müller–Meiningen, *Der Weltkrieg und das Völkerrecht*, 68–9. Also Schütze, *Englands Blutschuld gegen die weiße Rasse*; and Stibbe, *German Anglophobia*, 38–43.

[75] *La Dépêche Coloniale*, 18 August 1914.

[76] Cited in Michel, *L'appel à l'Afrique*, 345.

[77] See, for example, Boussenot, La *France d'outre–mer*, 23.

[78] Alphonse Séché, 'Les Noirs: L'âme du Sénégalais', *L'Opinion* 8/41 (1915): 286–8.

[79] Gaillet, *Coulibaly*.

[80] See Gervereau, 'De bien trop noirs desseins'.

[81] Cited in Diallo, *Force–Bonté*, 113.

[82] Cousturier, *Des Inconnus chez moi*, 12–13.

[83] Melzer, 'The "Mise-en-Scène" of the "Tirailleurs Sénégalais"', 222–8. This is a play on words with the expressions *teutons* (Teutons, Germans) and *tétons* (tits).

[84] Tharaud and Tharaud, *La randonnée de Samba Diouf*, 100.

[85] 'L'utilisation des Troupes Noires', *Revue de Paris* 24 (1917): 872–94 (here 882).

[86] 'Troupes coloniales: Nos forces ignorés', *Revue de Paris* 17 (1915): 265–80 (here 266).

[87] 'Les Noirs: Soldats de la civilization', *Afrique Française* 27 (1917): 317–318 (here 317).

[88] Meynier and Thobie, *Histoire de le France Coloniale*, vol. 2, 424.

[89] See Vankoski, 'Letters Home'; Koller, 'Überkreuzende Frontlinien?'; idem, 'Krieg, Fremdheitserfahrung und Männlichkeit', 117–28; idem, 'Representing Otherness'; Omissi, 'Europe through Indian Eyes', 371–96.

[90] Omissi, *Indian Voices of the Great War*, 39.

[91] Ibid., 33–4.

[92] Ibid., 96–7.

[93] Diallo, *Force-Bonté*. On Diallo see also Midiohouan, 'Le tirailleur sénégalais', 133–51; Riesz, 'The *Tirailleur Sénégalais*'; idem, 'Die Probe aufs Exempel', 433–54.

[94] Lunn, *Memoirs of the Maelstrom*. See also idem, 'Kande Kamara Speaks'; Koller, '"Pourquoi pleurer pour des fils ingrats?"'.

[95] See Nelson, 'Black Horror on the Rhine'; Marks, 'Black Watch on the Rhine'; Lebzelter, 'Die "Schwarze Schmach"'; Koller, *"Von Wilden aller Rassen niedergemetzelt"*; idem, 'Die "Schwarze Schmach"', 155–69.

[96] Boelcke, *Kriegspropaganda*, 130.

[97] See Scheck, *Hitler's African Victims*.

[98] de Coquet, *Nous sommes les occupants*, 107.

[99] See, for example, Deroo, *La Force Noire*, 203–11.

The Punishment of War Crimes Committed against Prisoners of War, Deportees and Refugees during and after the First World War

Daniel Marc Segesser

University of Bern, Switzerland

In 1999 Howard S. Levie began his article on war crimes for the *Encyclopedia of Peace, Violence and Conflict* by saying that

> the trials of war crimes were very much in the forefront of the news during the years immediately after the end of World War II. They then ceased to be of news value except on rare occasions such as the My Lai Massacre, and even then much of the media did not really view that as a war crime. With the events in Bosnia-Herzegovina and in Rwanda, war crimes trials have once again become front-page material.[1]

What Levie says is not only true for the media, but also to some extent for the historiography of war crimes and war crimes trials. Until the 1990s most of the studies on this issue were either written by legal experts or focused on the Nuremberg and Tokyo war crimes trials after the Second World War.[2] Only a small number of studies expressly discussed the issue in relation to the First World War[3] and it is therefore hardly surprising that Levie only mentioned the execution of the merchant seaman Charles Algernon Fryatt and the Leipzig trials of 1921 in his article.[4] Only in more recent times has the issue of war crimes in the First World War become a topic of historical research, the pioneering studies being those of John Horne and Alan Kramer on the controversial German atrocities in Belgium in 1914.[5] Others followed in their footsteps and discussed different aspects of war crimes and their punishment during and after the First World War.[6] Yet – except for the special case of the Ottoman Armenians which will not be discussed here[7] – the issue of the punishment of the mistreatment of prisoners of war and civilian refugees and of those responsible for deportations has so far only been treated in summary form. This essay will therefore look at the extent to which jurists and publicists discussed the aforementioned issues during the First World War. It will also examine attempts to prosecute alleged war criminals in post-war trials.

War crimes and their punishment: issues of terminology and criminality

Before looking at the discussions on the treatment of prisoners of war, deportees and civilian refugees during the war, two issues need to be addressed. Firstly how did contemporaries define 'war crimes'? And secondly, to what extent did they believe that such 'crimes' were punishable under international law? The term itself was seldom used by legal specialists and other academic publicists before and during the First World War, although most of them agreed that crimes committed during wars could and had to be punished.[8] The term itself had been introduced into modern legal language by Johann Caspar Bluntschli, a Swiss professor at the University of Heidelberg, in 1872[9] and in the same year his compatriot Gustave Moynier had for the first time demanded that violations of the rules of the 1864 Geneva Convention should be tried in an international criminal court.[10] Neither the term nor the idea of an international criminal court were taken up by Bluntschli and Moynier's colleagues in the last part of the century. In 1882 the *Institut de Droit International* preferred to speak of infringements against the rules of the manual on the laws of war on land, while the 1884 *British Manual of Military* Law used the terminology 'offence against the customs of war'. Likewise the German *Kriegsbrauch im Landkriege* of 1902 referred to 'violations of the prohibitions contained in the regulations'.[11] Only Article 28 of the 1906 Geneva Convention included an obligation for the contracting parties to take the necessary steps to repress violations should their military penal laws prove to be insufficient.[12]

By that time Lassa Oppenheim, a German lawyer who had since become a British national and who was teaching at the London School of Economics and Political Science, tried to revive the term 'war crime' in the second volume of his seminal work *International Law: A Treatise* (1906).[13] The context in which he became active had changed, however. While Bluntschli and Moynier did not have internationally agreed rules of the laws of war, apart from the Geneva Convention, Oppenheim could fall back on the Hague Conventions of 1899. He therefore defined war crimes more precisely than Bluntschli as 'such hostile acts of soldiers or other individuals as may be punished by the enemy on capture of the offenders'[14] thereby clearly stating that such acts were to be legally considered as crimes. Amongst them Oppenheim classified violations of the recognised rules of war committed by members of the armed forces, all hostilities committed by individuals who were not members of the armed forces, espionage and war treason, and all marauding acts in general. For the first group of war crimes Oppenheim presented a list, which included, among other things, making use of poisonous or otherwise forbidden arms and ammunition, the ill-treatment of prisoners of war, the killing of harmless enemy civilians, the assault, siege and bombardment of open towns, violations of the Geneva Convention or the unlawful destruction of enemy prizes. No specific mention was made, however, of the Hague Conventions. Except for the killing of harmless non-combatants, Oppenheim's list did also not contain any act committed specifically in the context of deportations or against civilian refugees.[15] While he could have referred to the former based on Articles 44 and 52 of the Hague Regulations of 1899,[16] the situation was less clear in the context of refugees. Neither the Hague Regulations nor other written rules of the laws of war protected civilian refugees as such.[17] Articles 23b, 23 g, 46 and 47 of the regulations of 1899 (and 1907) prohibiting the treacherous killing or wounding of individuals belonging to a hostile nation, the destruction or seizure of enemy property and acts of pillage, and promising respect for family honours and rights as well as for individual lives would, however, also have been applicable to civilian refugees.[18] That Oppenheim – like all other specialists on the international laws of war – did not take up this issue was probably due to the fact that they were all aware that civilians could be forced to flee due to the necessities of war and that they believed or hoped that the laws and customs of war would stop invading armies from committing any acts against civilians – whether refugees or not – that were not absolutely necessary in the context of their military operations.[19]

At first there were almost no reactions to the war crimes section of Oppenheim's book.[20] During the Balkan Wars of 1912–13 and the first months of the First World War Oppenheim's term was not used. The Carnegie report on the causes and the conduct of the Balkan Wars mentioned a series of violations of international law committed against prisoners of war and civilian refugees, but did not call for their punishment by legal means and did not use the term 'war crime'.[21] During the first months of the First World War the term was not used either, not even in the context of the German atrocities in Belgium. It was only in 1915–16 that some lawyers and publicists in Britain and France, such as Hugh Bellot or Fernand Engerand began to speak of 'war crimes'.[22] While Engerand did not bother to define more specifically what he meant, Bellot made it clear that for him war crimes were 'those acts of the armed forces of a belligerent against the person or property of the enemy, combatant or non-combatant, which are deemed contrary to the established usages of war'.[23] Thereby he excluded two aspects that Oppenheim had explicitly included amongst war crimes, that is, espionage and wartime treason on the one hand and all hostilities by individuals who were not members of the armed forces on the other. Bellot gave no explicit reasons for his choice, but from the rest of his text it is possible to make some guesses. It seems that for him espionage and war treason were legal terms in their own right that differed too much from the rest to be subsumed under the same heading. On the other hand Bellot did not accept Oppenheim's statement that civilians who took up arms in the defence of their country should be criminalised, because a country has a 'right to resist belligerent violation of its territory by "any means in its power . . .".[24] It is not surprising therefore that Bellot's first list of German war crimes concentrated on criminal acts committed by the armed forces during the course of actual fighting, while except for the case of Captain Fryatt discussed in more detail below, not a single crime committed against occupied populations or prisoners of war was mentioned.[25]

Most other legal professionals such as Louis Renault, Elihu Root, James Brown Scott or Thomas Erskine Holland did not at first take up Bellot or Oppenheim's use of the term 'war crimes' in their statements on violations of the laws of war.[26] Nevertheless at least amongst jurists and publicists in the Entente countries there was a change in the perception of such violations, which by 1916 were not only understood to be (punishable) violations of the laws of war, but criminal acts.[27] In Germany on the other hand there was a great debate as to whether captured enemy officers and soldiers could be brought to trial for crimes which they had committed before being captured. Neither jurists, the military courts, the officials of the Prussian Ministry of War, nor the Supreme Command agreed on this issue. While some, like Ernst Beling, Bernhard Coester, Richard Giessner and Friedrich Oppler stated that prisoners of war were liable to stand trial in German military courts,[28] others like Adolf Arndt, Josef Kohler, Ernst Müller-Meiningen or Karl Strupp did not accept such an interpretation.[29]

Only in the summer of 1918 did the term 'war crime' became more common in the context of the initial preparations by the British government for a post-war peace conference. On 17 October 1918 a Committee on War Crimes, as the *Law Journal* called it, was set up.[30] At first Attorney-General Frederick Smith tried to avoid the term created by Bellot, who was the secretary of the committee. Nevertheless he also sought to stress the criminal character of the violations committed by Germany and its allies: 'Many great crimes against International Law have been committed. The very origin of the war, the violation of Belgium, [will] for all time be remembered as one of the greatest crimes against civilisation'.[31]

Fernand Larnaude and Albert de Lapradelle, two French lawyers who prepared a memorandum on the issue for the French prime minister Georges Clemenceau, agreed with Smith and also called for the criminal prosecution of such acts. In this context they also used the term 'crimes de guerre' (war crimes) and included among them not only crimes committed by the armed forces during military operations, such as the German atrocities in Belgium and Northern France in 1914, but also crimes committed during the occupation of parts of Belgium and France, such as deportations of harmless civilians.[32] In January 1919 the Preliminary Peace Conference set up a commission composed of 15 members to inquire and report on the question of responsibility for the outbreak of war, the facts as to breaches of the laws and customs of war, the degree of responsibility of individuals for those offences and the appropriate manner for the trial of those accused.[33] Based on the definitions of Oppenheim, Bellot, Larnaude and Lapradelle as well as on reports submitted to it by the governments of the Allied states the committee created its own list of the violations of the laws and customs of war by the Central Powers, the term 'war crimes' being avoided.[34] In contrast to Oppenheim and Bellot, but in agreement with Larnaude and Lapradelle the list not only contained violations committed in the course of military operations, but also included a large number of occupation crimes, such as the abduction of girls and women for the purpose of enforced prostitution, the deportation of civilians, forced labour, the usurpation of sovereignty and the debasement of the currency of an occupied state.[35]

Although the term 'war crime' had not been used in the report of the Commission to the Preliminary Peace Conference it became more and more common in the inter-war period. Even in Germany, where the criminality of violations of the laws of war had been hotly debated during the war, the government used the term 'Kriegsverbrechen' (war crimes) when it submitted its bills for the prosecution of violations of the laws of war to the Reichstag in order to forestall the endeavours of the Allies against alleged German war criminals.[36] While academics from the former Allied states embraced the term in the early 1920s,[37] it became acceptable among their German-speaking colleagues only by the end of the decade. Probably this was also due to the activities of Alfred Verdross, who in 1924 published a seminal article on the topic in Karl Strupp's *Wörterbuch des*

Völkerrechts und der Diplomatie, in which to a large extent he followed the definitions given by Hugh H. Bellot.[38]

Prisoners of war

As Geoffrey Best argued in his 1980 study, the protection of combatants – and in particular the wounded and prisoners of war – was at the centre of the debates on the laws of war during the latter part of the nineteenth and the early years of the twentieth century. While the Geneva Convention of 1864 for the first time established internationally accepted rules for the care of the wounded, the same happened for prisoners of war only in 1899. Thus Articles 4 to 20 of the Hague Regulations respecting the laws and customs of war on land (Hague IV) referred specifically to prisoners of war, Article 4 clearly stating that they had to be humanely treated.[39] When the First World War began, most of the warring parties had accepted these rules,[40] in part out of concern to protect the interests of their own servicemen in captivity, but also because none of them expected to hold large numbers of prisoners over long periods of time. Although there were regional differences that cannot be discussed in detail here, most countries followed the utilitarian principle of reciprocity, and therefore brought their own national legislation into line with the Hague Regulations.[41] Even so, the precise details of international law were open to interpretation and this to some extent provided scope for dealing with prisoners of war according to the perceived national interests of the countries concerned. Moreover the issue became mixed up with war propaganda and the enemy was accused of barbarity against defenceless prisoners by all sides. This again made it more difficult to reach compromises where the application of the Hague Regulations was in dispute. Many prisoners of war subsequently fell victim to reprisals or counter-reprisals undertaken by the respective governments, whether out of revenge or for reasons of prestige and propaganda.[42]

Propaganda was very important during the First World War, because as the German theologian Ernst Troeltsch explained in 1915 'democratic nations can only make war in the form of people's war if they have a moral cause that is clear to the general public'.[43] The French president Raymond Poincaré agreed with Troeltsch and therefore called on the academics of his country to support the war, especially by explaining the reason for it to the people. Most intellectuals – among them many jurists too – accepted their new role and international cooperation ended in most fields, a fact which induced German classical philologist Hermann Diels to speak of a 'catastrophe of international scholarship'.[44] Some, like French writer and pacifist Romain Rolland as well as the German jurists Hans Wehberg and Walther Schücking, refused to take part in propaganda campaigns launched by their governments, but they were a minority.

Yet interestingly, while the issue of the treatment of prisoners of war remained an important topic for propagandists, it was rarely taken up by jurists when talking about violations of the laws of war.[45] One of the few cases that did become an object of discussion was that of Lieutenant-General Karl Stenger, which was taken up by John Hartman Morgan, professor of constitutional law at University College, London. He had come across it during his field research for the Bryce Commission, which had investigated the German atrocities in Belgium and northern France.[46] According to French newspapers Stenger, who was commander of the 58th Brigade, had published an order not to take any prisoners and to put to death all Allied soldiers who fell into the hands of his troops. Because the German government had denounced the document as a forgery, Morgan decided to investigate the case. In this context he also visited the French Ministry of War in Paris, where he looked at diaries of German soldiers who had been captured or killed on the western front. There, and among other testimonies made before the British Intelligence Department, he found further evidence that orders existed in the German army to take no prisoners. The most important evidence for Morgan was a field notebook of a German prisoner of war, which explicitly confirmed the existence of such an order. Morgan quoted the passage in German and gave an English translation: 'Then came a brigade order that all French, whether wounded or not, who fell into our hands, were to be shot. No prisoners were to be made.'[47]

For Morgan it was therefore beyond doubt that the order had been given by Stenger and that German soldiers had not acted on their own initiative, when killing Allied prisoners of war.[48] Although Morgan was a jurist he did not call for trials in court, either immediately or at the end of hostilities. Rather he believed that the experience of the war

> must teach jurists to be aware of the opiate of words and sacramental phrases. The immediate enterprise is not for lawyers but for our gallant men in the field. They and they alone, can lay the foundations of an enduring peace by an unremitting and inexorable war. They are the true ministers of justice.[49]

The same case was also taken up in the same year by Joseph Bédier, Professor of Medieval French literature and languages at the Collège de France, in his short study *Les Crimes Allemands d'après des Témoignages Allemands* (1915), which was also published in English as *German Atrocities from German Evidence* and which became popular, especially in the United States. Stenger's order was only one of many documents that Bédier referred to in his study, but it was one of the few for which he did not produce any photographic evidence. This made it easier for his German counterparts to question its authenticity, just as the German government had done when the document first appeared in Allied newspapers.[50] Paul Pic, professor of international law at the University of Lyon, also mentioned and even partially quoted Stenger's order and claimed that it was a disgrace that such a general was maintained in a command position in the German army. In contrast to Morgan and Bédier, Pic believed that it would be possible to try those responsible for crimes against prisoners of war in national courts at the end of the war.[51]

Neither Stenger's order referred to by Morgan, Bédier and Pic nor any of the other documents discussed by the three academics seem to have been preserved in the records of the French Ministry of War. This makes it very difficult for today's historian to determine the extent to which the documents were selectively quoted and whether the German denial of the reality of Stenger's order was honest or not. As Sacha Zala has shown in his study on official publications of sources during the war, however, many of them were quoted very selectively and sometimes even published in a manner as to give a completely different impression to that which the author had originally intended. Therefore it is quite possible that Morgan, Bédier and Pic presented their sources in such a way as to support the mainstay of their argument, which was that the German army and its soldiers pursued a policy of deliberate atrocities against Allied combatants and civilians.[52] Apart from the studies by Morgan, Bédier and Pic, the International Committee of the Red Cross (ICRC) was one of the few bodies concerned with international law which took up the issue of the treatment of prisoners of war on the battlefield, although mostly without giving its own opinion. Certainly it steered clear of taking sides for fear of violating its neutral status.[53]

As opposed to propagandists, relatively little comment was made by jurists on the conditions in camps for prisoners of war. In 1915 Austin Harrison, an English publicist, called on his government to intervene on behalf of its soldiers in enemy captivity and to make it clear to the German government 'that in the event of the maltreatment of prisoners or of their slaughter the Allied powers will hold the crowned heads, the Princes, Generals, Ministers, and higher officials responsible, who will be tried accordingly'.[54]

Louis Dumont-Wilden, a Belgian journalist and member of the *Office de Documentation et de Propagande*, also pointed to the bad conditions in German camps in an article he published in Édouard Clunet's *Journal du*

Droit International. While Dumont-Wilden, with a touch of irony, pointed to the civilising mission that the German government claimed to have, Paul Pic was more sober. He acknowledged that conditions in the camps had improved due to the intervention of the ICRC and some neutral countries like Switzerland and the United States. Pic was almost the only jurist who pointed to the fact that prisoners of war from western Allied countries were treated much better than those from Russia and he also mentioned that the Russian government had now begun to collect all the information available on the issue.[55]

At the end of the war the Allied governments decided to order trials against all those on the Central Powers' side allegedly responsible for violations of the laws of war. The legal basis for this had been worked out by many Allied jurists during the war, as has been shown above. In a first phase the Allies sought to target the political and military leadership of the German Reich and the other Central Powers. When this failed and the German government refused to hand over any of the more than 800 men accused of war crimes on the basis of the Versailles Treaty, the Allies eventually agreed to trials of 45 exemplary cases before the German Supreme Court or Reichsgericht in Leipzig. Here the alleged mistreatment of prisoners of war was one of the main facts of the case.[56] In three trials Karl Heynen, Emil Müller and Robert Neumann were accused of such mistreatment, including physical cruelty as well as nutritional and medical neglect. All of them were convicted and sentenced to not more than ten months' imprisonment. The German court was convinced that there had been no systematic mistreatment of Allied prisoners of war, but that in all cases the violations of the law had been due to excesses of individual officers or soldiers.[57] In a fourth trial Oskar Michelssohn, a medical doctor, was cleared of the charge that he had mistreated Allied prisoners of war and neglected his duties, thereby causing the death of many POWs and civilian internees.[58]

Amongst those accused in Leipzig was also the aforementioned Lieutenant-General Karl Stenger, whose order not to take any prisoners had not only been part of Allied war propaganda, but had also been discussed by a couple of jurists. This case was therefore of particular importance to the French delegation in Leipzig. Stenger had to stand trial together with one of his subordinates, Major Benno Crusius, who was accused of having passed on and executed the order. The trial took place from 29 June to 6 July 1921. Stenger, who had lost a leg during the war and who presented himself in full uniform with all his decorations, made a deep impression on the German judges. They therefore treated him with great care and finally acquitted him, even though Crusius and another officer, who had fallen during the war, had justified their actions in front of their soldiers by pointing to an order from brigade headquarters. The German court argued that Crusius and his comrade, in their state of agitation, had believed that such an order existed, although this had never been the case. Crusius was therefore found guilty of killing by neglect and sentenced to two years' imprisonment.[59] No further main hearings were conducted on the issue of prisoners of war. After 1923 the Reichsanwaltschaft (the German office for public prosecutions) and the Reichsgericht gradually abandoned those cases that were still pending.[60]

The trials in Leipzig on the issue of prisoners of war were not often taken up by jurists and publicists. Of course the French delegation to the trials severely criticised the acquittal of Stenger. Likewise, the *New York Times* also believed that in any other country the general would have been convicted. Édouard Clunet was also surprised that Stenger had been acquitted and pointed to the fact that the Allies had retained the right to judge any person accused of war-related crimes in case they were not satisfied with the trials in Leipzig. The case against Stenger showed that the Germans were not willing to judge their own war criminals. Therefore the Allies had to take things into their own hands again.[61] In Great Britain the indignation at the light sentences of Heynen, Müller and Neumann was also great. The *Times* spoke of a scandalous failure of justice and British politicians spoke of a judicial farce. The Foreign Office was more sceptical than Ernest Pollock and Claud Mullins, who were both members of the British delegation in Leipzig.[62] These two in turn were less critical than the rest of the British public. They stressed the fact that, although the sentences were light, it was the first time that a German court had convicted German soldiers and officers for violations of the international laws of war. This would have a much stronger effect on German society and the military than if an Allied court had handed down the same sentence. A similar reaction on the part of the British Law Officers' Department was later published in the *American Journal of International Law*.[63]

Deportees from occupied countries[64]

In 1914 and 1915 German troops invaded large parts of Belgium, Poland and Russia which, according to Article 42 of the Hague Regulations respecting the laws and customs of war on land (Hague IV), became occupied territory as soon as it was actually placed under the authority of the German army. As no detailed plans for a long-term occupation had been made by the military authorities, the German occupation policy was at the beginning largely characterised by improvisation and ad hoc decision making. Several plans were made for the future of the occupied territory, which were administratively organised in so-called *Generalgouvernements* in August 1914. Although differing in many details they all intended to make use of the economic resources provided by these countries. This included raw materials as well as agricultural and some industrial products not available in Germany or Austria. Workers were also included. The latter were particularly important for some areas of German industry as well as for some agricultural estates, in order to fill the places left vacant by German workers who had been enlisted. At first the German authorities began to recruit labourers from the occupied eastern territories on a voluntary basis, but some also by force. Most of the Poles and Russians recruited in this manner were not deported to Germany,[65] but used in the surrounding areas for building roads and clearing forests. On the other hand, migrant workers from the Russian part of Poland already in Germany when the war began were not allowed to return home after their contracts had expired.

With regard to Belgium, the German authorities in Berlin and Brussels at first decided to recruit workers only on a voluntary basis, probably fearing after the controversy regarding German atrocities in 1914 that recruiting them forcefully might lead to another wave of indignation in neutral countries. As the war progressed the number of workers who could be persuaded to work in Germany became smaller and smaller. This was in spite of the imposition of tough penalties, including fines and imprisonment, for unemployed Belgians who refused to accept a job offer from a German company. On the other hand the policy of Governor-General von Bissing to place the products of Belgian industry at the disposal of the German war economy also failed. In this context the arguments of the military leadership in favour of forced recruitment of Belgian workers began to receive significant support.[66] In 1916 Carl Duisberg, director of the Bayer-Werke in Leverkusen in agreement with other industrialists such as Hugo Stinnes, Alfred Hugenberg, Gustav Krupp and Walther Rathenau, called on the Prussian Minister of War, Adolf Wild von Hohenborn:

> Open the 'labour basin Belgium'! We have taken thousands of workers from Poland, but we have not received a single one from Belgium, and those we got have run away, because conditions in Belgium are better than they are with us.[67]

Early in October 1916 the forced deportation of Belgian workers began. In spite of the claims and protests of the Belgian government-in-exile in Le Havre, there was no systematic or long-term planning behind it.

Rather it was the consequence of the so-called Hindenburg programme, proclaimed by the new commander-in-chief of the German army in autumn of that year. At first workers were only deported from the so-called 'Operations- und Etappengebiet', that is, the area of military operations, but soon workers from the *Generalgouvernement* were also included. Almost 60,000 Belgian workers were deported to Germany in the period down to February 1917, when the deportations were stopped at least for those people living in the *Generalgouvernement*. In the Operations- und Etappengebiet the deportations continued up to the end of the war.[68]

Amongst jurists and publicists crimes committed in the context of occupation and deportation did not receive the same attention as the atrocities committed in Belgium and northern France during the course of the invasion in the summer and autumn of 1914. German occupation policy in Belgium and more so in eastern Europe was seldom discussed either in the public press or in academic journals. Relief operations for the civilian population in Belgium – but not in Poland or the occupied parts of Russia – and debates surrounding this, were much more important, not least because the issue was connected with British blockade policy.[69] The forced deportation of Belgian workers in the autumn of 1916 changed this situation to a large extent, although Belgian authors, having been accused of exaggerating with regard to the atrocities of 1914/15, were sometimes faced with difficulties when trying to publish their accounts.[70] A number of Belgian authors became active in this context, amongst them Charles de Visscher, a law professor at the University of Ghent living in exile in France, Jules van den Heuvel, Minister of State in the Belgian government-in-exile, Fernand Passelecq, a lawyer from Brussels and head of the propaganda office of the same government, and the aforementioned Louis Dumont-Wilden. De Visscher's aim was primarily to show that the German occupation authorities had no right to deport Belgian workers under international law and that the local population did not owe any loyalty to them. De Visscher criticised his German colleague Christian Meurer for saying that the occupation authorities had far-reaching powers, a point in which he was supported by the British lawyer Alfred Hopkinson.[71] Jules van den Heuvel pointed out that even the German regulations outlined in the *Kriegsbrauch im Landkriege* of 1902 called the deportation of civilians a barbarity. Nevertheless the German authorities had acted in this way, first using the pretext that Belgian civilians had attacked German troops and later that the deportations were a necessary means to combat unemployment in Belgium. Van den Heuvel did not deny that the unemployment rate in Belgium was very high, but for him it was clear that the German authorities had themselves caused the problem by closing down all companies that did not agree to support the German war economy. Van den Heuvel also criticised neutral countries like the Netherlands or Switzerland for their lukewarm reactions, but also pointed to the fact that the harsh protest of the American government had not been very effective.[72] Similar criticism was also voiced by Demetrius C. Boulger in the *Contemporary Review.*[73]

Fernand Passelecq published a large volume on the deportations in 1917, which contained an imposing selection of documents dealing mainly with protests against the measures taken.[74] In the first part of the volume, Passelecq discussed the beginning of the deportations and the reaction of Belgian workers, before turning to the justifications given by the German authorities.[75] In the third part he discussed the reasons for unemployment in Belgium, reaching the same conclusions as van den Heuvel.[76] Looking at the Hague Regulations, the German manual *Kriegsbrauch im Landkriege* and the American Lieber Code of 1863 he further concluded that the German authorities had returned to a practice which the United States qualified as that of barbarian and uncivilised nations and that had been considered abolished for a long time.[77] The deportations therefore had to be considered a brutal blow against the principles of law and justice, a point in which Passelecq was supported by Paul Fauchille, who reviewed the book in the *Revue Générale de Droit International Public.*[78] For Dumont-Wilden legal aspects were not as important. His main aim was to point the readers of the *Journal du Droit International* to the many cases of crimes committed by the German occupation authorities against helpless Belgian civilians. In this context Dumont-Wilden also spoke of 'terrorism' or even 'judicial terrorism'.[79] He was also one of the few to discuss the issue of the punishment in relation to German violations of the laws of war. For him it was clear that the people responsible had to be brought to court, but in contrast to Alfred Hopkinson, who favoured trials before military courts,[80] Dumont-Wilden showed no particular preference, and instead limited himself to providing an overview of the opinions of politicians and legal experts discussed above.[81] The deportations of Belgian workers to Germany were of course also discussed in the public press. American, British and French newspapers in particular severely criticised the German policy, while the reaction from their Swiss and Dutch counterparts was more mixed.[82] The deportation of workers from occupied territories in Poland or Russia as well as in Italy and Greece was not often taken up by the public press and it was not discussed in academic journals. This was probably due to the fact that the numbers seemed to be much smaller than in the case of Belgium, but possibly also because in general what happened in eastern Europe received much less attention.[83]

Apart from the issue of German atrocities in 1914, the deportation of Belgian workers to Germany was the most important point of controversy between the governments of the two countries when the war ended. As mentioned above the deportation of civilians and forced labour were listed among the crimes for which German officials, officers and soldiers were to stand trial, according to the opinion of Allied statesmen and jurists at the Paris Peace Conference. It proved impossible, however, for Belgium and Germany to reach an agreement on what had happened, not least because none of those responsible for the forced deportation of Belgian workers were either extradited to Belgium, as called for in the Treaty of Versailles, or tried in the context of the Leipzig trials. This is not to say that the German Reichsanwaltschaft did not initiate legal proceedings against some individuals accused of war crimes in this context, simply that such cases never got to court. Some, like the former Chancellor Theobald von Bethmann Hollweg, died before a decision had been reached as to whether to put them on trial. In others, cases, for instance that of August Keim, the former military governor of the province of Limburg, the proceedings were abandoned, because the Reichsanwaltschaft did not find any indication that Keim had been personally involved in the deportations. The proceedings against Field Marshal Paul von Hindenburg were only dropped in 1925, just before he was elected president of the Reich. In this case, the Reichsanwaltschaft argued that the deportations had been justified by articles 43 and 52 of the Hague Regulations and that therefore no criminal act had taken place under international law.[84]

Civilian refugees

As mentioned above, when the First World War began there were no rules in international law specifically dealing with the situation of civilians or refugees. The effect of Articles 42 to 56 of the Hague Regulations respecting the laws and customs of war on land (Hague IV) was restricted to the limitation of the authority of the occupying power and to the safeguarding of private property in occupied territories.[85] Refugees were therefore only protected by international law under the Martens clause, which was not very precise and which declared that in all cases not provided for in the regulations the populations remained 'under the protection and empire of the principles of international law as they result from the usages established between civilised nations, from the laws of humanity, and the requirements of public conscience'.[86]

When the German troops marched into Belgium in August 1914 tales of atrocities ran ahead of them. This caused large parts of the Belgian civilian population, especially in the west and south of the country, to flee their towns and villages and to seek refuge on the coastal strip still under Belgian control, as well as in France, Britain and the Netherlands. It was not just the invasion itself, but the growing credibility of the stories of German atrocities that provoked this mass exodus. Similar things happened in northern France, where the population believed tales of German brutality more readily as a consequence of the memories of the Franco-Prussian war. Despite the best efforts by the civilian prefects and the military authorities, the exodus spread throughout the départements du Nord, of the Pas-de-Calais, of Aube, Meurthe-et-Moselle, Meuse, Seine-et-Marne and Vosges. In most other départements on the other hand the situation remained calm. It was only after the victory in the battle of the Marne in September 1914 that the mood calmed down in the north of France as well.[87]

Due to the sketchy and unsatisfactory French and British statistics it is difficult to establish the exact numbers of refugees from Belgium and northern France, especially for the first months of the war. According to Pierre Purseigle refugees in France totalled 560,000 by 1 January 1915, the number rising steadily until September of the same year, and continuing to do so, although at a slower pace, up to 1918. The number of Belgian refugees present in Britain at one time reached a maximum of about 210,000 to 250,000 people in 1915, falling to 160,000 at the end of 1916. John Horne and Alan Kramer are therefore probably right to put the overall number of displaced persons in Belgium and northern France in the first months of the war at more than a million people.[88] Some were able to go home after the Allied victory at the Marne, but many more remained in France, Britain and the Netherlands, in spite of efforts by the German occupation authorities to induce Belgian refugees to return to their country of origin.[89]

As Peter Gatrell and Vejas Gabriel Liulevicius have shown the situation in Russia was even worse. Hundreds of thousands of people had to leave their homes as a consequence of defeat on the battlefield, but also of deliberate measures taken by their own generals.[90] The flood of refugees in Russia became a challenge for the Tsarist authorities. Public organisations began to provide assistance to the displaced, but their hopes were quickly shattered by the ruling bureaucracy, whose aim was to uphold the power and authority of the state over its subjects. Tensions remained high between the public welfare organisations and the state. This accounts for the fact that the political framework for handling the refugee crisis in Russia remained unstable up to 1917.[91] In contrast to Belgium no outside help was received, which was probably also due to the fact that the crisis facing refugees in Russia went almost unnoticed in the western European press and none of the academic journals discussed the issue. Furthermore the

Russian refugees were not victims of enemy violations of the laws of war, but victims of the defeat of their own military forces and of (deliberate) measures enacted by their own government. The fate of Belgian refugees was different. In 1914–15 many charitable organisations as well as government bodies in their host country showed a great deal of solidarity, not least because the fate of 'gallant little Belgium' could well be used by the Allied governments to foster a hatred of the enemy necessary to mobilise war enthusiasm in countries as far away from the actual front-line as Australia.[92] As the war continued the reputation of Belgian refugees suffered, but they continued to be cared for by their government-in-exile, by relief organisations of their own, and by their host country, including some support received from the United States.[93]

During the first months of the war, however, those Belgians fleeing their home country were not primarily seen as refugees, but as victims of the German atrocities. The Bryce Committee in Britain, the Belgian government-in-exile in Le Havre and several French committees were eager to collect any information about what had happened in the first months of the war.[94] Although the German atrocities of 1914 were continually discussed in the public press, in academic journals other issues, such as U-boat warfare, the use of gas and other new weapons, and individual cases such as those of Captain Charles Algernon Fryatt and nurse Edith Cavell, began to play a more important role as the war wore on. These latter two British citizens were executed by the German occupation authorities in Belgium. Cavell, a British nurse working in a Red Cross hospital in Brussels, had hidden Allied soldiers from the occupation authorities and had helped them to flee to the Netherlands. She was arrested on 5 August 1915 and executed on 12 October after a trial in which she confessed to the charges against her.[95] Fryatt on the other hand, had been a captain in the British merchant navy, who had saved his ship from being sunk by a German submarine in March 1915 by trying to ram the attacker. In June 1916 he had been caught with his ship by a German destroyer and brought to the Belgian port of Zeebrugge, where he was court-martialled as a franc-tireur or guerrilla of the seas.[96] While both cases were widely discussed in the public press, which condemned the outcome as judicial murder, jurists in academic journals were more reserved, especially in relation to Cavell. Hers was acknowledged as a case of treason, although the sentence passed on her was criticised as disproportionate to the harm she had caused.[97]

Not least due to such cases, which were pushed to the fore by the propaganda efforts of the Allied governments, the issue of the 1914 atrocities and the refugees lost some of its importance during the war.

At the Paris Peace Conference the atrocities of 1914 played an important role again, but the harm done was only mentioned in the context of reparations.[98] It comes as no surprise, therefore, that the treatment of refugees played no role in the trials in Leipzig, a fate it shared with the issue of the atrocities in Belgium in 1914, where all legal proceedings were abandoned without any formal trial. As in the case of the deportations it proved impossible for the Belgian and German governments and their respective lawyers and historians to find common ground on the issue, and the crimes committed against Belgian, but also Polish and Russian civilians in the First World War went unpunished.[99]

Conclusions

Although the issue of the punishment of war crimes was an important one, at least for many jurists on the Allied side, the practical results of these endeavours turned out to be small. Although the term 'war crime' finally became accepted in the inter-war period, the war crimes trials that took place after the war before the Reichsgericht in Leipzig proved to be insufficient. Although there were some trials and convictions of persons responsible for the violation of the rules of war in regard to prisoners of war, crimes committed in the context of deportation and the forced displacement of civilians during the war were seldom prosecuted. In those cases where legal proceedings were initiated, they were abandoned earlier rather than later by the German public prosecutor. This was a reaction that was typical in Germany after the First World War. Many Germans, including German jurists, thought that they had been unfairly treated under the Treaty of Versailles, not least in relation to Articles 227 to 231, the so-called *Schmachparagraphen* ('shame paragraphs'). Rather than trying to analyse what went wrong, many opted for a strategy of denial. Strategic and operational matters aside, the German conduct of war – especially in relation to the treatment of civilians – was never questioned in the inter-war period. Leipzig was *Verliererjustiz* (losers' justice), as Harald Wiggenhorn has called it, where it was more important to clear the accused from the charges presented by the former enemy than to make sure that justice was done.[100] It can therefore come as no surprise that after the Second World War the victorious Allies looked for ways to take justice into their own hands rather than leaving such matters in the hands of those who had lost the war. Only then were crimes committed in the context of deportation or the forced displacement of civilians finally brought to court, some under the classical heading of 'war crimes', others under the new heading of 'crimes against humanity'.[101]

Notes

[1] Levie, 'War Crimes', 725.

[2] See, for example, Minear, *Victors Justice*; Smith, *The American Road to Nuremberg*; Conot, *Justice at Nuremberg*; Tusa and Tusa, *The Nuremberg Trial*; Buscher, *The US-War Crimes Trial Program*; Ginsburgs and Kudriavtsev, *The Nuremberg Trial*; Kopelman, 'Ideology and International Law'; and Wieviorka, *Les Procès de Nuremberg*.

[3] Kaul, 'Die Verfolgung deutscher Kriegsverbrecher'; Bailey, 'Dry Run for the Hangman'; Foltz, 'The War Crimes Issue'; Schwengler, *Völkerrecht, Versailler Vertrag und Auslieferungsfrage*; and Willis, *Prologue to Nuremberg*.

[4] Levie, 'War Crimes', 727.

[5] Horne and Kramer, 'German "Atrocities"'; idem, 'War between Soldiers and Enemy Civilians'; and idem, *German Atrocities, 1914*.

[6] Von Selle, 'Prolog zu Nürnberg'; Müller, 'Oktroyierte Verliererjustiz'; Hankel, *Die Leipziger Prozesse*; Zuckerman, *The Rape of Belgium*, 218–258; Wiggenhorn, *Verliererjustiz*; Segesser, 'The International Debate'; and Thiel, '*Menschenbassin Belgien*', 296–304.

[7] Cf. Dadrian, *The History of the Armenian Genocide*; Bloxham, *The Great Game of Genocide*; and Segesser, 'Dissolve or Punish?'.

[8] McCormack, 'From Sun Tzu to Sixth Committee'; and Segesser, '"Moralische Sanktionen reichen nicht aus!"'.

[9] Bluntschli, *Das moderne Völkerrecht*, 358 (§ 643a).

[10] Gustave Moynier, 'Note sur la Création d' une Institution Judicaire Internationale propre à prévenir et à réprimer les Infractions à la Convention de Genève', *Bulletin International des Sociétés de Secours aux Militaires Blessés* 11 (1872): 122–31.

[11] Gustave Moynier, 'Rapport sur la Réglementation des Lois et Coutumes de la Guerre', *Annuaire de l'Institut de Droit International* 5 (1882): 174; War Office, *Manual of Military Law*, 306; and German General Staff, *Kriegsbrauch im Landkriege*, 20.

[12] Article 28 of the Geneva Convention of 1906, printed in Schindler and Toman, *The Laws of Armed Conflict*, 239.

[13] Oppenheim, *War and Neutrality*, 263–70.

[14] Ibid., 263–4.

[15] Ibid., 265–6.

[16] Article 44 of the Hague Regulations of 1899 was modified in 1907 and some of its content placed into Article 23 h of the regulations of 1907. See Schindler and Toman, *The Laws of Armed Conflict*, 77 and 82–84.

[17] Such protection was granted for the first time under Convention IV relative to the Protection of Civilian Persons in Time of War signed at Geneva on 12 August 1949 and printed in Ibid., 427–523.

[18] The relevant articles are printed in ibid, 76–77 and 83.

[19] Cf. Best, *Humanity in Warfare*, 157–190 and 200–215; and Max Huber, 'Die kriegsrechtlichen Verträge und die Kriegsraison', *Zeitschrift für Völkerrecht und Bundesstaatenrecht* 7 (1913): 351–74.

[20] None of the following reviews mentioned the section on war crimes: Nicolas Politis, 'Review of Oppenheim: *War and Neutrality*', *Revue Générale de Droit International Public* 13 (1906): 236; John Westlake, 'Review of Oppenheim,

War and Neutrality', *Law Quarterly Review* 22 (1906): 222; Daniel Crick, 'Review of Oppenheim, *War and Neutrality*, 2nd edition (London 1912)', *Revue de Droit International et de Législation Comparée* 45 (1913), 150–1; and George Winfield Scott, 'Review of Oppenheim: *International Law* 2 Vols., (London 1905–1906)', *Political Science Quarterly* 23 (1908): 344–8.

[21] Carnegie Endowment for International Peace, *Report of the International Commission.*

[22] Anon., 'Reparation for War Crimes', *Law Journal* 50 (1915): 276–7; Hugh H. Bellot, 'War Crimes: Their Punishment and Prevention', *Nineteenth Century and After*, 80, no. l (1916): 636–60; and Fernand Engerand in the debate to Louis Renault, 'Dans quelle mesure le droit pénal peut-il s'appliquer à des faits de guerre contraires au droit des gens?', *Revue Pénitentiaire et de Droit Pénal* 39 (1915): 451–56.

[23] Bellot, 'War Crimes: Their Punishment and Prevention', 636.

[24] Hugh H. Bellot, 'War Crimes and War Criminals', *Canadian Law Times* 36 (1916), 763; idem, 'War Crimes: Their Punishment and Prevention', 647.

[25] Bellot, 'War Crimes: Their Punishment and Prevention', 636.

[26] Louis Renault, 'Dans quelle mesure le droit pénal peut-il s'appliquer à des faits de guerre contraires au droit des gens?', *Revue Pénitentiaire et de Droit Pénal* 39 (1915), 406–29 and 484–9; Elihu Root, 'The Outlook for International Law', *American Journal of International Law* 10 (1916): 1–11; [James Brown Scott], 'The Use of Poisonous Gases in War', *American Journal of International Law* 9 (1915): 697–8; idem, 'The Hague Conventions and the Neutrality of Belgium and Luxembourg', *American Journal of International Law* 9 (1915): 959–62; and Holland, *Letters to the 'The Times'*, 33–5, 69–75 and 97–8.

[27] See here in particular the change in the terminology used by Henri Prudhomme, 'Sanctions Pénales des Violations du Droit des Gens', *Revue Pénitentiaire et de Droit Pénal* 39 (1915): 280–1; idem, 'Les Sanctions aux Violations du Droit des Gens', *Revue Pénitentiaire et de Droit Pénal* 39 (1915): 386–9; idem, 'Les Atrocités comises en Serbie par les Armées Austro-Hongroises', *Revue Pénitentiaire et de Droit Pénal* 39 (1915): 535; idem, 'Crimes commis par les Armées Austro-Allemandes', *Revue Pénitentiaire et de Droit Pénal* 40 (1916): 361; and Amos J. Peaslee, 'The Sanction of International Law', *American Journal of International Law* 10 (1916): 328–36.

[28] Ernst Beling, 'Militärpersonen als Angeklagte im feindlichen Ausland', *Deutsche Juristen-Zeitung* 20 (1915): 129–35; Bernhard Coester, 'Anwendung des heimischen Strafrechts auf Militärpersonen fremder Staaten', *Deutsche Strafrechts-Zeitung* 2 (1915): 48–53; Richard Giessner, 'Die strafrechtliche Stellung der Kriegsgefangenen nach deutschem Strafrecht, insbesondere ihre Verantwortung für vor der Ergreifung begangener Straftaten', *Archiv für Strafrecht und Strafprozess* 65 (1918): 240–68; and Friedrich Oppler, 'Bestrafung Kriegsgefangener wegen vor ihrer Gefangennahme verübter Straftaten', *Zeitschrift für die gesamte Strafrechtswissenschaft* 37 (1916): 849–72.

[29] Adolf Arndt, 'Nichtverfolgbarkeit von Handlungen, welche Kriegsgefangene als Militärpersonen vor der Gefangennahme begangen haben', *Das Recht: Rundschau für den deutschen Juristenstand* 19 (1915): 3–6; idem, 'Strafgerichtsbarkeit im Kriege ueber Ausländer, insbesondere Kriegsgefangene', *Zeitschrift für Politik* 8 (1915): 513–31; idem, 'Zur Frage der Bestrafung Kriegsgefangener und über sogenanntes Kriegsstrafrecht', *Archiv für Strafrecht und Strafprozess* 66 (1919): 522–30; Josef Kohler, 'Strafrecht und Völkerrecht', *Archiv für Strafrecht und*

Strafprozess 62 (1916): 369; Müller-Meiningen, *Der Weltkrieg und das Völkerrecht*, 227–9; Karl Strupp, 'Gegenwartsfragen des Völkerrechts', *Niemeyers Zeitschrift für internationales Recht* 25 (1915): 357–62.

[30] Anon., 'Punishment of War Crimes', *Law Journal* 53 (1918): 381–2; idem, 'The Committee on War Crimes', *Law Journal* 53 (1918): 382.

[31] Anon., 'German Crimes in the War', *Law Journal* 53 (1918): 388.

[32] Fernand Larnaude and Albert Geouffre de Lapradelle, 'Examen de la Résponsabilité Pénale de l'Empereur Guillaume d' Allemagne', *Journal du Droit International* 46 (1919): 132–6.

[33] Commission on the Responsibility of the Authors of the War and the Enforcement of Penalties, 'Report presented to the Preliminary Peace Conference', *American Journal of International Law* 14 (1920): 95.

[34] de Lapradelle (ed.), *Responsabilités des Auteurs*, 40–260.

[35] Commission on the Responsibility of the Authors of the War and the Enforcement of Penalties, 'Report' (as note 33 above), 114–15.

[36] Wiggenhorn, *Verliererjustiz*, 42–71.

[37] Theodore S. Woolsey, 'Reconstruction and International Law', *American Journal of International Law* 13 (1919): 196–7; George A. Finch, 'Jurisdiction of Local Courts to try Enemy Persons for War Crimes', *American Journal of International Law* 14 (1920): 218; idem, 'Superior Orders and War Crimes', *American Journal of International Law* 15 (1921): 440; Schwengler, *Völkerrecht, Versailler Vertrag und Auslieferungsfrage*, 278–281; and Zander, 'Das Verbrechen im Kriege', 21–22.

[38] Verdross, 'Kriegsverbrechen und Kriegsverbrecher', 775–7. In his habilitation thesis, *Die völkerrechtswiedrige Kriegshandlung*, Verdross had not yet used the term 'war crime'.

[39] Best, *Humanity in Warfare*, 147–157; and Schindler and Toman, *The Laws of Armed Conflict*, 70–6.

[40] Cf. Strupp, *Das Internationale Landkriegsrecht*, 45–56; Hinz, *Gefangen im Großen Krieg*, 43–70; and Best, *Humanity in Warfare*, 217–24.

[41] Cf. Oltmer, *Kriegsgefangene im Europa des Ersten Weltkrieges*; Hinz, 'Kriegsgefangene'; and Stibbe, 'Prisoners of War'.

[42] Hinz, 'Kriegsgefangene', 642. See also Heather Jones's contribution to this volume.

[43] Troeltsch, 'Der Kulturkrieg', 218.

[44] Hermann Diels, 'Eine Katastrophe der internationalen Wissenschaft', *Internationale Monatsschrift für Kunst, Wissenschaft und Technik* 9 (1914): 127–34. On the position of European scholarship at the beginning of the war see von Ungern-Sternberg, 'Wissenschaftler'; Mommsen, 'Die europäischen Intellektuellen, Schriftsteller und Künstler und der Erste Weltkrieg'; and Wallace, *War and the Image of Germany*, 1–24.

[45] Cf. Segesser, *Recht statt Rache*.

[46] Cf. Horne and Kramer, *German Atrocities*, 227–237.

[47] John Hartman Morgan, 'German Atrocities in France, with unpublished records', *Nineteenth Century and After* 77 (1915): 1223.

[48] Ibid., 1221–4.

[49] Morgan, *German Atrocities*, 39.

[50] Bédier, *Les Crimes Allemands*, 39–40. On the positive reception of this study in the United States see Hanna, *The Mobilization of Intellect*, 75.

[51] Paul Pic, 'Violation Systématique des Lois de la Guerre par les Austro-Allemands: Les Sanctions Nécessaires', *Revue Générale de Droit International Public* 23 (1916): 253–68.

[52] Cf. Horne and Kramer, *German Atrocities*, 7–8 and 286; Zala, 'Farbbücher', 470–1; idem, *Geschichte unter der Schere*, 31–7.

[53] On the role of the ICRC during the First World War, especially in relation to prisoners of war see Durand, *From Sarajevo to Hiroshima*, 22–77; Riesenberger, *Für Humanität in Krieg und Frieden*, 61–82; and Segesser, *Recht statt Rache*.

[54] Austin Harrison, 'Our Duty to the Prisoners', *English Review* 20 (1915): 240.

[55] Louis Dumont-Wilden, 'Du Traitement des Prisonniers de Guerre en Allemagne', *Journal du Droit International* 45 (1918): 611–20; and Pic, 'Violation Systématique', 253–4 (see note 51 above).

[56] Cf. Hankel, *Die Leipziger Prozesse*, 21–73; Horne and Kramer, *German Atrocities 1914*, 341–55; Wiggenhorn, *Verliererjustiz*, 9–102; Willis, *Prologue to Nuremberg*, 150–63.

[57] Hankel, *Die Leipziger Prozesse*, 333–47; and Wiggenhorn, *Verliererjustiz*, 157–87.

[58] Hankel, *Die Leipziger Prozesse*, 347–51; and Wiggenhorn, *Verliererjustiz*, 332–41.

[59] Wiggenhorn, *Verliererjustiz*, 213–31; and Hankel, *Die Leipziger Prozesse*, 123–42.

[60] Wiggenhorn, *Verliererjustiz*, 349, 352–7 and 472–3; Hankel, *Die Leipziger Prozesse*, 356–71.

[61] Édouard Clunet, 'Les Criminels de Guerre devant le Reichsgericht à Leipzig', *Journal du Droit International* 48 (1921): 440–7; Wiggenhorn, *Verliererjustiz*, 230.

[62] Wiggenhorn, *Verliererjustiz*, 173–4, 182 and 196.

[63] Claud Mullins, 'The War Crimes Trials', *Fortnightly Review* 116 (1921): 417–30; idem, *The Leipzig Trials*; Law Officers' Department, 'German War Trials', *American Journal of International Law* 16 (1922): 628–40. Pollock presented his impression in his foreword to Mullins's book.

[64] The separate issue of the deportation of members of national minorities within the borders of the warring countries, such as Italians or Poles, will not be discussed here. The issue was in some cases taken up by the public press – for example, the *Corriere della Sera* of 21 May 1915 and *The Times* of 22 May 1915, both carrying articles on the deportation of Italians from the Küstenland (Littoral) province of Austria-Hungary – but it was never discussed by jurists in academic journals, most probably because this was not a matter of the international laws of war, but of the constitutions of the respective countries. For the jurists of the time such acts could therefore not be considered war crimes, although the majority would have condemned them as violations of the liberal principles that they held so dear. On the importance of liberal principles to jurists in the late nineteenth and early twentieth centuries, an issue that remains under-researched, see Bass, *Stay the Hand of Vengeance*, 7–8; Koskenniemi, *The Gentle Civiliser of Nations*, 70–4; and Segesser, *Recht statt Rache*.

[65] I would like to thank Jochen Oltmer for alerting me to the findings of a dissertation project on this theme which is currently being conducted under his direction.

[66] Thiel, "*Menschenbassin Belgien* ", 61–102; Zilch, 'Generalgouvernement'; Liulevicius, 'Besatzung (Osten)'; idem, *War Land on the Eastern Front*, 72–4 and 165; Kramer, 'Besatzung (Westen)'; Hankel, *Die Leipziger Prozesse*, 378–80.

[67] Carl Duisberg at the so-called Industriekonferenz of 16 September 1916 at the Prussian Ministry of War, quoted in Thiel, "*Menschenbassin Belgien* ", 111.

[68] Thiel, "*Menschenbassin Belgien* ", 103–9 and 123–62.

[69] Zuckerman, *The Rape of Belgium*, 136–41.

[70] Segesser, *Recht statt Rache*.

[71] Charles de Visscher, 'L'Occupation de Guerre', *Law Quarterly Review* 34 (1918): 72–81; Meurer, *Die völkerrechtliche Stellung*, 3–6 and 18–25; Alfred Hopkinson, 'The Treatment of Civilians in Occupied Territories', *Transactions of the Grotius Society* 2 (1917): 157–9.

[72] Jules van den Heuvel, 'De la Déportation des Belges en Allemagne', *Revue Générale de Droit International Public* 24 (1917): 261–300.

[73] Demetrius C. Boulger, 'The Agony of Belgium', *Contemporary Review* 111 (1917): 28–36.

[74] Passelecq, *Les Déportations Belges*, 283–424.

[75] Ibid., 3–103.

[76] Ibid., 107–278.

[77] Ibid., 210–12.

[78] Paul Fauchille, 'Review of Passelecq, Déportations Belges', *Revue Générale de Droit International Public* 24 (1917): 362–3.

[79] Louis Dumont-Wilden, 'Le Terrorisme Allemand dans les Pays d'Occupation', *Journal du Droit International* 43 (1916): 893–5; idem, 'Du Terrorisme Judiciaire en Pays d' Occupation Allemande', *Journal du Droit International* 44 (1917): 516–24; and idem, 'Traitement des Prisoniers', 611–20.

[80] Hopkinson, 'The Treatment of Civilians', 159.

[81] Louis Dumont-Wilden, 'Des Sanctions à établir pour la Répression des Crimes Commis par les Allemands en Violation du Droit des Gens et des Traités Internationaux', *Journal du Droit International* 44 (1917): 125–39.

[82] Thiel, "*Menschenbassin Belgien* ", 216–17, 220–5 and 231–6.

[83] Hankel, *Die Leipziger Prozesse*, 380; and Segesser, *Recht statt Rache*.

[84] Thiel, "*Menschenbassin Belgien* ", 296–319; and Hankel, *Leipziger Prozesse*, 385–95.

[85] Schindler and Toman, *The Laws of Armed Conflict*, 82–6.

[86] Ibid., 64.

[87] Horne and Kramer, *German Atrocities 1914*, 178–84.

[88] Kushner, 'Local Heroes', 4; Purseigle, '"A Wave on to Our Shores"', 429–31; Horne and Kramer, *German Atrocities 1914*, 184.

[89] Zuckerman, *The Rape of Belgium*, 85, 95, 105–6 and 145.

[90] Gatrell, *A Whole Empire Walking*, 15–32; and Liulevicius, *War Land on the Eastern Front*, 20–1. See also Peter Gatrell's contribution to this volume.

[91] Gatrell, *A Whole Empire Walking*, 33–48.

[92] Cf. Cahalan, *Belgian Refugee Relief*, 18–246; Kushner, 'Local Heroes', 3–17; Purseigle, '"A Wave on to Our Shores"', 432–7; Segesser, *Empire und Totaler Krieg*, 333–4; and Smart, '"Poor Little Belgium"'.

[93] Cahalan, *Belgian Refugee Relief*, 17, 59 and 180–8; Purseigle, '"A Wave on to Our Shores"', 441–3; and Zuckerman, *The Rape of Belgium*, 106.

[94] Cf. Bryce, *Report of the Committee*, 3–8 and 10–56; Gouvernement Belge, *La Violation*, 5–8, 43–74 and 106–149; and Paul Fauchille, 'Les Attentats Allemands contre les Biens et les Personnes en Belgique et en France d'après les Rapports des Commissions D'Enquête Officielles (Août 1914–Mai 1915)', *Revue Générale de Droit International Public* 22 (1915): 248–411.

[95] On Cavell see also Pickles, *Transnational Outrage*.

[96] Willis, *Prologue to Nuremberg*, 27–8 and 30–1.

[97] Anon., 'The Fryatt Outrage', *Law Journal* 51 (1916): 395–6; idem, 'L'Execution de Miss Cavell à Bruxelles', *Bulletin International des Sociétés de la Croix-Rouge*, 185 (1916): 91–2; Hugh H. Bellot, 'War Crimes and War Criminals', *Canadian Law Times* 37 (1917): 21–2; Holland: *Letters to 'The Times'*, 79–80 (Letter of 26 October 1915); Lassa Oppenheim, 'War Treason', *Law Quarterly Review* 33 (1917), 285; and James Brown Scott, 'The Execution of Captain Fryatt', *American Journal International Law* 10 (1916): 865–77.

[98] Cf. Article 232 of the Treaty of Versailles published by Brigham Young University at http://net.lib.byu.edu/~rdh7/wwi/versailles.html (accessed 16 October 2008). (accessed 19 May 2008).

[99] Hankel, Die *Leipziger Prozesse*, 105–300; Horne and Kramer, *German Atrocities 1914*, 329–418; Segesser, *Recht statt Rache*; and Zuckerman, *The Rape of Belgium*, 242–76.

[100] Wiggenhorn, *Verliererjustiz*, 140–7 and 475; and Willis, *Prologue to Nuremberg*, 150–63.

[101] On the origins of the term 'crime against humanity' see Segesser, 'Die historischen Wurzeln'.

The Repatriation and Reception of Returning Prisoners of War, 1918–22

Reinhard Nachtigal

Freiburg im Breisgau, Germany

When on 11 November 1918 the armistice on the western front ended the First World War, 9 million out of a total of 71 million mobilised soldiers had died, countless numbers had been wounded, and hundreds of thousands were missing in action.[1] Seven million out of approximately 9 million prisoners of war were still awaiting repatriation. Over 650,000 prisoners of war (POWs) had died in captivity. Most of these, around 400,000, had perished in Russia. A further 1.2 million former POWs had been repatriated during the war, in the period before October 1918. The main beneficiaries, including invalid POWs, medical personnel and priests, were released under international agreements reached before and during the course of the fighting. In addition, the conclusion of a peace treaty between Russia and the Central Powers at Brest-Litovsk on 3 March 1918 paved the way for the return of up to 1 million former prisoners from Russia to Germany and Austria-Hungary, as well as a few Turks and Bulgarians. The repatriation process was organised by special welfare committees sent by the German and Austro-Hungarian authorities to the European parts of Russia.

At the same time relatively few Russian POWs were able to return home from German or Austro-Hungarian captivity in the period down to October 1918, and the same applied to German and Austro-Hungarian prisoners after the armistice in November 1918. Indeed, whereas a more liberal policy on releases and repatriation had been noticeable in the final phases of the war, in the immediate post-war period this trend was put into reverse, so that about 1 million POWs remained in captivity until the years 1920 to 1922. The many different reasons for this delay will be discussed in more detail below. In part broader external factors were to blame, but political decisions made by the captor nations also played an important role, often with damaging and inhuman consequences.

The following essay will investigate the process of repatriation in rough chronological order, beginning with the releases on the eastern front after the end of fighting there in 1917/18, moving on to the stance adopted by the defeated powers Germany and Austria-Hungary in November 1918, and ending with the policy pursued by the victor nations, Britain, France, Italy and the United States, after November 1918. A final section will consider the separate but related issue of the reception of returning POWs in their home countries.

Repatriation from Russia

A variety of political processes affected how repatriation was implemented after November 1918, either directly by intergovernmental arrangements, or indirectly through secondary factors. In western Europe the political circumstances remained relatively stable. Frontiers were altered only to a small extent, and in theory France, Britain, Italy and Germany entered into negotiations in order to establish the terms of peace, although in practice the victorious western Allies dictated these terms alone. In eastern Europe, however, where the guns had already fallen silent in December 1917, a very different situation began to emerge from the spring of 1918 onwards. Here, alongside the upheavals of the October Revolution, a general disintegration of the Russian empire took place. This included the rapid collapse of state authority and a subsequent breakdown of transport facilities and other infrastructures.

It was these developments which finally encouraged the Central Powers to invade Russia's western periphery from February to April 1918, when new national states in these territories were emerging. In particular Germany wanted to win influence over this process at an early stage. Finland, the former Russian Grand Duchy, was the first of these new states to declare its independence early in December 1917. This was welcomed by the German government, which now saw its wartime policy towards non-Russian nationalities on its eastern borders (*Randstaatenpolitik*) finally coming to fruition. The Central Powers also encouraged the secession of Ukraine from Russia, a process that had already begun in April 1917. Early in February 1918 Ukraine finally declared its independence and signed a separate peace with the Central Powers, thus triggering military invasion by the Bolshevik government. The former Russian part of Poland, 'Congress Poland', had been occupied by the Central Powers in the summer of 1915. Administered by Germany and Austria together, Poland was declared a semi-autonomous state by the grace of Berlin and Vienna in November 1916. This, however, did not reduce the far-reaching influence both occupants exercised in Poland until the end of the war. Meanwhile, Russia's erstwhile Baltic provinces found themselves closely monitored by nearby German forces, not least out of concern to protect the interests of ethnic German communities still living there.

The Caucasian tribes also loosened their ties with the Russian empire and sought independence. Many of the fragmented Caucasian communities were confronted with massive threats of expansion by the Ottoman empire, now gravitating towards the Caspian Sea. At that time the Caucasians could not expect any support from the new Bolshevik regime against Turkey. In particular, in early June 1918 civil war broke out on all fronts of European Russia. This conflict continued to menace the existence of revolutionary Russia until the end of 1919. The young Bolshevik state had to concentrate all its powers on the struggle against internal and external foes closer to home, and the Caucasians were left to themselves.

During 1918/19 and 1920 the new successor states of central and eastern Europe gradually established themselves in a belt reaching from Finland in the North to Romania and Yugoslavia in the South. Nevertheless, due to ethnic and frontier disputes with neighbouring states the external and internal political situation of these countries remained unstable and tangled. Ethnic tensions, for instance, could destabilise not only one state, but neighbouring states too. Of the former empires of eastern and south-eastern Europe, only Russia and Germany remained after 1918, and both suffered extensive territorial losses, especially Russia on its western borders. Meanwhile, the First Austrian Republic was a small state which bore no resemblance to the former Habsburg empire. It retained only a small number of Russian POWs in comparison to the huge number of its own compatriots who were still in Russian captivity. For all of these reasons, the repatriation of at least 2 million POWs on either side of the former eastern front was stymied. After 1918 it functioned only periodically, according to political circumstances.

Since December 1917 the complex events on the former eastern front had affected the overwhelming majority of all First World War POWs, namely almost 60% of the total number. During the war Germany, Russia and Austria-Hungary became the largest detaining powers of POWs: altogether some 5.2 million soldiers found themselves in captivity in one of these countries. Of these 2.8 million were soldiers of the Tsarist army, with 1.5 million of them imprisoned in Germany, and 1.3 million in Austria-Hungary. Russia held 2.3 million German and Austrian POWs at the time of the armistice on the eastern front of December 1917. Most of them, about 2.1 million, were soldiers of the multi-ethnic Habsburg army, only 170,000 were Germans, and a remaining 80,000 were Turks and Bulgarians. Early in 1915 Russia introduced a system of privileges for Slavs, Romanians and Italians captured while fighting with the Habsburg army. On the other hand, there was a deliberate policy of discrimination against ethnic Germans, Magyars, Turks and Jews, who got a much rougher deal while in captivity.

The other fronts of the Great War had given rise to far fewer POWs. Thus a total of 1.5 million were taken prisoner on both sides of the western front. Of these about 770,000 British, French, Belgian, Portuguese and US soldiers ended up in German captivity, and some 740,000 Germans and Austrians were captured by the western Allies.[2]

Mass repatriations took place on the eastern front at a much earlier stage in the war than on other fronts: that is to say during the 12 months between the October Revolution in Russia and November 1918, when Soviet Russia renounced the Brest-Litovsk Peace Treaty after the surrender of the Central Powers. By this stage Soviet Russia was deeply involved in a war against anti-Bolshevik White Russians and foreign interventionists. It had experienced the peace settlement at Brest-Litovsk as a heavy burden, not least because of the territorial losses it had entailed on Russia's western border regions, which were to be annexed by new nominal states under the control or influence of the Central Powers.

Moreover, the victorious powers at Brest-Litovsk required Russia to release the prisoners it was holding without guarantee of reciprocity. At that time there were still some 1.9 million soldiers from the armies of the Central Powers in Russia, who found themselves in an increasingly delicate political situation. They were involuntarily pushed into roles which had direct effects on their repatriation.[3] The Soviet government took up the discriminatory policy towards enemy POWs introduced under the Tsar, and continued by the provisional government during summer 1917. However, under Soviet rule it was not ethnicity that determined who was to be privileged and who not, but social class. Against this background a cluster of conflicting interests emerged which could not be efficiently channelled, either by the Soviet state as the official detaining power, or by the home countries of the POWs.

The repatriation and return of POWs from revolutionary Russia has been a key focus of recent research. The reason for this lies in their home countries' well-grounded fears that soldiers returning from Russian captivity might import social unrest or revolutionary ideas into central Europe.[4] The distrust shown by the state authorities towards the returnees, and the resulting political discontent among the former POWs, contributed in some degree to the end of the war and the revolution in Germany and Austria. Also, the emergence of the Hungarian Soviet Republic in 1919, with the former POW Béla Kun as its leader, could be seen as a direct consequence of wartime captivity and repatriation from Russia. Therefore the Central Powers anxiously watched as hundreds of thousands of their compatriots returned from Russia, a country in turmoil. Not only were they apparently ragged and down at heel after years in captivity, but they also aroused suspicion because of their political views, which had often been radicalised. The 'germ of Bolshevism' seemed to have seized hold of them, threatening to infect the hinterland as well. In particular Austria-Hungary, which had been exposed to severe supply problems since 1916/17, as well as social unrest and a series of internal political crises from early 1918, reacted with hostility and suspicion towards the masses of its returning captives. Various state organs were activated for the internal protection of the country. For instance, instead of being sent back to their families the returning prisoners were channelled into a political and physical quarantine whereby they had to spend many weeks in military confinement. Most of them were subsequently sent directly to the reserve units of their regiments. There they were guarded by soldiers who had never experienced captivity, and they were subjected to a humiliating military investigation concerning the circumstances of their capture (a *Rechtfertigungsverfahren*). Their loyalty and attachment to the Dual Monarchy was then fostered by officers from the army staging areas through patriotic instruction (*vaterländischer Unterricht*). Meanwhile, the treatment of tens of thousands of Reich Germans who returned to Germany from Russia at the same time was scarcely less severe.

The deep distrust of the Austo-Hungarian state towards returning POWs has been amply demonstrated.[5] At that time the Dual Monarchy underwent heavy strains: it had to overcome food shortages in its hinterland and was confronted with the intensifying nationality issue. During this period of mostly one-way repatriation from December 1917 until November 1918, there were in fact two discernible sub-phases. The earliest mass repatriation of the Great War began with an initial wave of some 600,000 Central Powers' returnees, who moved totally chaotically from European Russia to occupied Poland. Most of these former POWs had been soldiers of the Habsburg army and flooded into Austria-Hungary between December 1917 and June 1918. The exact number in this first wave, which in historiography has been designated as a 'wild return' (*wilde Heimkehr*), could not be established even by the Habsburg authorities.[6]

Meanwhile, during the months immediately following the Brest-Litovsk Treaty, that is from April to June 1918, Austria-Hungary and Germany established official repatriation commissions in Petrograd and Moscow.[7] Germany dispatched its central repatriation commission, together with a diplomatic mission under Count Mirbach-Harff, to Moscow, from mid-March 1918 the new capital of Soviet Russia. Accredited to the Soviet government, these missions began their official function at a time in June and July 1918, when the fronts of the Russian civil war had separated the Soviet state from much of its territory. Indeed, for more than 18 months the area of Bolshevik rule was confined to the central parts of European Russia. None of the Central Powers' missions designed for territories held by the Russian Whites and the Allied interventionist troops, that is east of the Ural mountains and central Asia, were able to become active. On the contrary, some of the members of these commissions were imprisoned by the Whites. As pointed out before, the Russian Whites did not recognise the Brest-Litovsk peace treaty with the Central Powers. Encouraged in this by the western Allies, who wanted to erect a new eastern front against Germany and Austria-Hungary, the Russian Whites considered themselves as military opponents of the Central Powers until November 1918. Accordingly they sent all POWs in their reach back to the prison camps. As the western Allies did not repatriate their POWs on the western front before autumn 1919, all the POWs in Siberia and central Asia had to spend at least another year in captivity. Only those who came under American and Japanese custody in eastern Siberia fared slightly better, at least in comparison with their fellow prisoners under White Russian or Czech supervision.

France and Britain had been intervening in the Russian civil war by military action since summer 1918. Until November 1918 they worked intensely for the resurrection of the eastern front. Indeed, the Russian withdrawal from the war in winter 1917/18 had hurt the Allied cause and threatened to cancel out any advantages accrued by the intervention of the United States in the conflict in April 1917. Several German divisions had already been transferred to the western front even before the peace treaty at Brest-Litovsk was signed; they were part of a much bigger force used in the German offensive launched in March 1918. Furthermore, Britain was also concerned that the large numbers of German and Austrian POWs, politicised by the Soviets and recruited into a 'Red' army, could become a menace to British colonies in south Asia. These concerns were admittedly exaggerated and based on unconfirmed rumours about the numbers thus far 'liberated' by the Soviet authorities.[8] Whatever else, the Allied presence in White-held areas made it even less likely that the German and Austrian repatriation missions would be able to fulfil their appointed task of bringing former POWs home.

For all of these reasons, only the repatriation commissions in Bolshevik-held territory were able to achieve any successes in the summer and autumn of 1918. Even so, there were fewer returnees now than during the first wave, the 'wild return'. Estimates for the second half of 1918 run from 200,000 to a maximum of 300,000 returnees. These were generally sent home via the exchange station in Belo-Russian Orsha, the border-town between Soviet Russia and the demarcation line of the German eastern occupation zone. The Habsburg military authorities also registered some 670,000 repatriates from Russia during both waves of repatriation, from early 1918 to mid-October 1918.[9]

Repatriation from Ukraine, occupied by German and Austrian troops during the spring of 1918, proceeded very differently. By the autumn of 1917 roughly 660,000 POWs, or one-third of the total number still in Russian captivity, were being held on Ukrainian soil. Some were deployed in agriculture and industry as part of a new labour recruitment drive begun in 1916, but others had been called up into new anti-Habsburg military units mobilised from within the prison camp system. The largest of these units was the Czech Legion, made up of 40,000 Czech and Slovak POWs. Of all the national groups in Russian captivity, they were the easiest to win over, as they expected the Russians to grant them national independence after the war: until the final break-up of the Habsburg empire the Austrian government stubbornly denied them national rights. In the course of 1917 the Czech Legion recruited more and more former POWs, not least because their members had access to better food and clothing than the average prisoner. When German troops occupied western Ukraine in March 1918 and threatened the eastern part of that country too, the Czech Legion marched towards the East in order to be shipped from Russia's Pacific port Vladivostok to Europe's western front. They were accompanied by smaller detachments of former POWs who had chosen to change sides: Romanians from the Hungarian part of the Dual Monarchy, and Italians from the Trentino, Istria and Fiume. A military contingent of South Slavs and Serbs went to northern Russia in order to support the British forces of intervention there. At the same time the advance of Central Powers troops encouraged German and Austrian POWs concentrated in central European Russia to move westwards: in their hundreds of thousands they made their way into Ukraine, Belorussia and the Baltic provinces.

However, when it reached the Ural mountains in May 1918, the Czech Legion quickly became embroiled in the burgeoning civil war between Reds and Whites, not least because it swept along large numbers of anti-Bolshevik Russians in its path. Together the Czechs and the White Russians erected a new front in the Urals against Trotsky's Red Army, pushing into European Russia from the East. This meant that all POWs who were being held to the east of this new front line in the civil war were in effect trapped, including those who had already made the journey from Siberia to the Urals. Only after the end of the civil war, in the summer of 1920, was it possible to resume an organised repatriation programme for these particular prisoners. The Czech Legion, meanwhile, had swollen to 70,000 men, most of them Czechs and Slovaks, but some of them Sudeten Germans or members of the Hungarian minority in Slovakia who were also claimed as Czechoslovak citizens by the new national government in Prague in November 1918. The majority were volunteers, but some were forcibly conscripted into the Legion. They were eventually repatriated via Vladivostok, returning home to become a key element in the army of the new Czechoslovak republic.

Whether recruited voluntarily or forcibly, the 100,000 or so former POWs concentrated by the Russians into anti-Habsburg national military units were no longer counted as prisoners under the formal protection of international law. In addition to the Czech Legion, about 30,000 South Slav POWs had been mobilised for the 'Serbian Voluntary Division' in Ukraine in 1916/17. Many of these 'volunteers' had been forced to sign up, and owing to subsequent disciplinary problems the whole unit had to be pulled out of Russia in the autumn of 1917. These South Slavs too had to be subtracted from the overall number of Central Powers POWs in Russia, as well as several thousand Romanians, Italians and Alsace-Lorrainers.

Ukraine remained a sort of transit zone for POWs and returnees for most of the second phase of repatriation. The German and Austrian occupation forces, up to their departure in late 1918, were never able to register all of the former POWs, as their sheer number remained huge, and thus difficult to survey. In Ukraine food was more plentiful than in the blockaded nations of central Europe or in those parts of Russia ravaged by civil war. So while many POWs were repatriated through Ukraine, tens of thousands of other returnees decided to hide from their national repatriation organs. An additional motive was the fear of being sent to fight on other fronts after being returned home. This possibility existed until November 1918. Finally, the Austrian army was also confronted in Ukraine not only with deserters who had joined anti-Habsburg military units like the Czech Legion, but also with the emergence of a Ukrainian national army which began to appear in the summer of 1918. Under the nominal head of state, Hetman Pavel Skoropadsky, Ukrainians from various national backgrounds, some Austrian, some Russian, signed up to join the new Ukrainian force, which in theory was now allied to the Central Powers.

The Austrian repatriation committees were of course committed to laying their hands on Austrian citizens of Ukrainian ethnicity who had chosen to stay in Ukraine, whoever they were: former Austrian POWs or volunteers from the Ukrainian contingent recruited by Austria-Hungary, the 'grey-coaters' and 'blue-coaters'. However, since this would automatically give rise to political tensions with the friendly Ukrainian government, and because of the volunteers' strong wish to serve their new fatherland, which meant choosing not return to Austria-Hungary, the Austrian leadership refrained from demanding the repatriation of these particular categories of former POWs. Chaotic conditions within the Dual Monarchy itself, as well as lack of resources and technical means to carry through a forceful repatriation at that time, also helped to determine this decision.[10]

Later, after the retreat of German and Austrian occupation forces in 1918/19, a power vacuum opened up in Ukraine. Various Ukrainian factions, as well as the last White Russian troops, fought each other while also attempting to defend themselves against the advancing Red Army. Once again, stranded returnees from the Central Powers assembled in Ukraine, mostly from European Russia and northern Caucasus. The Ukraine thus continued to be a collecting point for large numbers of former POWs in the western part of the former Tsarist empire. Those congregating in the Black Sea region were, for various reasons, among the last prisoners of the Great War to be repatriated, arriving home only in 1921–22. In the final stage of the civil war the area to the north and east of the Black Sea had become a dead zone for repatriation, although it was occasionally visited by Austrian repatriation missions in 1919/20.

At a time in late 1920 when almost all POWs in Siberia had returned to central Europe – either by ship from Vladivostok, or by train from western Siberia via Moscow and the Baltic ports – over 13,000 subjects of the former Central Powers were still trapped in the coastal areas of the Black Sea. It is this particular group of late repatriates which most strikingly demonstrates the internal as well as external circumstances which prevented POWs from returning home. Soon after the revolution, and not later than the beginning of 1918, the Soviet leadership realised that it could take advantage of the repatriation process in order to further its aim of promoting revolution in neighbouring central Europe. Prisoners in Soviet-controlled areas were thus exposed to Bolshevik propaganda and agitation in favour of socialist revolution in their home countries. Chaotic post-war conditions in the successor states of Austria-Hungary and Germany were designated as part of the World Revolution, an object that the Bolsheviks did not give up until the end of the Polish-Soviet war in 1921. In the end, though, the revolutions failed to materialise, with the exception of the short-lived Hungarian Soviet Republic from March to August 1919.

In the meantime, though, Bolshevik agitation had an adverse effect on the repatriation of former POWs from spring 1918 onwards. In May 1918 a Soviet repatriation commission was created in Moscow, with branches in the provinces: the *Tsentroplenbezh* (Central Committee for POWs and Refugees). Its official function was to collect statistics on POWs and refugees as well as to care for them and direct the varied movement of returnees, from west to east and the other way round. The *Tsentroplenbezh* was in charge of all displaced persons in Russia as well as the Russian POWs still in central Europe. With regard to the former enemy POWs within their reach they unofficially launched a propaganda campaign and hampered the efforts of the Central Powers' repatriation missions in Russia. The *Tsentroplenbezh* was led by a group of high-ranking, experienced Bolsheviks who received their directives from the Kremlin: if the POWs had to be released from Russia, at least they should return home imbued with ideas of socialist world revolution, as the unspoken party line went.

Both the German and Austrian repatriation missions as well as the returning POWs themselves described the committee's activities as highly obstructive to repatriation. It could not prevent the return of some 500,000 Germans, Austrians and Hungarians. But when Moscow renounced the Brest-Litovsk Treaty on 13 November 1918 and ordered all foreign missions to leave the country, no further repatriations from Russia were effected for over a year. During this time, only a few thousand former POWs succeeded in reaching their home country by means of escape from Bolshevik-held territory. Most of them had been in the western provinces of Russia, allowing them easier access to the border with the Baltic states, Poland, Ukraine or Romania.

The figures for repatriations from Russia after 1919, when the civil war had come to an end on almost all fronts and communication networks were completely destroyed after six years of war, can only be estimated. About 30,000 Germans and 118,000 former Austrians were repatriated from Siberia and central Asia in 1920. In 1921/22 another 13,000, mostly Austrians, returned from Ukraine and southern Russia. By 1922 a further 6850 repatriates had returned via Vladivostok.[11] The number of former POWs who preferred to stay in Soviet Russia after this date cannot be established. Already during the war a few thousand pro-Russian POWs had been released or 'liberated' from captivity by Tsarist officials. Most of them were Slavs who found it easy to communicate with the locals, and they were allowed to live in relative freedom in the towns of the Russian empire, exercising their civic professions and skills. From 1917 onwards some of them had families in Russia, after the provisional government granted them permission to marry Russian partners. After the October Revolution and the December armistice, other POWs decided to stay in Soviet Russia for political rather than familial reasons. Thus the so-called internationalists sided with the Bolshevik cause and often joined the Red Army in their own national units. They fought against the Whites and the western interventionists, and after victory in the civil war, decided to stay in Soviet Russia rather than return to their 'capitalist' homelands. The Hungarian communist Béla Kun is the most prominent example of these former POW-internationalists. Taken prisoner as an officer in the Austro-Hungarian army during the Brusilov offensive of 1916, he returned to Hungary to lead the short-lived Soviet regime in 1919, before briefly being interned in Austria and then fleeing back to Moscow. Here he enjoyed a career in the Communist Party of the Soviet Union (CPSU) and the Comintern (Communist International), and is said to have taken part in a terrible massacre of White Russian prisoners in the Crimea in 1920, an event which invited condemnation even from Lenin.[12] Ten years later, in the 1930s, there were still cases of ex-POWs who applied to be repatriated from what was now Stalin's Soviet Union. Many of these late returnees had been supporters of the Bolsheviks who had subsequently become disillusioned with the realties of everyday life in a socialist dictatorship. Meanwhile, Béla Kun fell victim to Stalin's purges in 1937, and it can be assumed that this also happened to other former POWs who had chosen to remain in Russia, particularly if they had joined the CPSU.

Most former POWs, including those who had taken part, voluntarily or involuntarily, in the Russian Revolution and the civil war and who sympathised in some way with communism, still opted for repatriation at the earliest possible date. At home some took part in politics, while others became writers or artists, using their books or works of art to give voice to their wartime experiences in Russia.[13] In his literary works, for instance, the Czech author Jaroslav Hašek rendered his personal experience of captivity and the Russian civil war in a most direct way. His world-famous novel, *The Good Soldier Svejk*, brought to life some of the bizarre and wonderful characters he met during his five-year stay in Russia. Some former POWs later became famous or rose to high positions. The roll call of names such as Ernst Reuter, Roland Freisler and Edwin Erich Dwinger among the Germans, and Otto Bauer, Jaroslav Hašek, Heimito von Doderer or Josef Tito among the Austrians suggests how deep and politically relevant their experiences must have been in Russian captivity. A number of Hungarian politicians who figured prominently in the post-1945 communist regime had also been POWs in Russia during the First World War, including Ferenc Münnich and Imre Nagy. From war captives they were transformed into internationalists and finally into national leaders. In short, the phenomenon of wartime captivity and revolution in Russia triggered diverse reactions and wholly different ways of looking at the world, from political radicalisation und inhuman brutalisation to withdrawal into the sphere of art and literature, or to philanthropy of various kinds. Those who spent the war years in Russian captivity, as opposed to captivity in other countries, also seem to have been intensely effected by their experiences, and to have dealt with these experiences in a more intense way.

In the latter context it is also worth highlighting the role played by the Swedish Red Cross nurse Elsa Brändstrom, who enjoyed a huge profile in post-war Germany and Austria, especially among former prisoners and their families. Known affectionately as the 'Angel of Siberia' due to her philanthropic work among POWs in Russia between 1914 and 1920, she was a regular guest of honour at meetings of veteran POW groups like the *Reichsvereinigung ehemaliger Kriegsgefangener* and its Austrian equivalent, the *Bundesvereingung der ehemaligen österreichischen Kriegsgefangenen*. Yet interestingly the German and Austrian Red Cross nurses who also volunteered for missions to the camps in Russia and Siberia tended to be more marginalised in post-war commemorations, so that names like Countess Nora Kinsky or Countess Alexandrine von Uexküll are now almost forgotten in German and Austrian history.[14]

Repatriation from the Central Powers

The repatriation of the approximately 2.5 million Russian POWs who were still interned in Germany and Austria-Hungary in early 1918 differed in many ways from the aforementioned repatriation from Russia, although it was an equally difficult and painful process. By the beginning of the last year of the war, over 150,000 of them had died in German and Austrian custody and another 100,000 had escaped through neutral states like the Netherlands, Denmark or Switzerland to Russia. Some 2000 war-wounded Russians had been interned in neutral countries. Another 30,000 Russian POWs had been exchanged in the period before the Treaty of Brest-Litovsk. With the signing of the Treaty in March 1918, it could be expected that the repatriation of all remaining POWs from the eastern front – 4.5 million in total – was imminent. However, the German leadership henceforth suspended the principle of reciprocity with regard to prisoner releases and instead embarked on a more restrictive exchange programme. During the last year of the Great War, the German war economy, it was generally felt, could not afford to lose 1.3 million Russians as a vital contribution to its labour force. Therefore a 'head for head' exchange was offered to the Soviet side, that is 140,000 of the 1.3 million Russians in Germany would be repatriated in exchange for the 140,000 Germans in Russian captivity. This, it was hoped, would prevent a significant loss of much-needed manpower in German industry and agriculture.[15] For this and other reasons only a small percentage of the total number of Russian POWs in Germany, mostly those who were long-term sick, disabled or otherwise unfit for work, were able to return home. Those selected for repatriation also often faced unexplained delays, so that in the end far more Germans and Austrians returned from Russia than vice versa in the period down to November 1918.[16]

After the armistice on the western front on 11 November, the leaders of the new German Republic adopted an entirely different course, rushing to repatriate some 900,000 Russians within two months before a new POW commission, sent by the western Allies, arrived in Berlin. One of the main tasks of this commission was to prevent the return of any more Russian POWs.[17] In fact, by releasing the Russians prematurely the German government had acted contrary to the conditions laid down in the armistice, and had done so deliberately. Its motives were twofold. Firstly, it was anxious to appease the Soviet leadership, especially after the latter's annulment of the Treaty of Brest-Litovsk on 13 November 1918. If Germany did not meet Soviet demands for immediate and full repatriation of all Russian POWs, it could face reciprocal retention of the German POWs in Russia. Berlin wished to avoid any pretext for such retaliatory measures. As pointed out earlier, Soviet Russia suspended its POW exchange soon after the armistice on the western front, in spite of the liberation of many of the Russian POWs in Germany and Austria from November 1918 onwards.

The anarchic situation within Germany after the end of the war provided the second motive for quick repatriation. Millions of German soldiers were now returning from the fronts to their families. After their demobilisation they expected to earn a living. Since all the harvest labour had been completed shortly before, over one million Russian POWs would have placed an additional burden on existing food supplies, especially given the continuation of the Allied economic blockade even after the armistice. In short, Germany was unable to feed its Russian POWs while the western Allies in turn were unwilling to lift the blockade. The only solution was to send them home. Britain and France, on the other hand, had good reasons to prevent the return of one million POWs to Russia, as both were participants in the Russian civil war and feared that returning soldiers would be recruited into the Red Army. At the same time, Britain as well as France tried to recruit volunteers for the anti-Bolshevik White armies from Russian POWs held in Germany and the successor states of Austria-Hungary.

During the war the Dual Monarchy had more of its subjects in Russian captivity (over 2 million) than it held Russian POWs in its territory: in 1918 the figure was less than 1.2 million. As in Germany, no general POW exchange took place in the period down to November 1918 because the Habsburg state depended heavily on the labour performed by Russian POWs. In addition, the technical preconditions for repatriation were hampered by serious organisational chaos in Austria's hinterland. Indeed, the internal crisis was much worse than in Germany, and became worse still in 1918. When in the summer of 1918 a Soviet repatriation mission arrived in Vienna against the political wishes of the Austrian leadership, the government in Vienna came to believe that the mission's objective was not merely the quick repatriation of Russian prisoners, but political agitation. This presented a much bigger menace to the Habsburg state than to the German state because of the nationality issue.[18]

The Soviet mission was tightly monitored and whenever possible, hampered in its work. The eventual breakdown of the Dual Monarchy and the end of the war in the autumn of 1918 created a new situation, however. Reduced to the territory of the German-Austrian Republic (*Deutsch-Österreich*), Vienna retained control over only 120,000 Russian prisoners. The remainder, a few hundred thousand, were scattered across the successor states of the Habsburg empire. All of these states had disputes with their new neighbours over frontiers and territory, so their inherited POW problem did not appear at the top of their political agendas.[19] Most of these states did not even know the exact number of former POWs in their territory. Many of the latter went into hiding or crossed borders from one jurisdiction to another, making it even more difficult to count them. The Pan-Slavist notion of solidarity with 'Russian brothers', in the summer of 1914 one of the driving ideas which triggered the Great War, had been abandoned in 1918 in favour of more pragmatic views and new political orientations. Yet overriding even this was the general breakdown of state authority, which meant that in many cases POWs were left to fend for themselves, and/or to organise their own repatriation.

In this scenario, the Italians were the first to go home. In November 1918, some 350,000 of them were in Austrian hands, making them the second largest group of prisoners in the Dual Monarchy. Admittedly most of them were being held in areas close to the new frontier with Italy.

By February 1919 the last of them had left the territory of the former Habsburg empire. By contrast, Russian returnees heading eastwards could be found in almost all of the successor states, including Poland, Romania and Czechoslovakia. Mostly they were left to their own devices. Where conflicts did arise, this was usually between the 'host' governments and the local Soviet repatriation missions, rather than with the POWs themselves. From the perspective of the newly created states in central Europe, the Soviet repatriation missions were less interested in repatriation and more interested in political agitation and/or shady financial dealings. In one or two cases, members of these missions were even prosecuted for economic crimes.[20]

Fear of communism also hindered the establishment of proper relations with the Soviet authorities in Moscow for many years after the war. The experience of the Hungarian Soviet Republic was not one which any of the successor states wished to repeat. For instance, the new republic of Austria only established full diplomatic relations with the Soviet Union in 1922, when the last Russians had already left Austrian soil.[21] A few thousand Russians preferred to stay in the states of their former detaining power. They had the same reasons for doing so as some 50,000 to 80,000 of their compatriots who chose to remain in Germany, namely opposition to communism or membership of a social class exposed to persecution in the Soviet Union. Marriage was the most obvious and direct reason for staying in central Europe. However, as the populations of Germany and Austria were still suffering from the economic consequences of the war, these former POWs were often regarded with suspicion and hostility as rivals for jobs or as extra mouths to feed – as indeed were the hundreds and thousands of refugees who were unable to return to their homes in former war zones.[22]

Thus, to summarise: with the exception of the relatively smooth return of some 1 million POWs from Russia during the revolutionary year 1918, the story of repatriation on the former eastern front is rather complex. Even the movement of former German and Austrian POWs out of Russia was at first 'wild' and chaotic, and it was only for a few months in the second half of 1918 that official repatriation organs were able to channel home their compatriots in something approaching an orderly fashion. The sudden and total break-up of two former empires, Austria-Hungary and Russia, caused huge disruption to transportation networks as well as the emergence of new nation states on their former territories. The frontiers of these new nation states remained uncertain until 1920/21, and their internal political structures for many years after that. Countries like Poland and Czechoslovakia also had large national minorities to contend with

(Germans, Hungarians and Ukrainians) at the same time as dealing with the issue of POW repatriation on the former eastern front.

On the Russian side repatriation was hampered by the fact that the Soviet leadership embarked on a policy subordinated to its revolutionary aims: this directly affected the return of the former POWs. Repatriation was seen as a Trojan horse to bring about revolution and social upheaval in central and eastern Europe. Returning prisoners were thus used as a means of intervening in the internal affairs of their home countries. This had several direct effects on them: they were confronted with a radical ideology and political agitation in the camps, and many of them were prevented from returning home by the Soviet detaining power. On top of this the civil war was responsible for ensuring that a further 600,000 POWs were unable to leave Russia until 1920. Of these, around 180,000 took part in the fighting itself, either as volunteers or as forced conscripts. Thus roughly 80,000 Czechs and Slovaks, and some 10,000 other legionaries such as Italians, Romanians, Poles and South Slavs, aligned themselves with the Whites. Another 90,000 or so fought for the Red Army, the majority of these being Hungarians.

Repatriations from other detaining powers

The process of repatriation on other fronts of the First World War was equally varied and complex. On both sides of the most contested front, the western front, there were still some 1.3 million POWs in November 1918, and on the Italian front in the Alps there were around 1 million. The numbers were of course lower than on the eastern front, and transport networks were generally in better shape, although minor complications occurred when state frontiers were altered to the losing states' disadvantage. Alsace-Lorraine, for instance, went from Germany to France, and Trieste, Istria, Trentino and South Tyrol from Austria to Italy. Having said this, the relative stability of state frontiers in western Europe, as well as a greater respect for diplomatic tradition, ensured that there was less anarchy in the repatriation process. This did not mean, however, that German and Austrian POWs would be discharged to their home countries any earlier than their comrades on the eastern front.

The other theatres of the Great War generated far fewer POWs. In the Near East, in the African colonies and in Asia there was a combined total of less than 300,000 POWs at the time of the armistice, mostly from the Central Powers. Much less is known about the fate and repatriation of POWs on these 'side stages' of the war. Meanwhile, the largest groups in western Europe were subjected to a variety of patterns of repatriation, with no one experience standing out as the norm.

In 1917 and 1918 France and Britain on the one side, and Germany on the other, agreed to a series of prisoner exchanges negotiated at Berne and at The Hague which represented something of a humanitarian breakthrough. As a result, around 100,000 disabled POWs were sent home or were interned in a neutral country for the rest of the war. Among the beneficiaries were also those who were suffering from 'barbed-wire disease', those with large families, and those who had spent 18 months or more in captivity. Indeed, such large-scale concessions would not be repeated during the Second World War, when only the severely wounded had a chance of being repatriated before the cessation of hostilities. The mutual exchanges, helped along by teams of medical inspectors from neutral countries, continued at a slow pace until the autumn of 1918, when they were unilaterally suspended by the French in the run up to the 11 November armistice.[23] During the armistice negotiations France insisted that Germany had to release all French subjects in its custody immediately and without guarantee of reciprocity. The intention was to retain as many German POWs as possible until (or even beyond) the formal conclusion of a peace treaty. The reasons for this policy were peculiar to the western front: the French nation had had to carry the heaviest burden of the war of all the western Allies, and needed all the manpower it could get in order to recover. The French people and economy had been bled white. Hundreds of thousands of French soldiers had been killed, maimed or captured. Loss of civilian life had been enormous too, and almost one-quarter of French territory had been severely damaged by the war. Now the former war zone was retaken, and hundreds of thousands of French war refugees returned to it.

Germany acted quickly and sent back most of its French POWs in the expectation that France would soon respond by returning its German prisoners. This would have been in line with the procedure recommended by the Hague Conventions of 1907. The new republican government of Germany was also determined not to provide any pretext for a delay in the repatriation of its citizens, or for inhuman or brutal treatment of those who now belonged to the losing side. Subsequent developments proved, however, that these hopes and expectations were in vain. By mid-January 1919 the repatriation of some 500,000 Frenchmen and 40,000 Belgians from Germany was completed with just a few exceptions, such as hospitalised, diseased and non-transportable POWs.[24]

Of the 420,000 German POWs held by France during the war, some 350,000 were still in detention in November 1918. In the end, the French government refused to allow their repatriation until the spring of 1920, mainly, as discussed above, so that they could be used as forced labour.

In addition, the German captives were seen as a bargaining tool to force Germany to accept the Versailles Treaty in the summer of 1919, which itself came into effect only in January 1920. In the meantime, the prisoners were drafted to clear unexploded mines and bombs on northern France's battlefields and for heavy reconstruction work more generally.[25] Both of these actions – the retention of POWs for over a year after the cessation of hostilities, and their deployment in types of work which seriously endangered their lives – were a clear breach of the 1907 Hague Convention on Land Warfare.

The French policy was motivated by emotions of hatred and revenge, but it was generally popular in post-war French society. In Germany the French conduct launched a wave of indignation and protest, first with the families of the POWs, then in the media. Outrage was also expressed in some neutral countries, and by the Red Cross. Finally, from late 1919 public opinion exercised increasing pressure on the French government over its continued refusal to repatriate the POWs. The French government resisted international condemnation until the spring of 1920, when it eventually released its political hostages. The story of France's behaviour towards its First World War captives remains an obscure chapter in its history even today, and we still lack a comprehensive scholarly treatment of this issue. However, some details are beginning to emerge about the exceptionally harsh treatment of German POWs after November 1918, which in turn gave rise to mutinies, violent labour strikes and even suicides among the retained prisoners themselves.[26]

Apart from this, France also had some other, rather peculiar issues to contend with in relation to repatriation. For instance, how did the French authorities react to the decision of some 1000 former French POWs to stay in Germany after the war, mainly because they had married German women? How did they treat some 17,000 soldiers of the Tsarist army who had been sent to France as an auxiliary force during the war to make up for French losses in the bloody battles of the western front?[27] In the spring of 1917, just after the February Revolution in Russia, this Russian expeditionary force in France had mutinied, and after the revolt had been suppressed by French troops the surviving mutineers had been held as POWs. Nonetheless, their fate after November 1918 remains unclear. Finally, what eventually happened to thousands of – mostly Austrian – deserters who had fought in Czech, Slovak, Polish and other 'national' units under French command? What policy did France apply with regard to POWs on the Balkan and the Turkish fronts? Such questions still await serious, systematic investigation.

As detaining powers the Anglo-Saxon countries proceeded quite differently with their POWs, although admittedly they held fewer of them. The POWs captured on the western front were of course predominantly Germans. Britain and the United States stuck closely to the liberal tradition of captivity and to the requirements of international law, though Britain retained more than half of its POWs in the communications zone of northern France for use as labour, and the United States transferred its POWs to the French army for the same purpose, at least temporarily. German POWs held in France by British and American troops were also forced to clear mines and undertake reconstruction work after November 1918. However, unlike the French, both Britain and America were inclined to send these POWs home as early as possible. Since Germany had repatriated almost all of its 180,000 British POWs and 2000 American soldiers by early 1919, reciprocity could no longer be used as an argument for continuing to detain German prisoners. Of course, psychological circumstances favoured early repatriation with the Anglo-Americans: neither of the two countries had a devastated war zone which had to be made habitable again. The USA had been at war for only one and-a-half years and had not sustained human losses and material damage on the same scale as any of the European powers, let alone France. Therefore, the American military, like its Japanese counterpart, called for the quick repatriation of its rather small number of POWs. Public opinion in both Anglo-Saxon countries also favoured sending the German prisoners back. In the event, releases were only postponed because the British and American governments were unwilling to break ranks with the French. Since the French government was stubbornly determined to use its 350,000 POWs for clearing and reconstruction tasks for as long as possible, it could not allow its wartime allies to repatriate their German POWs at an earlier date. Thus, the victorious powers on the western front agreed to the provisional retention of all their POWs. The USA and Britain repatriated their Germans only after the Treaty of Versailles in the summer of 1919, a process which lasted until the autumn of the same year.[28] Japan followed suit with its own releases a little later, while France, as we have seen, held out until the spring of 1920.

To some extent, Italy as a detaining power represented a special case. By a political mistake of the Austrian leadership during the armistice talks at Villa Giusti on 1 November 1918, some 330,000 Austrian soldiers on the Austrian-Italian front fell into Italian hands. These soldiers assumed the armistice had already come into force, when officially a state of war still existed. Until October 1918 Italy had captured some 180,000 enemy soldiers, the great majority of whom were Austrians. At the same time the

Dual Monarchy had taken around 400,000 Italians prisoner; the exact number of Italians in Austrian captivity has still not been firmly established. The parity in POW numbers, achieved by a quirk of fate in November 1918, did not last for long, as most of Austria's Italian POWs had returned to Italy by February 1919.[29] Of all repatriated POWs after 1918 they were received by their fatherland with the strongest distrust: many of them soon found themselves in prison camps or gaols, this time Italian ones. The reason for this distrust was the extremely high battlefield losses experienced by the Italian army during the war, particularly in terms of the number of soldiers captured. The Italian leadership therefore suspected mass defection and desertion, the more so as the military leadership was blissfully unaware of the severe conditions of Alpine warfare and did not bear in mind that Austrian resistance on the Alpine front was particularly stubborn. Moreover, in 1915 Italy's entry into the war had been deeply controversial among the Italians; many suspected the country's ruling elite of having pushed for war against Austria in pursuit of territorial gains secretly promised by Britain and France in the Treaty of London of April 1915. The working classes, the socialist movement and the Catholic church had opposed the war against Austria-Hungary, and there clearly were at least some cases of front-line troops choosing to surrender at the first opportunity rather than fight against the enemy. Unfortunately, this meant that all POWs were suspected of cowardice or desertion. Only Mussolini's Fascist party sought to heal these wounds by launching a big movement of social integration for all veterans of the war, including former Italian POWs. By contrast, Austrian POWs in Italy were treated much more respectfully. In fact, Rome sent its 500,000 POWs home as early as the summer of 1919, well before the signature of the Treaty of St Germain in the autumn of that year. Politically this was possible because Austria did not contest Italy's claim to the former Habsburg territories of Trieste, Istria, Trentino and South Tyrol, while Italy now saw Yugoslavia, and not Austria, as its main enemy and rival for influence in the Adriatic.[30]

The Reception of former POWs/returnees in their home countries

Former French POWs after 1918 faced similar problems of rejection and isolation in post-war society. This was in spite of the fact that the French government had previously been very keen to emphasise the terrible suffering and brutal treatment of their compatriots in German captivity.[31] Thus French military leaders treated their repatriated prisoners, as well as POWs captured from 're-gained' Alsace-Lorraine, with the utmost distrust, accusing them of collective disloyalty and defection. Like their

Italian counterparts, the 500,000 former French POWs had to fight a continuous battle for social respect and recognition into the 1930s and beyond, at a time when the war-wounded and other veterans could take such respect – and the social advantages that went with it – for granted.[32]

Initial research seems to indicate that the Russian leadership under the Tsar embarked on a similar policy towards its POWs in German and Austrian captivity. However, no published studies are available on this issue to date, as Russia's role in the First World War, and in particular conditions on the Russian home front, leave many questions open. Both the French and the Russian attitude towards their compatriots in captivity was characterised by hypocrisy. The Russian authority in charge of POW affairs, the Head Administration of the General Staff in Petrograd, alleged time and again in the period down to 1917 that Russian POWs in German and Austrian hands were being exposed to undernourishment, cold, and wanton mistreatment (meaning torture). The Central Powers' POWs in Russia, however, supposedly fared much better.[33] In fact, this was true only for a small minority of captives privileged by the Russian government. It was definitely not true for the overwhelming mass of POWs who had to bear terrible hardships caused by the complete disorganisation of the Russian hinterland, particularly during the early years of the war. At the same time, the Russian leadership prevented public charities from launching collections for Russian POWs in German and Austrian captivity and forbade the sending of food parcels by Russian families, setting it at odds with the policy pursued by its allies Britain, France and the USA. The German government had agreed to allow in food parcels for the masses of its Russian POWs in 1916, and in fact invited the Russian authorities to organise a steady flow of relief. The Austrian government did likewise in 1918.[34] But still the Russian leadership refused.

The repatriation policy of the Soviet leadership has to be seen in the same light. Towards the end of 1918 some 2.4 million Russians were still being held in the countries of the Central Powers. However, they had no effective body to assist or represent them, since neither their captors, nor the western Allies, nor the Bolshevik government, seemed to know what to do with them. In this their fate differed significantly from that of most other prisoners in Europe at this time. Moreover, if they did succeed in getting home, they could not expect much of a welcome from the new Soviet state. Official Leninist historiography interpreted the Great War as an imperialist conflict that had to end in the eventual triumph of communism. The victory of the Red Army after the civil war was presented as a foundation myth for the Soviet state, while the defeated Whites became the villains of history who had fought on the side of 'reaction'.[35]

Russia's important role in the First World War only became a topic of scholarly debate after the end of the Soviet Union in the 1990s. Even then, few studies devoted themselves to the issue of wartime captivity and repatriation. What more than 2.5 million Russians experienced in central Europe as POWs, and what consequences these experiences had when most of them returned to the socialist fatherland, has only recently become a subject of historic research.[36]

Worse still, during the years of Stalin's ascendancy in the Kremlin it became dangerous for any Russian who 'had seen the West' with his or her own eyes to speak about their impressions. The new 'paradise of the working class', whipped into shape by terror and compulsion, could not tolerate having foreign countries and societies as objects for comparison. Whoever had suffered and lived undernourished for several years between 1914 and 1920 in Germany or Austria knew that it was better to remain silent about this episode in their lives.

Thus in the aftermath of the war two powers with very different social and political systems, France and the Soviet Union, proceeded to adopt illiberal and inhumane policies towards foreign prisoners still within their control *and* towards their own compatriots returning home from enemy captivity. Ironically, both of these powers also produced prominent military leaders who had themselves been POWs during the First World War: the famous French general and resistance leader Charles de Gaulle (1893–1970), who went on to become President of the Fifth Republic, and the equally famous Red Army commander Mikhail Tukhachevsky (1893–1937), who was murdered in Stalin's purge of the Soviet military in the late 1930s. However, an important clue in explaining their later success is that neither of these men had been typical prisoners: both had belonged to the small minority of die-hard escapees among the officers in German captivity, and both had ended up being imprisoned in the high-security Bavarian military fortress at Ingolstadt.[37]

By contrast, Britain, Germany and the USA had a more benevolent attitude towards their subjects in captivity. All three countries organised relief and food parcels for their prisoners in enemy countries, and after repatriation they received them, by and large, with open arms and minds. The USA, it has to be admitted, was much less concerned about issues of loyalty and patriotism in 1918 than it was to become in subsequent years. It was only after the Second World War, during the conflicts in Korea and Vietnam, that signs of distrust appeared from the United States' authorities towards Americans taken prisoners by the communist enemy. The American leadership developed doubts about the political loyalty of their compatriots, who were supposedly subjected to 'brainwashing' techniques while in North Korean or Vietnamese captivity. Such doubts were of course hidden from the American public, and have only recently become the object of research by contemporary historians. Since the end of the Second World War, however, the problem of prisoner loyalty has concerned the USA as a universal political and omnipresent military power. Here too there are some interesting parallels with the multi-ethnic empires of the First World War.

The way in which returnees from captivity were treated and received in their home countries therefore tells us a lot about the different war cultures which emerged in the belligerent nations of the First World War. Another area which requires further study – and which unfortunately cannot be discussed in detail here – is the contribution of repatriated prisoners themselves to the process of cultural demobilisation after the war. Suffice it to say that associations of former POWs – like veterans' associations in general – were organised on national lines, and there is little evidence of any communication across borders and frontiers. For this and other reasons it proved impossible to establish any international consensus on the pressing issue of how well or how badly prisoners had been treated during their time in enemy captivity.[38]

Conclusion

Repatriation on all the fronts of the Great War was shaped by a number of different internal and external factors, including issues of time and place. Two elements that were absent on the western front had a crucial impact on the eastern front. Firstly, in Tsarist Russia the overwhelming majority of POWs were categorised along ethnic criteria, and this was highly significant in determining their experience of captivity. It was the first time in modern history that such a selection of POWs was carried out, and on such a large scale. From the beginning of 1918 the POWs in Bolshevik-controlled Russia were again categorised, but this time according to ideological and social, rather than ethnic criteria. Moreover, now they were exposed to attempts at political indoctrination which were not wholly unsuccessful. Given the chaotic situation within Russia, stricken with civil war and political terror, the Bolshevik leadership saw in the foreign POWs it had inherited not subjects of international law, but rather tools of the coming world revolution, a revolution which took precedence over any humanitarian considerations. This in turn explains why some of the German and Austrian prisoners held on the eastern front were among the last POWs of the Great War to be repatriated.

Historiography in both the East and West has previously ignored these prisoners, just as it has failed to take into account over 200,000 former

POWs on both sides of the eastern front who for political or personal reasons preferred to stay in the detaining country. Many of the latter were unwilling to return to their homes in what had become new states following the redrawing of national frontiers. Others had married local women. The 90,000 Russians who stayed behind in the successor states of the Habsburg Monarchy and in Germany probably accounted for the majority of such *Bleiber* (remainees). By contrast, the number of former Central Powers' captives who remained in Soviet Russia after the civil war is unknown. By default, they went into the calculation of losses and missed personnel of Germany and Austria, for instance in the statistics produced by the Austrian researchers Leopold Kern and Hans Weiland in their 1931 study. This in turn brought the apparent death rate in Russian captivity to 40%, or 600,000 men, a figure which is definitely too high.[39]

In France, too, there were many deaths in captivity, particularly among the retained POWs after the armistice who were forced to spend a period of over one year in miserable conditions. Here it was not so much difficult external circumstances, for instance food shortages or civil war that account for the ruthless exploitation of POWs. Nor can French policy here be explained as a deliberate decision to renounce international treaties for the sake of military advantage in the sense meant by the German Chancellor Bethmann Hollweg in 1914 when he famously said that 'Not kennt kein Gebot' (necessity knows no law).[40] None of these reasons can account for the French decision to send the POWs into the devastated war zone, where in addition they were exposed to an embittered, revengeful population which had returned impoverished from years of exile in unoccupied France. In fact, the reconstruction work which had to be done in the former war zone could easily have been organised in a more humane and more efficient way, even with the use of POW labour. In November 1918 France of all the detaining powers broke with the liberal tradition of captivity typical of the West; admittedly the other Allied countries had not been faced with the devastation of their territory on the same scale or over the same length of time, with the partial exception of Italy.

In fact it was the American historian Richard B. Speed who first explored some of these issues relating to captivity and repatriation on a comparative international level.[41] He divided the treatment of First World War POWs into three main patterns of behaviour: the 'liberal', the 'illiberal' and the 'radical'. By this classification he rightly characterises the ethnic selection of Habsburg prisoners in Russian captivity as a complete and radical break with the past. The POW policy of France, particularly after 1918, is seen as 'illiberal'. Britain and America, by contrast, remained 'liberal'.

Continuing with this analysis, it was the aftermath of the Second World War, rather than the First, which saw the complete abandonment of the liberal tradition by the victorious powers, including the Anglo-Saxons. The absence of a formal peace treaty with Germany after 1945 allowed Britain and America as well as France to retain POWs, this time for up to three years after the end of hostilities. Germans in Soviet captivity were retained for even longer, in some cases until 1955. Here again POWs from the losing side were used as pawns and even as a direct means of putting pressure on politicians in the now divided Germany. Meanwhile, illiberal and radical patterns of captivity continued from the Second World War into the Cold War era.[42] Indeed, many of the 'proxy wars' fought between the superpowers from the 1950s to the 1980s ended without a clear victory for one side or the other, and therefore without official peace treaties to ensure the smooth return of prisoners. In historical terms, the French redefinition of the idea of the 'just war' in 1918 to allow retribution against a defeated and 'barbaric' enemy may therefore have marked the beginning of a breach with older European traditions whose consequences can still be felt in many of today's regional wars, and especially in the US-led war against terror.

With regard to repatriation after the Great War there are some issues that remain to be explored. Repatriation policies in the Balkan states and Turkey are largely unknown, as is the history of wartime captivity in these regions. All of these countries had post-war military conflicts with their neighbours, some of them lasting until 1922/23. Initial findings suggest that the governments of these new states were even less concerned to stick within the bounds of international law than their predecessors. A long and painful period of readjustment and reintegration was, however, the most common experience for all former POWs, whichever front they fought on. Returnees from Russia in particular were held under suspicion as witnesses or even participants in the Russian Revolution and the civil war. Some converted their experiences into works of fine art or belles-lettres, others rose to prominence as politicians and military leaders. The long-term consequences of First World War captivity for the period that followed, and in particular for the treatment of POWs during the Second World War and after, have only just begun to be researched.

Notes

[1] Overmans, 'Kriegsverluste', 663–6.

[2] For statistical data see Nachtigal, 'Zur Anzahl der Kriegsgefangenen im Ersten Weltkrieg'.

[3] In no other detaining power of the First World War was the position and experience of POWs so varied as in Russia. Thus Slav prisoners could be liberated

early from captivity. Volunteers in the Czech Legion served as a military police in the Ukraine during 1917/18. Others were drafted into national legions fighting the Central Powers. In this way they lost their legal status as POWs, and sometimes their lives. See Nachtigal, 'Privilegiensystem und Zwangsrekrutierung', 167–93.

[4] In particular this refers to Austria-Hungary where this phenomenon became increasingly relevant because of the huge number of returnees during 1918. See Leidinger and Moritz, 'Österreich-Ungarn und die Heimkehrer'; idem, 'Im Schatten der Revolution'; idem, 'Otto Bauer 1914–1919'; and idem, *Gefangenschaft, Revolution, Heimkehr*.

[5] For the most detailed studies of this issue see Plaschka, *Cattaro – Prag*; idem, *Avantgarde des Widerstands*; Plaschka, Haselsteiner and Suppan, *Innere Front*; Kreiner, 'Von Brest-Litowsk nach Kopenhagen'; Przybilovszki, 'Die Rückführung der österreichisch-ungarischen Kriegsgefangenen'; and Wassermair, 'Die Meutereien der Heimkehrer'. See also the publications listed in note 3 above.

[6] For rough figures see the studies cited in notes 4 and 5 above.

[7] Nachtigal, 'Die Repatriierung der Mittelmächte-Kriegsgefangenen', 248.

[8] Schwarz, 'Divided Attention', 103–22. See also Leidinger and Moritz, *Gefangenschaft, Revolution, Heimkehr*, 364.

[9] Leidinger and Moritz, *Gefangenschaft, Revolution, Heimkehr*, 463. This figure relates only to registered Austro-Hungarian returnees. For the total figure, non-registered ones would have to be added as well as about 100,000 Germans, Turks and Bulgarians. Altogether they made up some 1 million returnees from the East in November 1918.

[10] Leidinger and Moritz, *Gefangenschaft, Revolution, Heimkehr*, 344. Austria-Hungary's decision not to enforce the repatriation of its own subjects is a peculiarity in legal terms. Clearly it judged that it would not be in its interests to carry out an enforced repatriation of disloyal subjects held by the defeated detaining power. However, this did not carry any broader implications because of the general chaos on both sides of the former eastern front, and because in October 1918 the Dual Monarchy ceased to exist as a state.

[11] See Nachtigal, 'Die Repatriierung der Mittelmächte-Kriegsgefangenen', 259; and Montandon, *Im Schmelztiegel des Fernen Ostens*. Central Europeans returning from Russia in 1920/21 (Germans, Austrians, Hungarians, Slavs) were usually repatriated by the International Committee of the Red Cross and the League of Nations High Commissioner for Refugees, the Norwegian Polar explorer Fridtjof Nansen. The same institutions cared for the repatriation for some 250,000 Russians still left in central Europe. See R. Cramer, 'Rapatriement des prisonniers'; and L. Cramer, 'L'achèvement du rapatriement général'.

[12] Conquest, *The Great Terror*, 69 and 402–3.

[13] For narratives of war captivity in Russia and the conclusions or experiences of former POWs see, for example, Liebold, '"In allem zurück, weit zurück ..."'. The issue of how the German writer and former POW Edwin Erich Dwinger dealt with his wartime experiences is examined by Wurzer, 'Das Schicksal der deutschen Kriegsgefangenen', 363–84. Dwinger's 'Russian trilogy' is not a personal real-life account. Rather it is written in the form of belles-lettres enriched by fiction, as Wurzer emphasises here and in other of his studies.

This does not necessarily mean that Dwinger wrote purely invented stories; rather he seemed to have 'borrowed' them from tales he heard from other former POWs.

[14] See here Rachamimov, '"Female Generals" and "Siberian Angels"', 23–46. Also Nachtigal, *Russland und seine österreichisch-ungarischen Kriegsgefangenen*, 108–41. On the *Reichsvereinigung ehemaliger Kriegsgefangener* see Pöppinghege, '"Kriegsteilnehmer zweiter Klasse"?'.

[15] Pardon and Shurawljow, *Lager, Front oder Heimat*, vol. 1, 14.

[16] See the latest studies by Oltmer, 'Repatriierungspolitik', 267–294; and idem, 'Unentbehrliche Arbeitskräfte', 67–96.

[17] Schlesinger, *Erinnerungen eines Aussenseiters*, 51, gives practical, legal, humanitarian and political motives for this policy. Many Russian returnees had already been forced into misery and destitution, the more so as Soviet relief organisations were either unwilling or unable to care for their compatriots during and after their return. See also the details in Hinz, *Gefangen im Großen Krieg*, 335.

[18] Leidinger and Moritz, *Gefangenschaft, Revolution, Heimkehr*, 561.

[19] Moritz and Leidinger, *Zwischen Nutzen und Bedrohung*, 290.

[20] For further details see Leidinger and Moritz, *Gefangenschaft, Revolution, Heimkehr*, 453.

[21] Leidinger and Moritz, 'Der Weg zur Anerkennung'.

[22] According to Hinz, *Gefangen im Großen Krieg*, 346, about 30,000 former Russian POWs remained in Germany with official permission, and another 40,000 to 50,000 stayed on illegally.

[23] Agreements were also reached between the Central Powers and Russia, as we have seen. Indeed, on the eastern front the number of exchanges increased considerably during the second half of 1917. Yet on the other fronts in Europe, and especially on the western front, progress towards implementation was much slower. See Speed, *The Diplomacy of Captivity*, 34 and 48. Also the contributions of Heather Jones and Matthew Stibbe to this volume.

[24] Hinz, *Gefangen im Großen Krieg*, 330. See also Jones, 'The Enemy Disarmed', 310, who emphasises that the French – and at an early stage the British – were also concerned to screen returning POWs due to fears about Spanish Fever spreading in 1918. This epidemic was indeed at first ascribed to particularly bad treatment of POWs in Germany.

[25] Delpal, 'Zwischen Vergeltung und Humanisierung der Lebensverhältnisse', 147–64.

[26] Jones, 'The Enemy Disarmed', 357. See also the discussion in Delpal, 'Zwischen Vergeltung und Humanisierung der Lebensverhältnisse'; and Nachtigal, 'Zur Anzahl der Kriegsgefangenen im Ersten Weltkrieg'.

[27] Jones, 'The Enemy Disarmed'. See also Nachtigal, 'Loyalität gegenüber dem Staat'.

[28] Jones, 'The Enemy Disarmed', 352 and 362.

[29] On Italian POWs see Procacci, 'Les causes de la forte mortalité', 125–35; idem, 'Fahnenflüchtige jenseits der Alpen', 194–215; and Kramer, 'Italienische Kriegsgefangene', 247–58.

[30] MacMillan, *Paris 1919*, 247 and 290–2. See also Afflerbach, '"... nearly a case of Italy contra mundum?"', 159–73.

[31] Jones, 'The Enemy Disarmed', is partly impressed by the French historical research following this view.

[32] See Abbal, 'Die französische Gesellschaft der Zwischenkriegszeit', 295–308 and Jones, 'The Enemy Disarmed', 399–411. According to Jones, this inevitably encouraged former French POWs to present their captivity in Germany as particular hard and brutal, especially when addressing domestic audiences.

[33] This deep-seated view, which disguised and concealed the real problems in the Russian hinterland from the beginning of the war, is uncritically revived in a recent Russian study – see Ikonnikova, *Voyennoplennye Pervoi mirovoi voiny na Dalnem Vostoke Rossii*.

[34] Further evidence of this is expected to be produced in a forthcoming study by Oksana Nagornaya (South-Ural State University, Tchelyabinsk) on Russian POWs in Germany.

[35] See Moritz and Leidinger, *Zwischen Nutzen und Bedrohung*, 317; and Nikonova, '"Der Kult des Heldenmutes ist für den Sieg notwendig"', 185–99.

[36] See the study by Oksana Nagornaya mentioned in note 35 above.

[37] For further details see Treffer, *Die ehrenwerten Ausbrecher*. Another prominent POW who actually succeeded in escaping was the Russian general Lavr Kornilov, who got out of Austria via Romania (still neutral at that point). He played a certain role in the early stages of the Russian civil war in southern Russia, where he was killed. Like de Gaulle and Tukhachevsky, he was a hyper-patriot. See Moritz and Leidinger, *Zwischen Nutzen und Bedrohung*, 157.

[38] For a broader discussion see Jones, 'The Enemy Disarmed', 382–443.

[39] See Kern, 'Kriegsgefangene und Zivilinternierte in den wichtigsten kriegführenden Staaten', statistical appendix, and the critical discussion in Nachtigal, 'Zur Anzahl der Kriegsgefangenen im Ersten Weltkrieg'. For a similar analysis of death rates among POWs on the western front see also Jones, 'The Enemy Disarmed', 4.

[40] Bethmann Hollweg used this phrase when announcing the German invasion of Belgium in his Reichstag speech on 4 August 1914. See Kramer, 'Kriegsrecht und Kriegsverbrechen', 282.

[41] Speed, *Prisoners, Diplomats, and the Great War*, 1, 61 and 169. For Russia see also the studies by Davis, 'Deutsche Kriegsgefangene im Ersten Weltkrieg'; and idem, 'The Life of Prisoners of War in Russia 1914–1921', 163–96.

[42] Very useful here are the entries in Vance, *Encyclopedia of Prisoners of War and Internment*, especially on 'Forcible Repatriation', 137–9; 'The Korean War', 226–8; and 'The Vietnam War', 421–3.

LIST OF REFERENCES

References

Abbal, Odon. *Soldats oubliés: Les prisonniers de guerre français.* Bez-et-Esparon, 2001.

———. 'Die französische Gesellschaft der Zwischenkriegszeit und die ehemaligen Kriegsgefangenen'. In *Kriegsgefangene im Europa des Ersten Weltkriegs,* ed. Jochen Oltmer. Paderborn, 2006.

Afflerbach, Holger. '"... nearly a case of Italy contra mundum?": Italien als Siegermacht in Versailles 1919'. In *Versailles 1919: Ziele – Wirkung – Wahrnehmung,* ed. Gerd Krumeich with Silke Fehlemann. Essen, 2001.

Ageron, Charles-Robert, and Charles-André Julien. *Histoire de l' Algérie contemporaine.* Paris, 1964–79.

———. *Les Algériens musulmans et la France, 1871–1919.* 2 vols. Paris, 1968.

———. 'Clemenceau et la question coloniale'. In *Clemenceau et la justice: Actes du colloque de décembre 1979 organisé pour le cinquentenaire de la mort de G. Clemenceau.* Paris, 1983.

Anderson, Ross. *The Forgotten Front: The East African Campaign, 1914–1918.* Stroud, 2004.

Applebaum, Anne. *Gulag: A History of the Soviet Camps.* London, 2003.

Arendt, Hannah. *The Origins of Totalitarianism.* New ed. New York, 1973.

Asiwaju, A.I. 'Migration as Revolt: The Example of the Ivory Coast and the Upper Volta before 1945'. *Journal of African History* 27 (1976): 577–94.

Audoin-Rouzeau, Stéphane. *La guerre des enfants (1914–1918).* Paris, 1993.

———. 'Kinder und Jugendliche'. In *Enzyklopädie Erster Weltkrieg,* ed. Gerhard Hirschfeld, Gerd Krumeich, and Irina Renz. Paderborn, 2004.

Audoin-Rouzeau, Stéphane, and Annette Becker. *La Grande Guerre, 1914–1918.* Paris, 1998.

———. *1914–1918: Understanding the Great War.* London, 2002.

Auswärtiges Amt [German Foreign Office]. *Völkerrechtswidrige Verwendung farbiger Truppen auf dem europäischen Kriegsschauplatz durch England und Frankreich*. Berlin, 1915.

———. *Employment, Contrary to International Law, of Coloured Troops upon the European Theatre of War by England and France*. Berlin, 1915 [English translation of the above].

Baer, E.H., ed. *Der Völkerkrieg: Eine Chronik der Ereignisse seit dem 1. Juli 1914*. 18 vols. Stuttgart, 1914–1918.

Bailey, Gordon W. 'Dry Run for the Hangman: The Versailles-Leipzig Fiasco, 1919–1921: Feeble Foreshadow of Nuremberg'. Ph.D diss., University of Maryland, 1971.

Balesi, Charles John. *From Adversaries to Comrades-in-Arms: West Africans and the French Military, 1885–1918*. Waltham, 1979.

Banskota, Purushottam. *The Gurkha Connection. A History of the Gurkha Recruitment in the British Indian Army*. New Delhi, 1994.

Barbusse, Henri. *Le Feu: Journal d'une escouade*. Paris, 1916.

Barkey, Karen, and Mark von Hagen, eds. *After Empire. Multi-Ethnic Societies and Nation-Building: The Soviet Union and the Russian, Ottoman and Habsburg Empires*. Boulder, CO, 1997.

Baron, N.P. and Peter Gatrell. 'Population Displacement, State-Building and Social Identity in the Lands of the Former Russian Empire, 1917–1923'. *Kritika: Explorations in Russian and Eurasian History* 4, no. 1 (2003): 51–100.

———. eds. *Homelands: War, Population and Statehood in Eastern Europe and Russia, 1918-1924*. London, 2004.

Baron, Salo. *The Russian Jew under Tsars and Soviets*. New York, 1964.

Barrows, Leland Conley. 'L'influence des conquêtes algériennes et coloniales sur l'armée française (1830–1919)'. *Le Mois en Afrique* 192, no. 3 (1981–82): 97–127.

Bartov, Omer. *Murder in our Midst: The Holocaust, Industrial Killing and Representation*. Oxford, 1996.

Bass, Gary Jonathan. *Stay the Hand of Vengeance: The Politics of War Crimes Tribunals*. Princeton, NJ, 2000.

Becker, Annette. *War and Faith: The Religious Imagination in France, 1914–1930*. Oxford, 1998.

———. *Oubliés de la grande guerre: Humanitaire et culture de guerre: Populations occupées, déportés civils, prisonniers de guerre*. Paris, 1998.

———. 'Charles de Gaulle, Prisonnier'. In *De Gaulle soldat 1914–1918*, ed. Alain Lebougre and Véronique Harel. Paris, 1999.

————. 'Religion'. In *Enzyklopädie Erster Weltkrieg*, ed. Gerhard Hirschfeld, Gerd Krumeich, and Irina Renz. Paderborn, 2004.

Becker, Jean-Jacques. *Les Français dans la Grande Guerre*. Paris, 1980.

Beckett, Ian Frederick William. 'The Nation in Arms, 1914–1918'. In *A Nation in Arms: A Social Study of the British Army in the First World War*, ed. Ian Beckett and Keith Simpson. Manchester, 1985.

Bédier, Joseph. *Les Crimes Allemands d'après des Témoignages Allemands*. Paris, 1915.

Bekraoui, Mohamed. 'Les soldats marocains dans la bataille de Verdun'. *Guerres Mondiales et Conflits Contemporains* 46 (1982): 39–44.

Belfield, Herbert. 'The Treatment of Prisoners of War'. *Transactions of the Grotius Society* 9 (1923): 139–40.

Belius, Hans. *Die farbigen Hilfsvölker der Engländer und Franzosen*. Berlin, 1915.

Benamrane, D. *L'émigration algérienne en France*. Algiers, 1983.

Bernard, Augustin. *L'Afrique du Nord pendant la guerre*. Paris, 1926.

Besson, Maurice and Pierre Perreau-Pradier. *L'Effort Colonial des Alliés*. Nancy, Paris and Strasbourg, 1919.

Best, Geoffrey. *Humanity in Warfare: The Modern History of International Law of Armed Conflicts*. London, 1980.

Bezhenets, Editorial, 2, 18 October 1915.

Bianchi, Bruna, ed. *La violenza contro la popolazione civile nella grande guerra: Deportati, profughi, internati*. Milan, 2006.

————. 'I civili: vittime innocenti o bersagli legittimi?' In Bianchi, *La violenza contro la popolazione civile*.

Bideleux, Robert, and Ian Jeffries. *The Balkans: A Post-Communist History*. London, 2007.

Bidwell, Robin. *Morocco under Colonial Rule: French Administration of Tribal Areas, 1912–1956*. London, 1973.

Blackbourn, David. 'Das Kaiserreich transnational. Eine Skizze'. In *Das Kaiserreich transnational: Deutschland in der Welt, 1871-1914*, ed. Sebastian Conrad and Jürgen Osterhammel. Göttingen, 2004.

Bloxham, Donald. *The Great Game of Genocide: Imperialism, Nationalism and the Destruction of the Ottoman Armenians*. Oxford, 2005.

Bluntschli, Johann Caspar. *Das moderne Völkerrecht der civilisirten Staaten als Rechtsbuch dargestellt*. 2nd ed. Nördlingen, 1872.

Boelcke, Willi A., ed. *Kriegspropaganda 1939–1941: Geheime Ministerkonferenzen im Reichspropagandaministerium*. Stuttgart, 1966.

Bolt, David. *Gurkhas*. London, 1967.

Borchardt, Rudolf. 'Der Krieg und die deutsche Selbsteinkehr. Rede, öffentlich gehalten am 5. September 1914 in Heidelberg'. In idem, *Gesammelte Werke in Einzelbänden: Prosa V.* Stuttgart, 1979.

Borck, Karin and Lothar Kölm, eds. *Gefangen in Sibirien. Tagebuch eines ostpreußischen Mädchens 1914-1920.* Osnabrück, 2001.

Bourke, Joanna. *An Intimate History of Killing: Face-to-Face Killing in Twentieth-Century Warfare.* London, 1999.

Boussenot, Georges. *La France d'outre-mer participe à la guerre.* Paris, 1916.

Bradley, Keith. 'The 1914–18 Campaign'. In *The Story of the Northern Rhodesia Regiment,* ed. W. V. Brelsford. Lusaka, 1954.

Bramwell, Anna C., ed. *Refugees in the Age of Total War.* London, 1988.

Brown, James Scott, ed. *The Hague Conventions and Declarations of 1899 and 1907* Washington, DC and Oxford, 1915.

Bryce, James. *Report of the Committee on Alleged German Outrages.* London, 1915.

Buhrer, Jules. *L'Afrique orientale allemande et la guerre de 1914–1918.* Paris, 1922.

Buitenhuis, Peter. *The Great War of Words: Literature as Propaganda 1914–18 and After.* Vancouver, 1987.

Burdick, Charles, and Ursula Moessner. *The German Prisoners-of-War in Japan, 1914–1920.* Lanham and London, 1984.

Burleigh, Michael. Sacred Causes. *Religion and Politics from the European Dictators to Al Qaeda.* London, 2006.

———. *Blood and Rage: A Cultural History of Terrorism.* London, 2008.

Buscher, Frank M. *The US-War Crimes Trial Program in Germany, 1946–1955.* New York, 1989.

Cahalan, Peter. *Belgian Refugee Relief in England during the Great War.* New York, 1982.

Cahen-Salvador, Georges. *Les Prisonniers de Guerre (1914–1919).* Paris, 1929.

Caine, Hall, ed. *King Albert's Book.* London, 1914.

Carnegie Endowment for International Peace. *Report of the International Commission to Inquire into the Causes and Conduct of the Balkan Wars.* Washington, DC, 1914.

Carrington, C.E.H. 'The Empire at War'. In The Empire-Commonwealth, 1870–1919, ed. Ernest A. Benians, vol. 3 of *Cambridge History of the British Empire.* Cambridge, 1959.

Caucanas, Sylvie, Rémy Cazals, and Pascal Payen, eds. *Les prisonniers de guerre dans l'histoire: Contacts entre peuples et cultures* Toulouse, 2003.

Cecil, Hugh, and Peter H. Liddle, eds. *Facing Armageddon. The First World War Experienced.* London, 1996.

Cecotti, Franco. 'Internamenti di civili durante la prima guerra mondiale. Friuli austriaco, Istria e Trieste'. In *'Un esilio che non ha pari' 1914–1918: Profughi, internati ed emigranti di Trieste, dell'Isontino e dell'Istria*, ed. Franco Cecotti. Gorizia, 2001.

Cesarani, David, and Tony Kushner, eds. *The Internment of Aliens in Twentieth Century Britain*. London, 1993.

Chen, Ta. *Chinese Migrations, with Special Reference to Labor Conditions*. Washington, DC, 1923.

Cherniavsky, M., ed. *Prologue to Revolution*. Englewood Cliffs, NJ, 1967.

Chernovich, S. 'Problemy "novoi charty"', Evreiskaia zhizn', 15, 11 October 1915.

Chickering, Roger. *The Great War and Urban Life in Germany: Freiburg, 1914–1918*. Cambridge, 2007.

Christie, Agatha. *An Autobiography*. London, 1977.

Clarke, Peter Bentley. *West Africans at War, 1914–18/1939–45: Colonial Propaganda and its Cultural Aftermath*. London, 1986.

Cochet, François. *Soldats sans armes: La captivité de guerre: une approche culturelle*. Brussels, 1998.

Cohen-Portheim, Paul. *Time Stood Still: My Internment in England, 1914–1918*. London, 1931.

Connes, Georges. *A POW's Memoir of the First World War: The Other Ordeal*. Trans. Marie-Claire Connes Wrages. Oxford, 2004.

Conot, Robert E. *Justice at Nuremberg*. London, 1983.

Conquest, Robert. *The Great Terror. A Reassessment*. New ed. London, 1990.

Cornevin, Robert. *La République populaire du Benin des origines Dahoméens à nos jours*. Paris, 1981.

Cornwall, Mark. *The Undermining of Austria-Hungary: The Battle for Hearts and Minds*. Basingstoke, 2000.

Cousturier, Lucie. *Des Inconnus chez moi: Tirailleurs Sénégalais*. Paris, 1920.

Cramer, Lucien. 'L'achèvement du rapatriement général des prisonniers de guerre par le Comité international de la Croix-Rouge'. *Revue internationale de la Croix-Rouge* 4, no. 1 (1922): 383–7.

Cramer, Renée M. 'Rapatriement des prisonniers de guerre centraux en Russie et en Sibérie et des prisonniers de guerre russes en Allemagne'. *Revue internationale de la Croix-Rouge* 2, no. 1 (1920): 526–56.

Crowder, Michael. 'The 1914–1918 European War and West Africa'. In *History of West Africa*, ed. Michael Crowder and Jacob Festus Ade Ajayi. 2 vols. London, 1974.

———. 'Blaise Diagne and the Recruitment of African Troops for the 1914–1918 War'. In idem, *Colonial West Africa. Collected Essays*. London, 1978.

Dadrian, Vahakn N. *The History of the Armenian Genocide: Ethnic Conflict from the Balkans to Anatolia to the Caucasus*. 4th ed. Providence, 2003.

D'Almeida-Topor, Hélène. 'Les populations dahoméens et le recrutement militaire pendant la première guerre mondiale'. *Revue française d'histoire d'outre-mer* 60 (1973): 196–241.

D'Anthouard, Baron. *Les Prisonniers Allemands au Maroc*. Paris, 1917.

D'Arcy, Fergus. *Remembering the War Dead: British Commonwealth and International War Graves in Ireland since 1914*. Dublin, 2007.

Davenport, Timothy R.H. 'The South African Rebellion, 1914'. *English Historical Review* 78 (1963): 73–94.

Davis, George H. 'Deutsche Kriegsgefangene im Ersten Weltkrieg in Russland'. *Militärgeschichtliche Mitteilungen* 31 (1982): 27–49.

———. 'The Life of Prisoners of War in Russia 1914–1921'. In *Essays on World War I: Origins and Prisoners of War*, ed. Samuel R. Williamson and Peter Pastor. New York, 1983.

———. 'National Red Cross Societies and Prisoners of War in Russia, 1914–1918'. *Journal of Contemporary History* 28 (1993): 31–52.

De Coquet, James. *Nous sommes les occupants*. Paris, 1945.

Delafosse, Louise. *Maurice Delafosse, le Berrichon conquis par l'Afrique*. Paris, 1976.

de Jastrzebski, T. 'The register of Belgian refugees', *Journal of the Royal Statistical Society*, 79 (1916): 133–58.

De Lapradelle, Albert, ed. *Responsabilités des Auteurs de la Guerre et Sanctions*. Vol. 3, *La Paix de Versailles*. Paris, 1930.

Delpal, Bernard. 'Zwischen Vergeltung und Humanisierung der Lebensverhältnisse. Kriegsgefangene in Frankreich 1914–1920'. In *Kriegsgefangene im Europa des Ersten Weltkriegs*, ed. Jochen Oltmer. Paderborn, 2006.

Deppe, Ludwig. *Mit Lettow-Vorbeck durch Afrika*. Berlin, 1919.

De Rivières, Edmond Seré. *Histoire du Niger*. Paris, 1965.

Deroo, Eric, and Antoine Champeaux. *La Force Noire: Gloire et infortune d'une légende coloniale*. Paris, 2006.

De Roodt, Evelyn. *Oorlogsgasten. Vluchtelingen en krijgsgevangenen in Nederland tijdens de Eerste Wereldoorlog*. Zaltbommel, 2000.

De Schaepdrijver, Sophie. *De groote oorlog: Het koninkrijk België tijdens de Eerste Wereldoorlog*. Amsterdam, 1997.

Diallo, Bakary. *Force-Bonté*. Paris, 1926.

Diamond, Hanna. *Fleeing Hitler: France 1940*. Oxford, 2007.

Di Giovanni, Janine. *Madness Visible: A Memoir of War*. London, 2004.

Djurović, Gradimir. *L'Agence Centrale de Recherches du Comité International de la Croix-Rouge: Activité du CICR en vue du soulagement des souffrances morales des victimes de guerre.* Geneva, 1981.

Doegen, Wilhelm. *Kriegsgefangene Völker: Der Kriegsgefangenen Haltung und Schicksal in Deutschland, herausgegeben im amtlichen Auftrage des Reichswehrministeriums.* Berlin, 1921.

———. ed. *Unter fremden Völkern: Eine neue Völkerkunde.* Berlin, 1925.

Dunn, Seamus, and T. G. Fraser, eds. *Europe and Ethnicity: World War I and Contemporary Ethnic Conflict.* London, 1996.

Duomg, Van Giao. *L'Indochine pendant la Guerre de 1914–1918: Contribution à l'étude de la colonisation indochinoise.* Paris, 1925.

Durand, André. *From Sarajevo to Hiroshima: History of the International Committee of the Red Cross.* Geneva, 1984.

Echenberg, Myron Joël. 'Paying the Blood Tax: Military Conscription in French West Africa 1914–1929'. *Canadian Journal of African Studies* 9 (1975): 171–92.

———. 'Les Migrations militaires en Afrique Occidentale Française, 1900–1945'. *Canadian Journal of African Studies* 14 (1980): 429–50.

———. *Colonial Conscripts: The Tirailleurs Sénégalais in French West Africa, 1857–1960.* Portsmouth, 1991.

Eisterer, Klaus, and Rolf Steininger, eds. *Tirol und der Erste Weltkrieg.* Innsbruck, 1995.

Elkins, Caroline. *Britain's Gulag: The Brutal End of Empire in Kenya.* London, 2005.

Ellinwood, DeWitt Clinton, and Satyendra Dev Pradham, eds. *India and World War 1.* New Delhi, 1978.

———. 'Ethnicity in a Colonial Asian Army: British Policy, War and the Indian Army, 1914–1918'. In *Ethnicity and the Military in Asia*, ed. DeWitt Clinton Ellinwood and Cynthia Holden Enloe. New Brunswick and London, 1981.

Ermacora, Matteo. 'Assistance and Surveillance: War Refugees in Italy, 1914–1918'. *Contemporary European History* 16, no. 4 (2007): 445–60.

Evans, Andrew D. 'Capturing Race: Anthropology and Photography in German and Austrian prisoner-of-war camps during World War I'. In *Colonialist Photography: Imagining Race and Place*, ed. Eleanor M. Hight and Gary D. Simpson. London, 2002.

Evans, Suzanne. *Mothers of Heroes, Mothers of Martyrs: World War I and the Politics of Grief.* Montreal, 2007.

Farcy, Jean-Claude. *Les camps de concentration français de la première guerre mondiale, 1914–1920.* Paris, 1995.

Farwell, Byron. *The Gurkhas*. London, 1984.

———. *Armies of the Raj: From the Mutiny to Independence, 1858–1947*. London, 1990.

Favez, Jean-Claude. *The Red Cross and the Holocaust*. Trans. and ed. John and Beryl Fletcher. Cambridge, 1999.

Fellner, Fritz, ed. *Schicksalsjahre Österreichs, 1908–1919: Das politische Tagebuch Josef Redlichs*. 2 vols. Vienna, 1953–54.

Ferguson, Niall. *The Pity of War*. London, 1998.

———. 'Prisoner Taking and Prisoner Killing in the Age of Total War: Towards a Political Economy of Military Defeat'. *War in History* 11, no. 2 (2004): 134–78.

———. *The War of the World: History's Age of Hatred*. London, 2006.

Fogarty, Richard. *Race and War in France: Colonial Subjects in the French Army, 1914–1918*. Baltimore, 2008.

Föllmer, Moritz. 'Der Feind im Salon: Eliten, Besatzung und nationale Identität in Nordfrankreich und Westdeutschland 1914-1930'. *Militärgeschichtliche Zeitschrift* 61, no. 1 (2002): 1–24.

Foltz, David A. 'The War Crimes Issue at the Paris Peace Conference, 1919–1920'. PhD diss., College of Arts and Sciences of the American University, Washington, DC, 1978.

Fournier, L. *Historique du 2ᵉ Régiment de Tirailleurs Sénégalais 1892–1933*. Paris, 1934.

Frerk, Willy. *Kriegsgefangen in Nordafrika. Aus dem Tagebuche des deutschen Gardegrenadiers Eduard von Rohden: Ein Dokument französischer Schmach*. Siegen, 1917.

Fry, Ruth. *A Quaker Adventure: The Story of Nine Years' Relief and Reconstruction*. London, 1926.

Fryer, C.E.J. *The Destruction of Serbia in 1915*. New York, 1997.

Gaillet, Léon. *Coulibaly: Les Sénégalais sur la terre de France*. Paris, 1917.

Gainer, Bernard. *The Alien Invasion: The Origins of the Aliens Act of 1905*. London, 1972.

Garcia, Luc. 'Les mouvements de résistance au Dahomey (1914–1917)'. *Cahiers d'Etudes Africaines* 10 (1970): 144–78.

Gardner, Brian. *German East: The Story of the First World War in East Africa*. London, 1963.

Garson, Noël G. 'South Africa and World War I'. *Journal of Imperial and Commonwealth History* 8 (1979): 68–85.

Gärtner, August. 'Einrichtung und Hygiene der Kriegsgefangenenlager'. In *Handbuch der Ärztlichen Erfahrungen im Weltkriege 1914/18*, Band VII, ed. Wilhelm Hoffmann. Leipzig, 1922.

Gatrell, Peter. *A Whole Empire Walking: Refugees in Russia during World War I*. Bloomington, 1999.

———. *Russia's First World War: A Social and Economic History*. Harlow, 2005.

———. 'Introduction: World Wars and Population Displacement in Europe in the Twentieth Century', special guest-editor Peter Gatrell, *Contemporary European History* 16, no. 4 (2007): 415–26.

———. 'War after the War: Conflicts 1919-1923'. In *Blackwell Companion to the First World War*, ed. John Horne. London, forthcoming.

Gatrell, Peter, and Jo Laycock. 'Armenia: the 'nationalisation', internationalisation and representation of the refugee crisis'. In *Homelands: War, Population and Statehood in Eastern Europe and Russia, 1918-1924*, ed. Nick Baron and Peter Gatrell. London, 2004.

German Army Supreme Command. *Kriegsgefangene, 1914/18: Auf Grund der Kriegsakten bearbeitet beim Oberkommando der Wehrmacht*. Berlin, 1939.

German General Staff, ed. *Kriegsbrauch im Landkriege*. Berlin, 1902.

German Reichstag. *Verhandlungen des Reichstages: Stenographische Berichte. Berlin, 1871–1939*.

———. *Völkerrecht im Weltkrieg: Dritte Reihe im Werk des Untersuchungsausschusses der Verfassunggebenden Deutschen Nationalversammlung und des Deutschen Reichstages 1919–1928*. 4 vols. Berlin, 1927.

Gertjejanssen, Wendy Jo. 'Sexual Violence'. In *Encyclopedia of Prisoners of War and Internment*, ed. Jonathan F. Vance. 2nd ed. Millerton, NY, 2006.

Gervereau, Laurent. 'De bien trop noirs desseins'. In *'Tirailleurs sénégalais': Zur bildlichen und literarischen Darstellung afrikanischer Soldaten im Dienste Frankreichs*, ed. Jànos Riesz and Joachim Schultz. Frankfurt am Main, 1989.

Gerwarth, Robert. 'The Central European Counterrevolution: Paramilitary Violence in Germany, Austria and Hungary after the Great War'. *Past and Present* 200, no. 1 (2008): 175–209.

Gilbert, Adrian. *POW: Allied Prisoners in Europe, 1939-1945*. London, 2007.

Gilbert, Martin. *The First World War*. London, 1994.

Gill, Rebecca. 'Calculating Compassion in War: The "New Humanitarian" Ethos in Britain, 1870-1918'. PhD diss., University of Manchester, 2005.

Ginsburgs, George, and Vladimir N. Kudriavtsev. *The Nuremberg Trial and International Law*. Dordrecht, 1990.

Glenny, Misha. *The Balkans, 1804-1999: Nationalism, War and the Great Powers*. London, 1999.

Glinga, Werner. 'Ein koloniales Paradoxon. Blaise Diagne und die Rekrutierungsmission 1918'. In *'Tirailleurs sénégalais': Zur bildlichen und literarischen Darstellung afrikanischer Soldaten im Dienste Frankreichs*, ed. Jànos Riesz and Joachim Schultz. Frankfurt am Main, 1989.

Gnankambary, Blamy. 'La révolte bobo de 1916 dans le cercle du Dedougou'. *Notes et Documents voltaïques* 3 (1970): 56–87.

Goldstein, Daniel. *Libération ou annexion aux chemins croisés de l'histoire tunisienne (1914–1922)*. Tunis, 1978.

Golos Rossii, 5, 3 April 1916.

Gourko, B. *Memories and Impressions of War and Revolution*. London, 1918.

Gouvernement Belge. *La Violation du Droit des Gens en Belgique*. Paris, 1915.

Grandhomme, Jean-Noël. 'Internment Camps for German Civilians in Finistère, France, 1914–1919.' *The Historian* 68, no. 12 (2006): 792–811.

Greenhut, Jeffrey. 'The Imperial Reserve. The Indian Corps on the Western Front, 1914–15'. *Journal of Imperial and Commonwealth History* 12 (1983): 54–73.

Greenstein, Lewis J. 'The Impact of Military Service in World War I on Africans: The Nandi of Kenya'. *Journal of Modern African Studies* 16 (1978): 495–507.

Grove, Eric J. 'The First Shots of the Great War: The Anglo-French Conquest of Togo, 1914'. *The Army Quarterly and Defence Journal* 106 (1976): 308–23.

Grundy, Kenneth William. *Soldiers without Politics: Blacks in the South African Armed Forces*. Berkeley, CA, 1983.

Haller, Oswald. 'Das Internierungslager Katzenau bei Linz. Die Internierung und Konfinierung der italienischsprachigen Zivilbevölkerung des Trentinos zur Zeit des Ersten Weltkrieges'. Masters diss., University of Vienna, 1999.

Hanák, Peter. 'Die Volksmeinung während des letzten Kriegsjahres in Österreich-Ungarn'. In *Die Auflösung des Habsburgerreiches. Zusammenbruch und Neuorientierung im Donauraum*, ed. Richard Georg Plaschka and Karlheinz Mack. Vienna, 1970.

Hankel, Gerd. *Die Leipziger Prozesse: Deutsche Kriegsverbrechen und ihre strafrechtliche Verfolgung nach dem Ersten Weltkrieg*. Hamburg, 2003.

Hanna, Marta. *The Mobilization of Intellect: French Scholars and Writers during the Great War*. Cambridge, MA, 1996.

Haste, Cate. *Keep the Home Fires Burning: Propaganda in the First World War*. London, 1977.

Healy, Maureen. *Vienna and the Fall of the Habsburg Empire: Total War and Everyday Life in World War I*. Cambridge, 2004.

Hebert, Jean. 'Révoltes en Haute Volta de 1914 à 1918'. *Notes et Documents voltaïques* 3 (1970): 3–54.

Herbert, Ulrich. *A History of Foreign Labor in Germany, 1880-1980: Seasonal Workers/Forced Laborers/ Guest Workers*. Ann Arbor, MI, 1990.

Hiery, Hermann Joseph, *The Neglected War: The German South Pacific and the Influence of World War I*. Honolulu, 1995.

Hill, Robert A., ed. *The Marcus Garvey and Universal Negro Improvement Association Papers*, vol 9 of *Africa for the Africans*, 1921–1922. Berkeley, Los Angeles and London, 1995.

Hinz, Uta. 'Die deutschen "Barbaren" sind doch die besseren Menschen. Kriegsgefangenschaft und gefangene "Feinde" in der Darstellung der deutschen Publizistik, 1914–1918'. In *In der Hand des Feindes: Kriegsgefangenschaft von der Antike bis zum Zweiten Weltkrieg*, ed. Rüdiger Overmans. Cologne, 1999.

———. 'Internierung'. In *Enzyklopädie Erster Weltkrieg*, ed. Gerhard Hirschfeld, Gerd Krumeich and Irina Renz. Paderborn, 2004.

———. 'Kriegsgefangene'. In *Enzyklopädie Erster Weltkrieg*.

———. 'Zwangsarbeit'. In *Enzyklopädie Erster Weltkrieg*.

———. *Gefangen im Großen Krieg: Kriegsgefangenschaft in Deutschland 1914–1921*. Essen, 2006.

———. 'Humanität im Krieg? Internationales Rotes Kreuz und Kriegsgefangenenhilfe im Ersten Weltkrieg'. In *Kriegsgefangene im Europa des Ersten Weltkriegs*, ed. Jochen Oltmer. Paderborn, 2006.

Historial de la Grande Guerre, Péronne. 'Démobilisations culturelles après la Grande Guerre'. Special issue guest editor John Horne *14–18 Aujourd'hui, Today, Heute*, 5 (2002).

History of the 5th Royal Gurkha Rifles (Frontier Force), 1858 to 1928. Aldershot, 1930.

Hobsbawm, Eric. *Globalisation, Democracy and Terrorism*. London, 2007.

Hodges, Geoffrey W.T. 'African Manpower Statistics for the British Forces in East Africa'. *Journal of African History* 19 (1978): 101–16.

———. The Carrier Corps. *Military Labour in the East African Campaign of 1914 to 1918*. Westport, CT, 1986.

Hoffmann-Holter, Beatrix. 'Abreisendmachung'. *Jüdische Kriegsflüchtlinge in Wien 1914 bis 1923*. Vienna, 1995.

Holland, Thomas Erskine. *Letters to the 'The Times' upon War and Neutrality (1881-1920)*. 3rd ed. London, 1921.

Holquist, Peter. *Making War, Forging Revolution: Russia's Continuum of Crisis, 1914–1921*. Cambridge, MA and London, 2002.

Hong, Young-Sun. 'World War I and the German Welfare State: Gender, Religion and the Paradoxes of Modernity'. In *Society, Culture and the State in Germany, 1870-1930*, ed. Geoff Eley. Ann Arbor, MI, 1996.

Honig, Jan Willem, and Norbert Both. *Srebrenica. Record of a War Crime*. London, 1996.

Höpp, Gerhard. *Muslime in der Mark. Als Kriegsgefangene und Internierte in Wünsdorf und Zossen, 1914–1924*. Berlin, 1997.

Horne, Alistair. *The Price of Glory: Verdun 1916*. London, 1962.

Horne, John, and Alan Kramer. 'German "Atrocities" and Franco-German Opinion, 1914: The Evidence of German Soldiers' Diaries'. *Journal of Modern History* 66 (1994): 1–33.

———. 'War between Soldiers and Enemy Civilians, 1914–1915'. In *Great War – Total War: Combat and Mobilization on the Western Front, 1914–1918*, ed. Roger Chickering and Stig Förster. Cambridge, 2000.

———. *German Atrocities 1914: A History of Denial*. New Haven, CT and London, 2001.

Huebner, Todd. 'The Internment Camp at Terezín, 1919'. *Austrian History Yearbook* 27 (1996): 199–211.

Hull, Isabel. *Absolute Destruction. Military Culture and the Practices of War in Imperial Germany*. Ithaca, 2005.

Ikonnikova, Tat'iana. *Voennoplennye pervoi mirovoi voiny na Dal'nem Vostoke Rossii (1914–1918 gg.)*. Khabarovsk, 2004.

Iliffe, John. *A Modern History of Tanganyika*. London, 1979.

Inglis, Brian. *Roger Casement*. London, 1973.

International Committee of the Red Cross. *Rapport general du Comité International de la Croix-Rouge sur son activité de 1912 à 1920*. Geneva, 1921.

Jahr, Christoph. 'Zivilisten als Kriegsgefangene. Die Internierung von "Feindstaaten-Ausländern" in Deutschland während des Ersten Weltkrieges am Beispiel des "Engländerlagers Ruhleben".' In *In der Hand des Feindes: Kriegsgefangenschaft von der Antike bis zum Zweiten Weltkrieg*, ed. Rüdiger Overmans. Cologne. 1999.

———. 'Keine Feriengäste: "Feindstaatenausländer" im südlichen Bayern während des Ersten Weltkrieges'. In *Der Erste Weltkrieg im Alpenraum. Erfahrung, Deutung, Erinnerung/La Grande Guerra nell' arco alpino: Esperienze e memoria*, ed. Hermann J. W. Kuprian and Oswald Überegger. Innsbruck, 2006.

Jeismann, Michael, 'Propaganda'. In *Enzyklopädie Erster Weltkrieg*, ed. Gerhard Hirschfeld, Gerd Krumeich and Irina Renz. Paderborn, 2004.

Johnson, R.W. and Anne Summers. 'World War I. Conscription and Social Change in Guinea'. *Journal of African History* 19 (1978): 25–38.

Jones, Heather. 'Encountering the "Enemy": Prisoner of War Transport and the Development of War Cultures in 1914'. In *Warfare and Belligerence: Perspectives in First World War Studies*, ed. Pierre Purseigle. Leiden, 2005.

———. 'The Enemy Disarmed: Prisoners of War and the Violence of Wartime: Britain, France and Germany, 1914–1920'. PhD diss., Trinity College, Dublin, 2005.

———. 'The Final Logic of Sacrifice? Violence in German Prisoner of War Labour Companies in 1918'. *The Historian* 68, no. 4 (2006): 770–91.

———. 'The German Spring Reprisals of 1917: Prisoners of War and the Violence of the Western Front'. *German History* 26, no. 3 (2008): 335–56.

Kahleyss, Margot. *Muslime in Brandenburg – Kriegsgefangene im Ersten Weltkrieg. Ansichten und Absichten*. Berlin, 1998.

Kamian, Bakari. *Des tranchées de Verdun à l'église Saint–Bernard: 80'000 combattants maliens au secours de la France (1914–18 et 1939–45)*. Paris, 2001.

Katzenellenbogen, Simon E. 'Southern Africa and the War of 1914–1918'. In *War and Society: Historical essays in Honour and Memory of J. R. Western 1928–1971*, ed. M.R.D. Foot. London, 1973.

Kaul, Friedrich Karl. 'Die Verfolgung deutscher Kriegsverbrecher nach dem Ersten Weltkrieg'. *Zeitschrift für Geschichtswissenschaft* 14 (1966): 19–32.

Kazanskii, P.E. *Galitsko-russkie bezhentsy v Odesse v 1915-1916g*. Odessa, 1916.

Keegan, John. *The First World War*. London, 1998.

Kennan, George F. *The Decline of Bismarck's European Order: Franco-Russian Relations, 1875–1890*. Princeton, NJ, 1979.

Kern, Leopold. 'Kriegsgefangene und Zivilinternierte in den wichtigsten kriegführenden Staaten' (appendix). In *In Feindeshand. Die Gefangenschaft im Weltkriege in Einzeldarstellungen*, ed. Hans Weiland and Leopold Kern. 2 vols. Vienna, 1931.

Kershaw, Ian. *Hitler, 1889-1936*. Vol. 1, *Hubris*. London, 2001.

Ketchum, John Davidson. *Ruhleben: A Prison Camp Society*. Toronto, 1965.

Kettlitz, Eberhardt. *Afrikanische Soldaten aus deutscher Sicht seit 1871: Stereotype, Vorurteile, Feindbilder und Rassismus*. Frankfurt am Main, 2007.

Killingray, David. 'The Idea of a British Imperial African Army'. *Journal of African History* 20 (1979): 421–36.

King, Jeremy. *Budweisers into Czechs and Germans: A Local History of Bohemian Politics, 1848-1948*. Princeton, NJ, 2002.

Koestler, Arthur. *The Scum of the Earth*. London, 1941.

Koller, Christian. 'Überkreuzende Frontlinien? Fremdrepräsentationen in afrikanischen, indischen und europäischen Selbstzeugnissen des Ersten Weltkrieges'. *War and Literature* 6 (2000): 33–57.

——. *'Von Wilden aller Rassen niedergemetzelt': Die Diskussion um die Verwendung von Kolonialtruppen in Europa zwischen Rassismus, Kolonial– und Militärpolitik (1914–1930)*. Stuttgart, 2001.

——. 'Enemy Images: Race and Gender Stereotypes in the Discussion on Colonial Troops – A Franco-German Comparison, 1914–1923'. In *Home/Front. The Military, War and Gender in Twentieth-Century Germany*, ed. Karen Hagemann and Stefanie Schüler–Springorum. Oxford, 2002.

——. '"Pourquoi pleurer pour des fils ingrats?" Erinnerungen westafrikanischer Soldaten des Ersten Weltkriegs'. *Arbeitskreis Militärgeschichte Newsletter* 19 (2003): 15–20.

——. 'Krieg, Fremdheitserfahrung und Männlichkeit: Alterität und Identität in Feldpostbriefen indischer Soldaten des Ersten Weltkrieges'. In *Erfahrung – Alles nur Diskurs? Zur Verwendung des Erfahrungsbegriffes in der Geschlechtergeschichte*, ed. Marguérite Bos Bettina Vincenz and Tanja Wirz Zurich, 2004.

——. 'Die 'Schwarze Schmach' – afrikanische Besatzungssoldaten und Rassismus in den zwanziger Jahren'. In *AfrikanerInnen in Deutschland und schwarze Deutsche – Geschichte und Gegenwart*, ed. Marianne Bechhaus-Gerst and Reinhard Klein–Arendt. Münster, 2004.

——. 'Representing Otherness. African, Indian, and European Soldiers' Letters and Memoirs'. In *Race, Empire and First World War Writing*, ed. Santanu Das. Cambridge, forthcoming.

Kopelman, Elizabeth. 'Ideology and International Law: The Dissent of the Indian Justice at the Tokyo War Crimes Trial'. *New York University Journal of International Law and Politics* 23 (1991): 373–444.

Koskenniemi, Martti. *The Gentle Civiliser of Nations: The Rise and Fall of International Law 1870-1960*. Cambridge, 2002.

Kotek, Joël, and Pierre Rigoulot. *Das Jahrhundert der Lager. Gefangenschaft, Zwangsarbeit, Vernichtung*. Berlin, 2001. Originally published as *Le siècle des camps: détention, concentration, extermination*. (Paris, 2000).

Kouandété, Maurice Iropa. *Un aspect de l'insurrection nationaliste au Dahomey*. Cotonou, 1971.

Kramer, Alan. '*Wackes* at War: Alsace-Lorraine and the Failure of German National Mobilization, 1914–1918'. In *State, Society and Mobilization in Europe during the First World War*, ed. John Horne. Cambridge, 1997.

——. 'Kriegsrecht und Kriegsverbrechen'. In *Enzyklopädie Erster Weltkrieg*, ed. Gerhard Hirschfeld, Gerd Krumeich and Irina Renz. Paderborn, 2004.

————. 'Besatzung (Westen)'. In Hirschfeld, Krumeich and Renz, *Enzyklopädie Erster Weltkrieg.*

————. 'Deportationen'. In Hirschfeld, Krumeich and Renz, *Enzyklopädie Erster Weltkrieg.*

————. 'Italienische Kriegsgefangene im Ersten Weltkrieg'. In *Der Erste Weltkrieg im Alpenraum: Erfahrung, Deutung, Erinnerung/La Grande Guerra nell'arco alpino: Esperienze e memoria*, ed. Hermann J. W. Kuprian and Oswald Überegger. Innsbruck, 2006.

————. *Dynamic of Destruction: Culture and Mass Killing in the First World War.* Oxford, 2007.

Krebs, Gerhard. 'Die etwas andere Kriegsgefangenschaft. Die Kämpfer von Tsingtau in japanischen Lagern 1914–1920'. In *In der Hand des Feindes: Kriegsgefangenschaft von der Antike bis zum Zweiten Weltkrieg*, ed. Rüdiger Overmans. Cologne, 1999.

Krech, Hans. *Die Kampfhandlungen in den ehemaligen deutschen Kolonien in Afrika während des 1. Weltkrieges (1914–1918).* Berlin, 1999.

Kreiner, Judith. 'Von Brest-Litowsk nach Kopenhagen: Die österreichischen Kriegsgefangenen in Russland im und nach dem Ersten Weltkrieg unter besonderer Berücksichtigung der Kriegsgefangenenmissionen in Russland'. Masters diss., University of Vienna, 1996.

Kruse, Wolfgang, ed. *Eine Welt von Feinden: Der große Krieg.* Frankfurt am Main, 1997.

Kuprian, Hermann J.W. '"Frontdienst redivivus im XX. Jahrhundert!" Arbeitszwang am Beispiel von Flucht, Vertreibung und Internierung in Österreich während des Ersten Weltkrieges'. *Geschichte und Region/storia e regione* 12, no. 1 (2003): 15–38.

Kuprian, Hermann J.W., and Oswald Überegger, eds., *Der Erste Weltkrieg im Alpenraum: Erfahrung, Deutung, Erinnerung /La Grande Guerra nell'arco alpino: Esperienze e memoria.* Innsbruck, 2006.

Kushner, Tony. 'Local Heroes: Belgian Refugees in Britain during the First World War'. *Immigrants & Minorities* 18, no. 1 (1999): 1–28.

Kushner, Tony, and Katharine Knox. *Refugees in an Age of Genocide: Global, National and Local Perspectives during the Twentieth Century.* London, 1999.

Latter, E. 'The Indian Army in Mesopotamia, 1914–18'. *Journal of the Society for Army Historical Research* 72 (1994): 92–246.

Lebzelter, Gisela. 'Die "Schwarze Schmach": Vorurteile – Propaganda – Mythos'. *Geschichte und Gesellschaft* 11 (1985): 37–58.

Leidinger, Hannes, and Verena Moritz. 'Im Schatten der Revolution: Die Heimkehrer aus russischer Kriegsgefangenschaft nach dem Ende des Ersten Weltkrieges'. *Wiener Geschichtsblätter* 51, no. 4 (1996): 229–64.

―――. 'Österreich-Ungarn und die Heimkehrer aus russischer Kriegsgefangenschaft im Jahr 1918'. *Österreich in Geschichte und Literatur* 41, no. 6 (1997): 385–403.

―――. 'Otto Bauer 1914–1919: Kriegsgefangenschaft und Heimkehr als Problem einer Biographie'. *Wiener Geschichtsblätter*, 54, no. 1 (1999): 1–21.

―――. *Gefangenschaft, Revolution, Heimkehr: Die Bedeutung der Kriegsgefangenenproblematik für die Geschichte des Kommunismus in Mittel- und Osteuropa 1917–1920.* Vienna, Cologne and Weimar, 2003.

―――. 'Der Weg zur Anerkennung: Die Beziehungen zwischen Wien und Moskau 1918–1924'. *Österreichische Osthefte* 46 (2004): 361–89.

―――. 'Verwaltete Massen: Kriegsgefangene in der Donaumonarchie, 1914–1918'. In *Kriegsgefangene im Europa des Ersten Weltkriegs*, ed. Jochen Oltmer. Paderborn, 2006.

Lejri, Mohammed-Salah. *L'histoire du mouvement national*, vol 1 of *Évolution du mouvement national des origines à la deuxième guerre mondiale.* Tunis, 1974.

Levene, Mark. 'Frontiers of Genocide: Jews in the Eastern War Zones, 1914-20 and 1941'. In *Minorities in Wartime: National and Racial Groupings in Europe, North America and Australia During the Two World Wars*, ed. Panikos Panayi. Oxford, 1993.

Levie, Howard S. 'War Crimes'. In *Encyclopedia of Peace, Violence and Conflict*, ed. Lester Kurtz and Jennifer Turpin, vol 3 of P_o-Z. San Diego, 1999.

Liebold, Jan, '"In allem zurück, weit zurück . . .": Russlandbilder deutscher Kriegsgefangener im Ersten Weltkrieg: Ihre Darstellung und Veränderung in der Erinnerungsliteratur 1916–1939'. Masters diss., Humboldt University Berlin, 2006.

Liulevicius, Vejas Gabriel. *War Land on the Eastern Front: Culture Identity, and German Occupation in World War I.* Cambridge, 2000.

―――. 'Besatzung (Osten)'. In *Enzyklopädie Erster Weltkrieg*, ed. Gerhard Hirschfeld, Gerd Krumeich and Irina Renz. Paderborn, 2004.

Lohr, Eric. *Nationalizing the Russian Empire: The Campaign Against Enemy Aliens during World War I.* Cambridge, MA, 2003.

Lombard, Jacques. *Structures de type féodal en Afrique Noire: Etude des dynamismes internes et des relations sociales chez les Bariba du Dahomey.* Paris, 1965.

Long, P.W. *Other Ranks of Kut.* London, 1938.

Loth, Heinrich. *Geschichte Afrikas: Von den Anfängen bis zur Gegenwart*, vol 2 of *Afrika unter imperialistischer Kolonialherrshaft und Formierung der antikolonialen Kräfte 1884–1945.* East Berlin, 1976.

Lucassen, Leo. 'The Great War and the Origins of Migration Control in Western Europe and the United States (1880-1920)'. In *Regulation of Migration. International Experiences*, ed. Anita Böcker, Kees Groenendijk, Tetty Havinga and Paul Minderhoud. Amsterdam, 1998.

Lunn, Joe Harris. 'Kande Kamara Speaks: An Oral History of the West African Experience in France 1914–18'. In *Africa and the First World War*, ed. Melvin E. Page. London, 1987.

———. *Memoirs of the Maelstrom. A Senegalese Oral History of the First World War*. Portsmouth, Oxford and Cape Town, 1999.

———. "Les Races Guerrières': Racial Preconceptions in the French Military about West African Soldiers during the First World War'. *Journal of Contemporary History* 34 (1999): 517–36.

Lüsebrink, Hans-Jürgen. "'Tirailleurs Sénégalais" und "Schwarze Schande": Verlaufsformen und Konsequenzen einer deutsch–französischen Auseinandersetzung'. In *'Tirailleurs sénégalais': Zur bildlichen und literarischen Darstellung afrikanischer Soldaten im Dienste Frankreichs*, ed. Jànos Riesz and Joachim Schultz. Frankfurt am Main, 1989.

MacKenzie, S.P. *The Colditz Myth. British and Commonwealth Prisoners of War in Nazi Germany*. Oxford, 2004.

———. 'The Ethics of Escape: British Officer POWs in the First World War'. *War in History* 15, no. 1 (2008): 1–16.

MacMillan, Margaret. *Paris 1919: Six Months that Changed the World*. New York, 2003.

MacMunn, George F. *The Martial Races of India*. London, 1933.

McCormack, Timothy L.H. 'From Sun Tzu to Sixth Committee: The Evolution of an International Criminal Law Regime'. In *The Law of War Crimes: National and International Approaches*, ed. Timothy L. H. McCormack and Gerry J. Simpson. The Hague, 1997.

McPhail, Helen. *The Long Silence. Civilian Life under the German Occupation of Northern France, 1914–1918*. London, 1999.

Madley, Benjamin. 'From Africa to Auschwitz: How German South West Africa Incubated Ideas and Methods Adopted and Developed by the Nazis in Eastern Europe.' *European History Quaterly* 35, no.3 (2005): 429-64.

Maglen, Krista. 'Importing Trachoma: The Introduction into Britain of American Ideas of an "Immigrant Disease", 1892–1906'. *Immigrants & Minorities* 23, no. 1 (2005): 80–99.

Mahrenholz, Jürgen-K. 'Zum Lautarchiv und seiner wissenschaftlichen Erschliessung durch die Datenbank IMAGO'. In *Berichte aus dem ICTM-Nationalkomitee Deutschland, Band XII, Bericht über die*

Jahrestagung des Nationalkomitees der Bundesrepublik Deutschland im International Council for Traditional Music [Unesco] am 08. und 09. März 2002 in Köln, ed. Marianne Bröcker. Bamberg, 2002.

Malkki, Liisa. *Purity and Exile: Violence, Memory, and National Cosmology among Hutu Refugees in Tanzania*. Chicago, 1995.

Mangin, Charles Marie Emmanuel. *La Force Noire*. Paris, 1911.

———. *Lettres de Guerre, 1914–1918*. Paris, 1950.

Margueritte, Paul. *L'immense effort, 1915–1916*. Paris, 1916.

Marks, Sally. 'Black Watch on the Rhine: A Study in Propaganda, Prejudice and Prurience'. *European Studies Review* 13 (1983): 297–333.

Marrus, Michael R. *The Unwanted: European Refugees in the Twentieth Century*. New ed. Philadelphia, PA, 2003.

Martin, Gregory. 'German and French Perceptions of the French North and West African Contingents, 1910–1918'. *Militärgeschichtliche Mitteilungen* 56 (1997): 31–68.

Mason, Philip A. *A Matter of Honour: An Account of the Indian Army, its Officers and Men*. London, 1974.

Mayer, L. 'Die Flüchtlingsfürsorge'. In *Die Wiederaufbau Preussens*, ed. Erich Göttgen. Königsberg, 1928.

Mayerhofer, Lisa. 'Making Friends and Foes: Occupiers and Occupied in First World War Romania (1916-1918)'. Unpublished paper presented at the third conference of the International Society for First World War Studies, Trinity College, Dublin, September 23–25, 2005.

———. 'Making Friends and Foes: Occupiers and Occupied in First World War Romania, 1916–1918'. In *Untold War: New Perspectives in First World War Studies*, eds Heather Jones, Jennifer O'Brien and Christopher Schmidt-Supprian. Leiden: 2008 (Published version of the paper mentioned above).

Mazohl-Wallnig, Brigitte, and Marco Meriggi, eds. *Österreichisches Italien – Italienisches Österreich? Interkulturelle Gemeinsamkeiten und nationale Differenzen vom 18. Jahrhundert bis zum Ende des Ersten Weltkrieges*. Vienna, 1999.

Mazower, Mark. *The Balkans*. London, 2000.

———. *Hitler's Empire. Nazi Rule in Occupied Europe*. London, 2008.

Melzer, Annabelle. '"The Mise–en–Scène" of the "Tirailleurs Sénégalais" on the Western Front, 1914–1920'. In *Borderlines. Genders and Identities in War and Peace, 1870–1930*, ed. Billie Melman. New York, 1998.

Mentzel, Walter. 'Weltkriegsflüchtlinge in Cisleithanien 1914–1918'. In *Asylland wider Willen: Flüchtlinge in Österreich im europäischen*

Kontext seit 1914, ed. Gernot Heiss and Oliver Rathkolb. Vienna, 1995.

Mercier, Paul. *Tradition, changement, histoire: Les 'Somba' du Dahomey septentrional.* Paris, 1968.

Merewether, C.I.E., and Frederick Smith. *The Indian Corps in France.* London, 1917.

Meurer, Christian. *Die völkerrechtliche Stellung der vom Feind besetzten Gebiete.* Tübingen, 1915.

Meynier, Gilbert. *L'Algérie révélée: La guerre de 1914–1918 et le premier quart du XXe siècle.* Geneva, 1981.

Meynier, Gilbert, and Jacques Thobie. *Histoire de le France Coloniale.* Paris, 1991.

Michalka, Wolfgang, ed. *Der Erste Weltkrieg: Wirkung, Wahrnehmung, Analyse.* Munich, 1994.

Michel, Marc. 'La genèse du recrutement de 1918 en Afrique noire française'. *Revue française d'histoire d'outre-mer* 58 (1971): 433–50.

———. 'Le recrutement des tirailleurs en A.O.F. pendant la première guerre mondiale'. *Revue française d'histoire d'outre-mer* 60 (1973): 645–60.

———. *L'appel à l'Afrique: Contributions et réactions à l'effort de guerre en A. O. F.* Paris, 1982.

———. '"Intoxication ou brutalisation". Les représailles de la grande guerre'. *14-18. Aujourd'hui, Today, Heute* 4 (2001): 175–97.

Michels, Stefanie. 'Askari – treu bis in den Tod? Vom Umgang der Deutschen mit ihren schwarzen Soldaten'. In *AfrikanerInnen in Deutschland und schwarze Deutsche – Geschichte und Gegenwart*, ed. Marianne Bechhaus-Gerst and Reinhard Klein-Arendt. Münster, 2004.

Midiohouan, Guy Ossito. 'Le tirailleur sénégalais du fusil à la plume: La fortune de "Force-Bonté" de Bakary Diallo'. In *'Tirailleurs sénégalais': Zur bildlichen und literarischen Darstellung afrikanischer Soldaten im Dienste Frankreichs*, ed. Jànos Riesz and Joachim Schultz. Frankfurt am Main, 1989.

Miller, Charles. *Battle for the Bundu: The First World War in East Africa.* London, 1974.

Minear, Richard. *Victors Justice: The Tokyo War Crimes Trial.* Princeton, NJ, 1971.

Mitrany, David. *The Effect of the War in South-Eastern Europe.* New Haven, CT, 1936.

Mitrović, Andrej. *Serbia's Great War, 1914–1918.* London, 2007.

Mollo, Boris. *The Indian Army.* Poole, 1981.

Mommsen, Wolfgang J., ed. *Kultur und Krieg: Die Rolle der Intellektuellen, Künstler und Schriftsteller im Ersten Weltkrieg.* Munich, 1996.

————. 'Die europäischen Intellektuellen, Schriftsteller und Künstler und der Erste Weltkrieg'. In *Bürgerliche Kultur und politische Ordnung: Künstler, Schriftsteller und Intellektuelle in der deutschen Geschichte 1830-1933*, ed. Wolfgang J. Mommsen. Frankfurt am Main, 2000.

Montandon, George. *Im Schmelztiegel des Fernen Ostens: Geschichte der sibirischen Mission des Internationalen Komitees vom Roten Kreuze zu Gunsten der österreichischen und ungarischen Kriegsgefangenen (Mai 1919 bis Juni 1921)*. Vienna, 1923.

Morgan, John Hartman. *German Atrocities: An Official Investigation*. London, 1916.

Moritz, Verena (with Hannes Leidinger). *Zwischen Nutzen und Bedrohung: Die russischen Kriegsgefangenen in Österreich 1914–1921*. Bonn, 2005.

Mosse, George L. *Toward the Final Solution: A History of European Racism*. New York, 1978.

Müller, Herbert Landolin. *Islam, gihad ('Heiliger Krieg') und Deutsches Reich*. Frankfurt am Main, 1991.

Müller, Kai. 'Oktroyierte Verliererjustiz nach dem Ersten Weltkrieg'. *Archiv des Völkerrechts* 39 (2001): 202–22.

Müller-Meiningen, Ernst. *Der Weltkrieg und das Völkerrecht: Eine Anklage gegen die Kriegführung des Dreibundes*. 2nd ed. Berlin, 1915.

Mullins, Claud. *The Leipzig Trials: An Account of the War Criminals' Trial and a Study of German Mentality*. London, 1921.

Mundro, J. Forbes, and Donald C. Savage. 'Carrier Corps Recruitment in the British East Africa Protectorate 1914–1918'. *Journal of African History* 7 (1966): 313–42.

Mundschütz, Reinhard. 'Internierung im Waldviertel. Die Internierungslager und – stationen der BH Waidhofen an der Thaya, 1914–1918'. PhD diss., University of Vienna, 2002.

Nachtigal, Reinhard. 'Seuchen unter militärischer Aufsicht in Rußland: Das Lager Tockoe als Beispiel für die Behandlung der Kriegsgefangenen 1915/16'. *Jahrbücher für Geschichte Osteuropas* 48 (2000): 363–87.

————. *Russland und seine österreichisch-ungarischen Kriegsgefangenen (1914–1918)*. Remshalden, 2003.

————. 'Seuchenbekämpfung als Probleme der russischen Staatsverwaltung: Prinz Alexander von Oldenburg und die Kriegsgefangenen der Mittelmächte'. *Medizinhistorisches Journal* 39 (2004): 135–63.

————. *Kriegsgefangenschaft an der Ostfront 1914 bis 1918: Literaturbericht zu einem neuen Forschungsfeld*. Frankfurt am Main, 2005.

————. 'Privilegiensystem und Zwangsrekrutierung: Russische Nationalitätenpolitik gegenüber Kriegsgefangenen aus Österreich-Ungarn'.

In *Kriegsgefangene im Europa des Ersten Weltkriegs*, ed. Jochen Oltmer. Paderborn, 2006.

———. 'Die Repatriierung der Mittelmächte-Kriegsgefangenen aus dem revolutionären Russland: Heimkehr zwischen Agitation, Bürgerkrieg und Intervention 1918-1922'. In Oltmer, *Kriegsgefangene im Europa*.

———. 'Loyalität gegenüber dem Staat oder zur Mère-Patrie? Die deutschen Kriegsgefangenen aus Elsaß-Lothringen in Rußland während des Ersten Weltkrieges'. *Zeitschrift für die Geschichte des Oberrheins* 154 (2006): 395–428.

———. 'Zur Anzahl der Kriegsgefangenen im Ersten Weltkrieg'. *Militärgeschichtliche Zeitschrift* 67 (forthcoming).

Nagler, Jörg. *Nationale Minoritäten im Krieg: 'Feindliche Ausländer' und die amerikanische Heimatfront während des Ersten Weltkrieges*. Hamburg, 2000.

Nagler, Jörg, and Stig Förster, eds. *On the Road to Total War: The American Civil War and the German Wars of Unification, 1861–1871*. Cambridge, 1997.

Nathans, Eli. *The Politics of Citizenship in Germany: Ethnicity, Utility and Nationalism*. Oxford, 2004.

Neave, Dorina L. *Remembering Kut: 'Lest we forget'*. London, 1938.

Nelipovich, S.G. 'V poiskakh "vnutrennogo vraga"'. In *Pervaia mirovaia voina*. Vol. 1 Moscow, 1994.

Nelson, Keith S. 'Black Horror on the Rhine. Race as a Factor in post–World War I Diplomacy'. *Journal of Modern History* 42 (1970): 606–27.

Nelson, Robert L. '"Ordinary Men" in the First World War? German Soldiers as Victims and Participants'. *Journal of Contemporary History*, 39, no. 3 (2004): 425–35.

Némirovsky, Irène. *Suite Française*. Trans. Sandra Smith. London. 2007.

Netesin, Iu. N. *Promyshlennyi kapital Latvii 1860-1917*. Riga, 1980.

Neutatz, Dietmar. *Die 'deutsche Frage' im Schwarzmeergebiet und in Wolhynien. Politik, Wirtschaft, Mentalitäten und Alltag im Spannungsfeld von Nationalismus und Modernisierung (1856–1914)*. Stuttgart, 1993.

Nikonova, Olga. '"Der Kult des Heldenmutes ist für den Sieg notwendig" – Sowjetisches Militär und Erfahrungen des Ersten Weltkrieges'. In *Kriegsniederlagen, Erfahrungen und Erinnerungen*, ed. Horst Carl, Hans-Henning Kortüm, Dieter Langewiesche and Friedrich Lenger. Berlin, 2004.

Nivet, Philippe. *Les réfugiés français de la grande guerre: Les 'Boches du Nord'*. Paris, 2004.

Nogaro, Bertrand, and Lucien Weil. *La main-d'œuvre étrangère et coloniale pendant la guerre*. Paris, 1926.

Oltmer, Jochen. *Bäuerliche Ökonomie und Arbeitskräftepolitik im Ersten Weltkrieg: Beschäftigungsstruktur, Arbeitsverhältnisse und Rekrutierung von Ersatzarbeitskräften in der Landwirtschaft des Emslandes, 1914–1918*. Emsland, Bentheim, 1995.

————. 'Zwangsmigration und Zwangsarbeit: Ausländische Arbeitskräfte und bäuerliche Ökonomie im Deutschland des Ersten Weltkriegs'. *Tel Aviver Jahrbuch für deutsche Geschichte* 27 (1998): 135–68.

————. 'Arbeitszwang und Zwangsarbeit – Kriegsgefangene und ausländische Zivilarbeitskräfte im Ersten Weltkrieg'. In *Der Tod als Maschinist: Der industrialisierte Krieg, 1914–1918*, ed. Rolf Spilker and Bernd Ulrich. Bramsche, 1998.

————. 'Schreckbild Migration? Ausländerbeschäftigung und Ausländerpolitik in Preußen-Deutschland vom späten 19. Jahrhundert bis zum Ende der Weimarer Republik'. In *Probleme der Migration und Integration im Preussenland vom Mittelalter bis zum Anfang des 20. Jahrhunderts*, ed. Klaus Militzer. Marburg, 2005.

————. ed. *Kriegsgefangene im Europa des Ersten Weltkriegs*. Paderborn, 2006.

————. 'Unentbehrliche Arbeitskräfte. Kriegsgefangene in Deutschland 1914–1918'. In Oltmer, *Kriegsgefangene im Europa*.

————. 'Repatriierungspolitik im Spannungsfeld von Antibolschewismus, Asylgewährung und Arbeitsmarktentwicklung: Kriegsgefangene in Deutschland 1918–1922'. In Oltmer, *Kriegsgefangene im Europa*.

Omissi, David. *The Sepoy and the Raj: The Indian Army, 1860–1940*. London, 1994.

————. ed. *Indian Voices of the Great War: Soldiers' Letters, 1914–18*. London, 1999.

————. 'Europe Through Indian Eyes: Indian Soldiers Encounter England and France, 1914–1918', *English Historical Review*, 122 (2007).

Opfer, Björn. *Im Schatten des Krieges: Besatzung oder Anschluss – Befreiung oder Unterdrückung? Eine komparative Untersuchung über die bulgarische Herrschaft in Vadar-Makedonien 1915–1918 und 1941–1944*. Münster, 2005.

Oppenheim, Lassa. *War and Neutrality*. Vol. 2, *International Law: A Treatise*. London, 1906.

Osherovskii, L.Ia. *Tragediia armian-bezhentsev*. Piatigorsk, 1915.

Osterhammel, Jürgen, and Niels P. Petersson. *Globalization: A Short History*. Princeton, NJ, 2005.

Otchet tsentral'nogo evreiskogo komiteta pomoshchi zhertvam voiny. Petrograd, 1918.

Overmans, Rüdiger. '"Hunnen" und "Untermenschen" – deutsche und russisch/sowjetische Kriegsgefangenschaftserfahrungen im Zeitalter der Weltkriege'. In *Erster Weltkrieg, Zweiter Weltkrieg: Ein Vergleich. Krieg, Kriegserlebnis, Kriegserfahrung in Deutschland*, ed. Bruno Thoß and Hans-Erich Volkmann. Paderborn, 2002.

———. 'Kriegsverluste'. In *Enzyklopädie Erster Weltkrieg*, ed. Gerhard Hirschfeld, Gerd Krumeich and Irina Renz. Paderborn, 2004.

Paget, Murial. *With Our Serbian Allies*. London, 1915.

Paice, Edward. *Tip and Run: The Untold Tragedy of the Great War in Africa*. London, 2007.

Paléologue, Maurice. *La Russie des Tsars pendant la grande guerre*. 3 vols. Paris, 1922.

Palla, Luciana. *Il Trentino orientale e la grande guerra: Combattenti, internati, profughi di Valsugana, Primiero e Tesino (1914–1920)*. Trento, 1994.

Panayi, Panikos. *The Enemy in Our Midst: Germans in Britain During the First World War*. Oxford, 1991.

———. 'Normalität hinter Stacheldraht: Kriegsgefangene in Großbritannien, 1914–1919'. In *Kriegsgefangene im Europa des Ersten Weltkriegs*, ed. Jochen Oltmer. Paderborn, 2006.

Pardon, Inge, and Waleri W. Shurawljow, eds. *Lager, Front oder Heimat: Deutsche Kriegsgefangene in Sowjetrussland 1917–1920*. Munich, 1994.

Passelecq, Fernand. *Les Déportations Belges à la Lumière des Documents Allemands*. Paris, 1917.

Pershing, John J. *My Experiences in the World War*. New York, 1931.

Petrovich, Michael Boro. *A History of Modern Serbia, 1804-1918*. 2 vols. London, 1976.

Pickles, Katie. *Transnational Outrage: The Death and Commemoration of Edith Cavell*. Basingstoke, 2007.

Pircher, Gerd. *Militär, Verwaltung und Politik in Tirol im Ersten Weltkrieg*. Innsbruck, 1995.

Plaschka, Richard G. *Cattaro – Prag. Revolte und Revolution*. Graz, 1963.

———. *Avantgarde des Widerstands: Modellfälle militärischer Auflehnung im 19. und 20. Jahrhundert*. 2 vols. Vienna, 2000.

Plaschka, Richard G., Horst Haselsteiner, and Arnold Suppan. *Innere Front, Militärassistenz, Widerstand und Umsturz in der Donaumonarchie 1918*. 2 vols. Vienna, 1974.

Polner, Tikhon. *Russian Local Government during the War and the Union of Zemstvos*. New Haven, CT, 1930.

Popik, Sergii. *Ukraintsi v Avstrii 1914–1918*. Kiev, 1999.

Pöppinghege, Rainer. "'Kriegsteilnehmer zweiter Klasse'? Die Reichsvereinigung ehemaliger Kriegsgefangener 1919-1933'. *Militärgeschichtliche Zeitschrift* 64 (2005): 391–423.

———. *Im Lager unbesiegt: Deutsche, englische und französische Kriegsgefangenen-Zeitungen im Ersten Weltkrieg.* Essen, 2006.

Pörzgen, Hermann. *Theater ohne Frau: das Bühnenleben der Kriegsgefangenen Deutschen, 1914–1920.* Königsberg, 1933.

Powell, Allan Kent. *Splinters of a Nation: German Prisoners of War in Utah.* Salt Lake City, 1989.

Pradhan, Satyendra Dev. 'The Indian Army and the First World War'. In *India and World War 1*, ed. DeWitt Clinton Ellinwood and Satyendra Dev Pradhan. New Delhi, 1978.

———. 'The Sikh Soldier in the First World War'. In Ellinwood and Pradhan, *India and World War 1*.

Procacci, Giovanna. *Soldati e prigionieri italiani nella grande guerra.* New ed. Turin, 2000.

———. 'Les causes de la forte mortalité des prisonniers de guerre italiens en Allemagne et en Autriche au cours des deux guerres mondiales'. In *Les prisonniers de guerre dans l'histoire: Contacts entre peuples et cultures*, ed. Sylvie Caucanas, Rémy Cazals and Pascal Payen. Toulouse, 2003.

———. 'Fahnenflüchtige jenseits der Alpen: Die italienischen Kriegsgefangenen in Österreich-Ungarn und Deutschland'. In *Kriegsgefangene im Europa des Ersten Weltkriegs*, ed. Jochen Oltmer. Paderborn, 2006.

Prusin, Alexander Victor. *Nationalizing a Borderland. War, Ethnicity and Anti-Jewish Violence in East Galicia, 1914–1920.* Tuscaloosa, 2005.

Przybilovszki, Inge. 'Die Rückführung der österreichisch-ungarischen Kriegsgefangenen aus dem Osten in den letzten Monaten der k.u.k. Monarchie'. PhD diss., University of Vienna, 1965.

Purseigle, Pierre. "'A Wave on to Our Shores": The Exile and Resettlement of Refugees from the Western Front, 1918-1918'. *Contemporary European History* 16, no. 4 (2007): 427–44.

———. 'A Very French Debate: The 1914–1918 "War Culture"'. *Journal of War and Cultural Studies*, 1, no. 1 (2008): 9–14.

Quataert, Jean H. 'Women's Wartime Services under the Cross: Patriotic Communities in Germany, 1912–1918'. In *Great War, Total War. Combat and Mobilization on the Western Front, 1914–1918*, ed. Roger Chickering and Stig Förster. Cambridge, 2000.

Rachamimov, Alon. *POWs and the Great War: Captivity on the Eastern Front.* Oxford, 2002.

————. 'Arbiters of Allegiance: Austro-Hungarian Censors during World War I'. In *Constructing Nationalities in East Central Europe*, ed. Pieter M. Judson and Marsha L. Rozenblit. Oxford, 2005.

————. '"Female Generals" and "Siberian Angels": Aristocratic Nurses and the Austro-Hungarian POW Relief'. In *Gender and War in Twentieth-Century Eastern Europe*, ed. Nancy M. Wingfield and Maria Bucur. Bloomington and Indianapolis, 2006.

————. 'The Disruptive Comforts of Drag: (Trans)Gender Performances among Prisoners of War in Russia, 1914–1920'. *American Historical Review*, 111, no. 2 (2006): 362–82.

Rapports des Délégués du gouvernement espagnol sur leurs visites dans les camps de prisonniers français en Allemagne, 1914-1917. Paris, 1917.

Rawe, Kai. '*Wir werden sie schon zur Arbeit bringen!' Ausländerbeschäftigung und Zwangsarbeit im Ruhrkohlenbergbau während des Ersten Weltkrieges*. Essen, 2005.

Ray, Joanny. *Les Marocains en France*. Paris, 1937.

Read, James Morgan. *Atrocity Propaganda 1914–1919*. Chicago, 1945.

Recham, Belkacem. *Les musulmans algériens dans l'armée française (1919–1945)*. Paris, 1996.

Rechter, David. 'Galicia in Vienna: Jewish Refugees in the First World War'. *Austrian History Yearbook* 28 (1997): 113–30.

————. *The Jews of Vienna and the First World War*. London, 2000.

RGVIA f. 2005, op. 1, d. 44, 11.

Riesenberger, Dieter. *Für Humanität in Krieg und Frieden: Das Internationale Rote Kreuz 1863-1977*. Göttingen, 1992.

Riesz, Jànos. 'The *Tirailleur Sénégalais* Who Did Not Want to Be a "Grand Enfant". Bakary Diallo's *Force Bonté* (1926) Reconsidered'. *Research in African Literatures* 27 (1996): 157–97.

————. 'Die Probe aufs Exempel: Eine afrikanische Autobiographie als Zivilisations–Experiment'. In *Identität und Moderne*, ed. Herbert Willems and Alois Hahn. Frankfurt am Main, 1999.

Robert, Tristan. 'Les prisonniers civils de la grande guerre: Le cas de la Picardie'. *Guerres mondiales et conflits contemporains*, 190 (1998): 61–78.

Rosen, Erwin. *England: Ein Britenspiegel. Schlaglichter aus der Kriegs-, Kultur- und Sittengeschichte*. Stuttgart, 1916.

Roshwald, Aviel, ed. *Ethnic Nationalism and the Fall of Empires: Central Europe, Russia and the Middle East, 1914-1923*. London, 2005.

Roth, Andreas. '"The German Soldier is not tactful": Sir Roger Casement and the Irish Brigade in Germany during the First World War'.

The Irish Sword: The Journal of the Military History Society of Ireland,
19, no. 78 (1995).

Rozenblit, Marsha L. 'For Fatherland and Jewish People. Jewish Women in
Austria During the First World War'. In *Authority, Identity and the
Social History of the Great War,* ed. Frans Coetzee and Marilyn
Shevin-Coetzee. Oxford, 1995.

———. *Reconstructing A National Identity: The Jews of Habsburg Austria
during World War I.* New York, 2001.

Ruf, Werner. 'Politische und ökonomische Ursachen und Folgen der
Migration am Beispiel Algerien'. In *Rassismus und Migration in
Europa: Beiträge des Kongresses 'Migration und Rassismus in Europa'.*
Hamburg, 1992.

Samson, Anne. *Britain, South Africa and the East Africa Campaign,
1914–1918: The Union Comes of Age.* London, 2006.

Sarraut, Albert. *La mise en valeur des colonies françaises.* Paris, 1923.

Scharnagl, Hermann. *Kurze Geschichte der Konzentrationslager.* Wiesbaden,
2004.

Scheck, Raffael. *Hitler's African Victims: The German Army Massacres of
Black French Soldiers in 1940.* Cambridge, 2006.

Schindler, Dietrich and Jirí Toman, eds. *The Laws of Armed Conflict:
A Collection of Conventions, Resolutions and Other Documents.*
Alphen aan den Rijn, 1981.

Schlesinger, Moritz. *Erinnerungen eines Aussenseiters im diplomatischen
Dienst.* Cologne, 1977.

Schoenberner, Gerhard and Mira Bihaly, eds. *House of the Wannsee
Conference. Permanent Exhibit, Guide and Reader* [English language
version]. Berlin, 2000.

Schor, Ralph. *Histoire de l'immigration en France de la fin du XIXe. siècle
à nos jours.* Paris, 1996.

Schulin, Ernst. 'Die Urkatastrophe des zwanzigsten Jahrhunderts'. In *Der Erste
Weltkrieg. Wirkung, Wahrnehmung, Analyse,* ed. Wolfgang Michalka.
Munich, 1994.

Schulze, Reinhard. *Die Rebellion der ägyptischen Fallahin, 1919.* West
Berlin, 1981.

Schütze, Woldemar. *Englands Blutschuld gegen die weiße Rasse.* Berlin,
1914.

Schwarz, Benjamin. 'Divided Attention: Britain's Perception of a Threat to
her Eastern Position in 1918'. *Journal of Contemporary History* 28,
no. 1 (1993): 103–22.

Schwengler, Walter. *Völkerrecht, Versailler Vertrag und Auslieferungsfrage: Die Strafverfolgung wegen Kriegsverbrechen als Problem des Friedenss-chlusses 1919/20.* Stuttgart, 1982.

Scott, Peter T. 'Captive Labour: The German Companies of the B.E.F., 1916-1920'. *The Army Quarterly and Defence Journal* 110, no. 3 (1980): 319–31.

Segesser, Daniel Marc. *Empire und Totaler Krieg: Australien 1905-1918.* Paderborn, 2002.

———. 'The International Debate on the Punishment of War Crimes During the Balkan Wars and the First World War'. *Peace & Change: Journal of Peace Research* 31 (2006): 533–54.

———. 'Die historischen Wurzeln des Begriffs "Verbrechen gegen die Menschlichkeit"'. *Jahrbuch der Juristischen Zeitgeschichte* 8 (2007): 75–101.

———. 'Dissolve or Punish? The International Debate amongst Jurists and Publicists on the Consequences of the Armenian Genocide for the Ottoman Empire, 1915-1923'. *Journal of Genocide Research* 10 (2008): 95–110.

———. '"Moralische Sanktionen reichen nicht aus!": Die Bemühungen um eine strafrechtliche Ahndung von Kriegsverbrechen auf nationaler und internationaler Ebene'. In *Kriegsgreuel: Die Entgrenzung der Gewalt in kriegerischen Konflikten vom Mittelalter bis ins 20. Jahrhundert*, ed. Sönke Neitzel and Daniel Hohrath. Paderborn, forthcoming.

———. *Recht statt Rache oder Rache durch Recht? Die internationale fachwissenschaftliche Debatte zur Frage der Ahndung von Kriegsver-brechen, 1872-1945.* Paderborn, forthcoming.

Sergeev, Evgenij. 'Kriegsgefangenschaft aus russischer Sicht: Russische Kriegsgefangene in Deutschland und im Habsburger Reich 1914–1918'. *Forum osteuropaische Ideen- und Zeitgeschichte* 1, no. 2 (1997): 113–34.

Siebrecht, Claudia. 'The Mater Dolorosa on the Battlefield – Mourning Mothers in German Women's Art of the First World War'. In *Untold War: New Perspectives in First World War Studies*, ed. Heather Jones, Jennifer O'Brien and Christoph Schmidt-Supprian. Leiden, 2008.

Silber, Laura, and Allan Little. *The Death of Yugoslavia.* London, 1995.

Simms, Brendan. *Unfinest Hour. Britain and the Destruction of Bosnia.* London, 2001.

Smart, Judith. '"Poor Little Belgium" and the Australian Popular Support for War 1914–1915'. *War and Society* 12 (1994): 31–7.

Smith, Bradley F. *The American Road to Nuremberg: The Documentary Record 1944-1945.* Stanford, CA, 1982.

Smith, Eric David. *Britain's Brigade of Gurkhas: The 2nd K.E.O. Gurkha Rifles, the 6th Q.E.O. Gurkha Rifles, the 7th D.E.O. Gurkha Rifles and the 10th P.M.O. Gurkha Rifles*. London, 1984.

Smith, Richard. *Jamaican Volunteers in the First World War: Race, Masculinity and the Development of National Consciousness*. Manchester, 2004.

Snyder, Timothy. *The Red Prince: The Fall of a Dynasty and the Rise of Modern Europe*. London, 2008.

Speed III, Richard B. *Prisoners, Diplomats, and the Great War: A Study in the Diplomacy of Captivity*. Westport, CT, 1990.

Spoerer, Mark. 'The Mortality of Allied Prisoners of War and Belgian Civilian Deportees in German Custody during World War I: A Reappraisal of the Effects of Forced Labour'. *Population Studies* 60, no. 2 (2006): 121–36.

Stampler, Katharina. 'Flüchtlingswesen in der Steiermark, 1914–1918'. Masters diss., University of Graz, 2004.

Stargardt, Nicholas. *Witnesses of War. Children's Lives under the Nazis*. London, 2005.

Stengers, Jean. 'Pre-war Belgian Attitudes to Britain: Anglophilia and Anglophobia'. In *Europe in Exile: European Exile Communities in Britain 1940-1945*, ed. Martin Conway and José Gotovitch. Leamington Spa, 2001.

Sterckx, Claude. *La tête et les seins. La mutilation rituelle des ennemis et le concept de l'âme*. Saarbrücken, 1981.

Stibbe, Matthew. *German Anglophobia and the Great War, 1914–1918*. Cambridge, 2001.

———. 'The Internment of Civilians by Belligerent States during the First World War and the Response of the International Committee of the Red Cross'. *Journal of Contemporary History* 41, no. 1 (2006): 5–19.

———. 'Prisoners of War during the First World War'. *Bulletin of the German Historical Institute London* 28, no. 2 (2006): 47–59.

———. 'Elisabeth Rotten and the "Auskunfts- und Hilfsstelle für Deutsche im Ausland und Ausländer in Deutschland", 1914–1919'. In *The Women's Movement in Wartime: International Perspectives, 1914–19*, ed. Alison S. Fell and Ingrid Sharp. Basingstoke, 2007.

———. *British Civilian Internees in Germany: The Ruhleben Camp, 1914–1918*. Manchester, 2008.

Stiehl, Otto. *Unsere Feinde: 96 Charakterköpfe aus deutschen Kriegsgefangenenlagern*. Stuttgart, 1916.

Stora, Benjamin. *Ils venaient d'Algérie: L'immigration algérienne en France (1912–1992)*. Paris, 1992.

Stovall, Tyler. 'The Color Line behind the Lines. Racial Violence in France during the Great War'. *American Historical Review* 103 (1998): 737–69.

Strachan, Hew, ed. *World War I: A History*. Oxford, 1998.

———. *The First World War in Africa*. Oxford, 2004.

Struck, Hermann. *Kriegsgefangene: ein Beitrag zur Völkerkunde im Weltkriege: 100 Steinzeichnungen*. Berlin, 1916.

Strupp, Karl. *Das Internationale Landkriegsrecht*. Frankfurt am Main, 1914.

Summershill, Michael. *China on the Western Front: Britain's Chinese Work Force in the First World War*. London, 1982.

Suret-Canale, Jean. *Schwarzafrika: Geschichte West- und Zentralafrikas, vol 2 of Geschichte West — und Zentralafrikas 1900–1945*. East Berlin, 1969.

Svoljšak, Petra. 'La popolazione civile nella Slovenia occupata'. In *La violenza contro la popolazione civile nella grande guerra: Deportati, profughi, internati*, ed. Bruna Bianchi. Milan, 2006.

Świętosławska-Zółkiewska, Janina. 'Działalność oświatowa polskich organizacji w Moskowie, 1915-1918'. *Przegląd Historyczno-Oświatowy* 32 (1989): 383–405.

Talha, Larbi. *Le salariat immigré dans la crise: La main-d'œuvre maghrébine en France (1921–1987)*. Paris, 1989.

Tatham, Mis M.I. 'The Great Retreat in Serbia in 1915'. In *Everyman at War: Sixty Personal Narratives of the War*, ed. C.B. Purdom. London, 1930.

Tharaud, Jérôme, and Jean Tharaud. *La randonnée de Samba Diouf*. Paris, 1922.

Thiel, Jens. *'Menschenbassin Belgien': Anwerbung, Deportation und Zwangsarbeit im Ersten Weltkrieg*. Essen, 2007.

Thurstan, Violetta. *The People Who Run: Being the Tragedy of the Refugees in Russia*. London, 1916.

Tiepolato, Serena. '"... und nun waren wir auch Verbannte. Warum? Weshalb?". Deportate Prussiane in Russia 1914–1918'. *Deportate, esuli, profughe. Rivista telematica di studi sulla memoria femminile* 1 (2004): 59–85.

———. 'L'internamento di civili prussiani in Russia (1914–1920)'. In *La violenza contro la popolazione civile nella grande guerra: Deportati, profughi, internati*, ed. Bruna Bianchi. Milan, 2006.

Tooley, T. Hunt. 'World War 1 and the Emergence of Ethnic Cleansing in Europe'. In *Ethnic Cleansing in Twentieth-Century Europe*, ed. Steven B. Várdy and T.H. Tooley. Boulder, CO, 2003.

Torpey, John. *The Invention of the Passport. Surveillance, Citizenship and the State.* Cambridge, 2000.

Treffer, Gerd. *Die ehrenwerten Ausbrecher: Das Kriegsgefangenenlager Ingolstadt im Ersten Weltkrieg.* Regensburg, 1990.

Trench, Charles Chenevix. *The Indian Army and the King's Enemies, 1900–1947.* London, 1988.

Troeltsch, Ernst. 'Der Kulturkrieg'. In *Deutsche Reden in schwerer Zeit*, ed. the Zentralstelle für Volkswohlfahrt and the Verein für Volkstümliche Kurse. No. 27. Berlin, 1915.

Tuker, Francis. *Gorkha: The Story of the Gurkhas of Nepal.* London, 1957.

Tusa, Ann, and John Tusa. *The Nuremberg Trial.* London, 1983.

Une ame de Chef. Le Gouverneur général J. Van Vollenhoven. Paris, 1920.

Valois, Victor. *Nieder mit England! Betrachtungen und Erwägungen.* Berlin, 1915.

Vance, Jonathan F., ed. *Encyclopedia of Prisoners of War and Internment.* 2nd ed. Millerton, NY, 2006.

Vankoski, Susan C. 'Letters Home, 1915–16. Punjabi Soldiers Reflect on War and Life in Europe and their Meanings for Home and Self'. *International Journal for Punjab Studies* 2 (1995): 43–63.

Varet, Pierre. *Du concours apporté à la France par ses Colonies et Pays de Protectorat au cours de la Guerre de 1914.* Paris, 1927.

Verdross, Alfred. *Die völkerrechtswidrige Kriegshandlung und der Strafanspruch der Staaten.* Berlin, 1920.

———. 'Kriegsverbrechen und Kriegsverbrecher'. In *Wörterbuch des Völkerrechts und der Diplomatie*, ed. Karl Strupp, vol. 1 of *Aachen - Lynchfall*, Berlin, 1924.

Vischer, Adolf Lukas. *Barbed Wire Disease: A Psychological Study of the Prisoner of War.* London, 1919. Also published in German as *Die Stacheldraht-Krankheit.* (Zurich, 1918).

von Hagen, Mark. *War in a European Borderland: Occupations and Occupation Plans in Galicia and Ukraine, 1914–1918.* Seattle, 2007.

von Lettow-Vorbeck, [Paul]. *Meine Erinnerungen aus Ostafrika.* Leipzig, 1920.

von Liszt, Franz. *Völkerrecht.* 10th ed. Berlin, 1915.

von Selle, Dirk. 'Prolog zu Nürnberg: Die Leipziger Kriegsverbrecherprozesse vor dem Reichsgericht'. *Zeitschrift für Neuere Rechtsgeschichte* 3, no. 4 (1997): 192–209.

von Ungern-Sternberg, Jürg. 'Wissenschaftler'. In *Enzyklopädie Erster Weltkrieg*, ed. Gerhard Hirschfeld, Gerd Krumeich and Irina Renz. Paderborn, 2004.

Waites, Bernard. 'Peoples of the Underdeveloped World'. In *Facing Armageddon: The First World War Experienced*, ed. Peter H. Liddle and Hugh Cecil. London, 1996.

Wall, Richard, and Jay Winter, eds. *The Upheaval of War. Family, Work and Welfare in Europe, 1914–1918*. Cambridge, 1988.

Wallace, Stuart. *War and the Image of Germany: British Academics 1914–1918*. Edinburgh, 1988.

Wang, Nora. 'Chinesische Kontraktarbeiter in Frankreich im Ersten Weltkrieg'. In *Enzyklopädie Migration in Europa vom 17. Jahrhundert bis zur Gegenwart*, ed. Klaus J. Bade, Pieter C. Emmer, Leo Lucassen and Jochen Oltmer. Paderborn, 2007.

War Office (British). *Manual of Military Law*. London, 1884.

———. *Statistics of the Military Effort of the British Empire during the Great War 1914–1920*. London, 1922.

Wassermair, Otto. 'Die Meutereien der Heimkehrer aus russischer Gefangenschaft bei den Ersatzkörpern der k.u.k. Armee im Jahre 1918'. PhD diss., Vienna, 1968.

Weiland, Hans, and Leopold Kern, eds. *In Feindeshand. Die Gefangenschaft im Weltkriege in Einzeldarstellungen*. 2 vols. Vienna, 1931.

Weindling, Paul. *Health, Race and German Politics between National Unification and Nazism, 1870-1945*. Cambridge, 1989.

Wendland, Anna Veronika. *Die Russophilen in Galizien: Ukrainische Konservative zwischen Österreich und Rußland 1848-1915*. Vienna, 2001.

———. 'Post-Austrian Lemberg: War Commemoration, Interethnic Relations and Urban Identity in L'viv, 1918–1939'. *Austrian History Yearbook*, 34 (2003): 83–102.

Wieviorka, Annette, ed. *Les Procès de Nuremberg et de Tokyo*. Brussels, 1996.

Wiggenhorn, Harald. *Verliererjustiz: Die Leipziger Kriegsverbrecherprozesse nach dem Ersten Weltkrieg*. Baden-Baden, 2005.

Willan, B.P. 'The South African Native Labour Contingent 1916–1918'. *Journal of African History* 9 (1978): 61–86.

Willcocks, James. *With the Indians in France*. London, 1920.

Willis, James F. *Prologue to Nuremberg: The Politics and Diplomacy of Punishing War Criminals of the First World War*. London, 1982.

Winter, Jay, and Antoine Prost. *The Great War in History. Debates and Controversies, 1914 to the Present*. Cambridge, 2005.

Wippich, Rolf-Harald. 'Internierung und Abschiebung von Japanern im Deutschen Reich im Jahr 1914'. *Zeitschrift für Geschichtswissenschaft* 55, no. 1 (2007): 18–40.

Wou, P. *Les travailleurs chinois et la grande guerre*. Paris, 1939.

Wurzer, Georg. 'Das Schicksal der deutschen Kriegsgefangenen in Russland im Ersten Weltkrieg: Der Erlebnisbericht Edwin Erich Dwingers'. In *In der Hand des Feindes: Kriegsgefangenschaft von der Antike bis zum Zweiten Weltkrieg*, ed. Rüdiger Overmans. Cologne, 1999.

Yčas, Martynas. *Pirmasis nepriklausomos Lietuvos dešimtmetis, 1918-1928*. London, 1955.

Yovanovitch, Dragolioub. *Les effets économiques et sociaux de la guerre en Serbie*. Paris, 1930.

Zahra, Tara. *Kidnapped Souls: National Indifference and the Battle for Children in the Bohemian Lands, 1900-1948*. Ithaca, NY, 2008.

Zala, Sacha. *Geschichte unter der Schere der politischen Zensur: Amtliche Aktensammlungen im internationalen Vergleich*. Munich, 2001.

———. 'Farbbücher'. In *Enzyklopädie Erster Weltkrieg*, ed. Gerhard Hirschfeld, Gerd Krumeich and Irina Renz. Paderborn, 2004.

Zander, Jens-Peter. 'Das Verbrechen im Kriege – Ein völkerrechtlicher Begriff: Ein Beitrag zur Problematik des Kriegsverbrechens'. PhD diss., University of Würzburg, 1969.

Ziemann, Benjamin. *War Experienes in Rural Germany, 1914-1923*. Oxford, 2007.

Zilch, Reinhard. 'Generalgouvernement'. In *Enzyklopädie Erster Weltkrieg*, ed. Gerhard Hirschfeld, Gerd Krumeich and Irina Renz. Paderborn, 2004.

Zimmerer, Jürgen. 'Kriegsgefangene im Kolonialkrieg: Der Krieg gegen die Herero und Nama in Deutsch-Südwestafrika'. In *In der Hand des Feindes: Kriegsgefangenschaft von der Antike bis zum Zweiten Weltkrieg*, ed. Rüdiger Overmans. Cologne, 1999.

———. 'The Birth of the "Ostland" out of the Spirit of Colonialism: A Postcolonial Perspective on the Nazi Policy of Conquest and Extermination'. *Patterns of Prejudice*, 39, no. 2 (2005): 197–219.

Zolberg, Aristide. 'The Formation of New States as a Refugee-Generating Process'. *Annals AAPSS* 467 (1983): 282–96.

Zuckerman, Larry. *The Rape of Belgium: The Untold Story of War War I*. New York, 2004.

Index

Made in the USA
San Bernardino, CA
19 July 2017